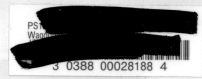

HAWTHORNE

HAWTHORNE

A Critical Study
By Hyatt H. Waggoner

Revised Edition

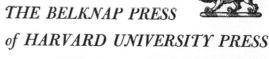

THE BELKNAP PRESS
of HARVARD UNIVERSITY PRESS
CAMBRIDGE · MASSACHUSETTS · 1963

For Louise

PREFACE TO THE SECOND EDITION

In revising this book almost a decade after first writing it, I have found much that no longer satisfies me, and some parts that positively embarrass me. This is no doubt as it should be: one likes to think that one grows in perceptiveness in a decade, and even if one has not, one learns from the work of others. Criticism needs to be redone every generation, even when it is written by better critics than I. So there are many extensive revisions in this new edition. A good deal has been added, and some material omitted. Chapter eight is entirely new: how I managed to miss the Faun's virtues almost completely ten years ago I cannot now understand, but I did. Here I had to start all over again.

Still, the experience was not all like this. There was satisfaction in noting that sometimes, where the points I made did not now seem so fresh as I once thought them, the reason was that they had been absorbed by younger students of the subject and made the basis of further explorations of Hawthorne's achievement. I take this to mean that criticism, though not a science, need not be wholly subjective or wholly evanescent. Even though criticism does need to be redone every so often, understanding of Hawthorne does not just change, it grows. Which is good, because Hawthorne deserves the very best understanding we can bring to him, and understanding grows best when personal insights are shared within the "magic circle" of those who care about his work.

Barrington, R. I., 1963   H. H. W.

ACKNOWLEDGMENTS

I am indebted to many people for help in the writing of this book. The students in English 511 at the University of Kansas City have contributed a great deal that can no longer be specifically identified and so cannot be acknowledged except in this way. I am grateful to Francis J. Polek for typing the manuscript; he worked at the task as though it were a labor of love and not an ill-paid job. I have tried to acknowledge my chief debts to other writers on Hawthorne as I have gone along in the body of this work, but I find that I have nowhere adequately noted my debt to Richard Fogle, whose articles I have long used and admired and whose book, *Nathaniel Hawthorne: The Light and the Dark,* is a significant landmark in the history of Hawthorne criticism. Finally, I am indebted to a number of people for making suggestions at various stages in the preparation of the manuscript, but especially, and most deeply, to Jeremy Ingalls, W. Stacy Johnson, and Randall Stewart.

Kansas City, 1953   H. H. W.

CONTENTS

1 THE MATERIAL OF ART   1

2 THE TALES: *The Use of the Past*   45

3 THE TALES: *The Discovery of Meaning*   71

4 THE TALES: *The Texture of Meaning*   105

5 THE SCARLET LETTER   126

6 THE HOUSE OF THE SEVEN GABLES   160

7 THE BLITHEDALE ROMANCE   188

8 THE MARBLE FAUN   209

9 THE LATE ROMANCES   226

10 CONCLUSION   247

INDEX   269

CHAPTER ONE

THE MATERIAL OF ART

When Nathaniel Hawthorne was born in 1804 the decline of his family's fortunes was already far advanced and the decline of Salem as a seaport was beginning. His father's death at sea when Hawthorne was four later seemed to Hawthorne to have completed the personal decline. Salem's loss of trade to Boston and New York, so that it took on some of those aspects of a ghost town that are recorded in the Custom House essay attached to *The Scarlet Letter,* connected foreground and background in a picture nearly monochromatic. When Hawthorne married at the age of thirty-eight, his life was more than half over and he wavered between a feeling that the best years were already gone and a feeling that his real life had just begun. When he was not yet sixty and while his children were still young, failing health and a premonition of early death made him both physically and psychologically an old man. A dream of lost power and innocence, a memory of Arcadia and Eden, runs through his works as a dominant theme.

Yet his life was not spectacularly unfortunate. The pathos felt by most of the biographers can hardly be fully accounted for by the outward facts. Though his family had declined in wealth and prestige, and Hawthorne himself struggled for twenty-five years to become a writer without getting any substantial encouragement, he lived to know full recognition, to be acclaimed by his own contemporaries as a great writer. Though he married late, yet he married the woman of his choice and was unusually happy in his marriage. Unlike Emerson, Longfellow, and Mark Twain, he never knew the grief brought by the death of wife and children or the desolation of outliving the friends he cared for. He was remarkably handsome, even, as some said, "beautiful," and, until the last several years of his life, enjoyed unusually good health. Even his financial problems were not, at any time in his life, to be compared with the struggles with poverty endured by many of the greatest writers. His outward life was relatively uneventful, serene, and fortunate.

There is a paradox here not easily to be resolved, but it is only one of many that become apparent when one contemplates the man and his work. When Hawthorne was a boy he suffered an injury to his foot. Though there is no evidence that the injury was especially severe, his family found the incident reason enough to account for the habit of withdrawal which boy and youth developed. The earlier biographies of Hawthorne are full of such attempts to account for aspects of the man by reference to youthful events which themselves need accounting for. After her husband's death Mrs. Hawthorne devoted herself to presenting to the world a proper picture of her famous husband, carefully altering the Notebooks and suppressing the facts to do her husband the service, as she supposed, of letting him appear in the role of the ideal Victorian man of letters, cheerful, confident, pious, refined, and optimistic. Yet there cannot be much doubt that she was right in supposing that her husband would in the main have approved of what she did to retouch the portrait.

Hawthorne wrote a good deal about his sense of isolation, his loneliness. He felt, before his marriage, imprisoned in a cell to which the key had been lost. He longed to "open an intercourse with the world." And many observers, then and later, noticed the painful shyness of the man, the "furtive" look noted by Lowell. Yet Randall Stewart, protesting against a "romanticized" picture of Hawthorne as lonely, aloof, and alienated, has underscored the evidence of his adjustment. His was a very "normal" college career, with the usual pranks and friendships and lack of distinction in most things. He liked to smoke cigars and to drink moderately with friends over cards. His best friends were politicians, sailors, journalists, all of whom he preferred to romantic poets and transcendental philosophers. His letters and notebook entries are "earthy," as realistic and occasionally "unrefined" as we should expect to find them in any normal man even in Victorian Salem and Concord. Mr. Stewart is undoubtedly justified in his correction of the picture of Hawthorne as recluse. But which is the "real" Hawthorne, the man of the self-estimate, the man Mrs. Hawthorne tried to make him, or the man Mr. Stewart presents?

There were in fact several Hawthornes and all of them are to some degree masks. There was the "man of sensibility," as sensibility was defined in the first half of the nineteenth century, the "man of feeling" who was contemporary with Irving and Longfellow. This was the Hawthorne of the tender fancies, the whimsical sentiments, the Hawthorne of some of the sketches who declared himself deeply moved by Longfellow's *Evangeline*. Now and then, in this phase, he skirts perilously close to what today seems sentimentality. This Hawthorne wrote "The Snow Image" and "Little Daffydowndilly," was properly reverent and lighthearted, had the conventional emotions in the presence of feminine purity, and created the blonde maidens who flit through the novels like sunbeams in a dark world. This Hawthorne was contemporary, correct, an approximation to the ideal of his time. Hawthorne liked this Hawthorne and tried to encourage him.

But not very successfully. The sense of irony, the cool skepticism, the detached, sometimes cruel sense of humor collaborated with the visions that came between sleep and waking to make it difficult for this admired Hawthorne to maintain himself. He found it difficult to feel as he knew he *ought* to feel. Often he found it difficult to feel at all, even to feel the wrong emotions. Hence, if we are searching for the "real" Hawthorne, we must take account of another Hawthorne, cold, isolated, detached, watchful, skeptical. If the picture thus presented seems quite untrue to the outlines of the public Hawthorne preserved in the records of family and friends, we need only keep two things in mind to correct the distortion: this is the most persistent shape of the self-portrayal in all of Hawthorne's writing, both fiction and non-fiction; and the self-image, though we may assume that it was created out of knowledge not available to others, could not have been the whole truth, for another part of Hawthorne very much disliked *this* Hawthorne.

Hawthorne must have been to some degree, in short, the man he saw himself as being; but he was also the man who did the seeing and passed the negative judgments on what he saw. He was the young man of "The Christmas Banquet," more unfortunate than the worst of life's unfortunates, whose tragedy lay in the fact that he could feel nothing, could not respond emotionally to life. He was the cold observer who could not muster enough faith to participate in what he observed: Coverdale peeping through the window into other lives in *The Blithedale Romance,* Paul Pry, Ethan Brand searching in every heart for the unpardonable sin, the man in the steeple looking down on those in the streets from a position remote enough to make him feel wholly detached. He was the Hawthorne of parts of the Notebooks. This Hawthorne, whose reactions to people were so frequently negative, found it easier to detect a sham than to discover a virtue in unpromising circumstances. The Hawthorne of the Notebooks comments on the Shakers, on American visitors to the Consulate in Liverpool, on abolitionists and other idealists, was so detached that he might easily be imagined using other people simply as the objects of study—the sin committed by Ethan Brand, Aylmer, Rappaccini, Westervelt.

But there was another Hawthorne too, the one who joined the Brook Farm community, that high-minded experiment in practical brotherhood. It was this Hawthorne, also, who helped a certain Miss Bacon publish a book which he felt sure would not succeed, because she needed the help and he believed her case, even if wrong, should get a hearing; who stood by his friend Pierce when to do so was almost tanta-mount to being judged guilty of treason; who was more generous with his practical aid than in his judgments, and who was as severe in judging himself as in judging anyone else.

And there was, after 1850, the famous man of letters who found it increasingly difficult to write anything which he thought worth while. In many respects this is the most puzzling mask of all. For twenty-five years after his gradua-tion from college Hawthorne persevered in a long apprentice-ship to his craft that brought neither fame nor money. Creating stories that we now recognize as great and being forced to sell them for trifling sums to obscure publications, he continued to write steadily in the face of discouragement and poverty. But after *The Scarlet Letter* had brought him immediate fame and more money than he had ever got from his writing, as well as an assured public for future works, he tended more and more to find excuses for not writing. The publishers pressed him for new books, and he went through stacks of old magazines and annuals, culling stories and sketches he had done twenty years before; or satisfied them with retelling classic legends for children; or put them off with promises of a novel to come when conditions were more propitious. He protested that he could not write in summer heat, or in winter cold. In the Berkshires the novelty of mountain scenery and air soon wore off and he longed for the air of the seaside and for a more luxurious home than the red farmhouse. Salem was intolerable—and he made it more so by his acid portrayal of it in the Custom House Letter but he could never feel at home anywhere else. England, Rome, Concord, all seemed places where it was almost im-possible to work.

A good deal of sympathy has been wasted on Hawthorne because he had to take political jobs to make a living. It is generally assumed that these jobs kept him from writing; this is indeed the impression that he himself had. But the adverse circumstances that kept him from writing, or that weakened his writing, were not outward but inward. Though his position in the Boston Custom House before his marriage may have been nearly as onerous as he portrayed it, his two later political jobs were of a very different character. Neither was sufficiently burdensome to have kept a different sort of man from writing. In the Salem position described in the essay prefacing *The Scarlet Letter* Hawthorne had to work only a few hours each morning, and even then, "work" is hardly the word for what he did. Mostly he read, or wrote book reviews, or just sat and thought. His problem was to pass the time. But he could write nothing more serious than book reviews until he had been fired and the need was desperate.

In the English Consulate, again, he put in at most several hours a day, with whole weeks and even months taken out entirely for sightseeing tours and other recreation. The job was essentially a sinecure in which a different sort of artist could have done voluminous writing, for the "work"— usually no more arduous than signing his name—demanded neither much time nor much thought. In the last twenty years of his life the only extensive period when Hawthorne worked continuously at his writing was in the four years before his death, when he tortured himself in the attempt to do one more novel but could produce nothing which he could complete or was willing to publish. Hawthorne worked hard at becoming a man of letters until he was recognized as being one. After that, he worked at it only when forced to by need for money or the demands of conscience.

These are only a few of the paradoxes that emerge when we contemplate the man who made an "ideal" marriage, yet who in his last miserable years found himself utterly alone in the midst of loving wife and children; who was simple in his tastes and requirements, yet contented nowhere; who longed all his life for a home, yet discovered reasons for rejecting every home he found or made; who took part in Brook Farm utopianism, yet despised reformers; who considered his Christian faith unshakable, yet never went to church, disliked theological writings, and usually was repelled by preachers of the gospel. It is perhaps partly because of the centrality of such paradoxes that all of the existing biographies are interesting and none of them wholly satisfactory. Hawthorne's friend Cilley once wrote, "I admire him: but I do not know him." Longfellow, also writing as a friend, put the matter succinctly: "He was a mysterious man." It is still true today that the student of Hawthorne who wishes to get a complete and rounded view of the man must read more than one biography, then supplement the biographies he has read with the Notebooks, sketches, letters, and stories, then finally understand the man, if at all, by a leap of intuitive sympathy.

If he has made the leap successfully—and there is no publicly demonstrable test of success here—he will perhaps be aware of nuances in the works that he would otherwise have missed, read them with another level of meaning in mind, or at least approach them with a sympathy not otherwise attainable. But no merely factual knowledge of the externals of Hawthorne's life will be of much use to one who is trying to understand his works. The Taine approach to literature, through the study of the writer's environment, is of some use, perhaps, in studying Whitman, who "expressed" his age and found his best material in the things he did and saw and felt. But it works so poorly as to be hardly worth attempting with Hawthorne, whose creative life was wholly inward, who usually wrote badly when he tried to write of the things he outwardly saw and actually did, and who was truest to himself when he wrote of others and truest to his own age when he ignored it and wrote of the past or the legendary and the mythical. This is true no doubt partly because much of his best work falls into the genre of historical fiction; but more profoundly perhaps for two other, related, reasons: because his work is concerned with the essentials of human experience and captures those essentials in art forms that have the timelessness of classic art; and because, to a peculiar degree, that which is most valuable in Hawthorne's writing springs from the depths of head and heart where newspaper headlines make no ripple.

2

A close look at Hawthorne's sketches will prepare us better for the tales and novels than any study of the externals of his life. It is fashionable at present to depreciate the sketches, and it is true that some of them come close to a kind of Irvingesque indulgence in sentiment for its own sake. But it is by no means true that there is no "thinking" in them, as some of Hawthorne's critics seem to believe. The thinking in them is casual, to be sure, even deliberately relaxed and apparently inconsecutive, masquerading as fancy and taste. This was the demand made by the genre and the time.

But it was also the kind of thinking that Hawthorne did best; and it would seem that we should know enough by this time about the processes of creative thought to know that it does not always, perhaps does not often, take the form of high-level ratiocination. The fact about the sketches that should be recognized is that, unlike both the sketches of Irving, who excelled in sentiment, and many of the essays of Macaulay, who excelled in a kind of reasoning, they run counter to the trend toward that dissociation of thought and feeling which marked so much nineteenth-century writing.

The paraphrasable content of "The Haunted Mind," to take one of the better early sketches for an example, is very slight, but a close look at the piece will take us far toward an understanding of Hawthorne's work. The sketch provides, first of all, a unique glimpse of the characteristically romantic approach to life and to art. It shows us that Hawthorne was not only, as we shall see, at odds with his time: he was also a part of it, sharing the romantic concern for that which can only be seen out of the corner of the eye, or in a half-light, or when the mind is relaxed. This concern with the strange, the half-known, the dimly seen, coming, as it is customary in literary histories to say, as a reaction against the rigidities and apparent superficialities of the age of common sense and limited reason, this concern with the verities which are no less important because they cannot be demonstrated by the methods favored by the age of the enlightenment—this is fully adumbrated in "The Haunted Mind."

Hawthorne asks us to consider what thoughts come to the mind halfway between sleep and waking when one starts up from midnight slumber. Then the mind is passive, the dreams are close, and the revelations that come may be "truer" than those that come to the concentrated and controlled intelligence. We think, perhaps, as we read this, of the use of drugs as an aid to creation, of Keats's praise of sleep, of the romantic tendency to prefer the night to the day and the sea to the land. But even an amateur knowledge of psychoanalysis should correct any tendency we may have to dismiss this approach to experience as simply "romantic" and of only historical interest.

The sketch reveals as much of Hawthorne's special concerns and the shape of his sensibility as it does of the outlook he shared with the writers of his youth. When you first wake up, he tells us, you are very close to your dream, and for a while its vivid illusions occupy you. But then you begin to "think," though not in a very "reasonable" way. You think various things, but principally of "how the dead are lying in their cold shrouds and narrow coffins." The long paragraph in the middle of the sketch devoted to the thoughts that come at this time is concerned wholly with death and frustration. "In the depths of every heart there is a tomb and a dungeon," it begins, introducing us both to Hawthorne's most characteristic metaphors, the tomb or dungeon of the heart, and to the feeling that pervades nearly all of his work except the deliberately light-hearted sketches he sometimes contrived to write.

"The lights, the music, and the revelry above" may, Hawthorne tells us, cause us to forget the existence of these tombs and dungeons and "the buried ones, or prisoners, whom they hide," but "sometimes, and oftenest at midnight, these dark receptacles are flung wide open. In an hour like this, when the mind has a passive sensibility, but no active strength; when the imagination is a mirror, imparting vividness to all ideas, without the power of selecting or controlling them;

then pray that your griefs may slumber, and the brotherhood of remorse not break their chain."

Then, with a characteristic turn to the abstract when the revelation threatens to become too personal, Hawthorne personifies the visitors who come with the "funeral train" that moves into the center of consciousness: Sorrow, Disappointment, and Fatality appear, the last "a demon to whom you subjected yourself by some error at the outset of life." On the face of another ghost you see "the writhed lip of scorn, the mockery of that living eye, the pointed finger, touching the sore place in your heart. Do you remember any act of enormous folly at which you would blush, even in the remotest cavern of the earth? Then recognize your Shame."

Though this has in part the "dated" air of the allegorical poem and the moral essay, the reader today, whether or not he submits to Hawthorne's effort to evoke in each his own "Shame," will recognize something else at any rate: the darkness that is always so much more impressive, so much more *felt*, than the light in Hawthorne's works; the artistic superiority of the dark guilty women of the tales and novels over the pale blonde innocent maidens, the Hesters and Miriams over the Phoebes and the Hildas; the shapes of all the "villains" in the works, with their features cold and mocking; the sense of fate, whether made explicit as in "Wakefield" or recognized and denied by a conscious effort to believe in freedom, as in *The House of the Seven Gables*.

But the sketch continues: "Sufficient, without such guilt, is this nightmare of the soul; this heavy, heavy sinking of the spirits; this wintry gloom about the heart; this indistinct horror of the mind, blending itself with the darkness of the chamber." Finding that the "visions" have become intolerable—as his waking vision became to Leonard Doane in "Alice Doane's Appeal"—"By a desperate effort you start upright, breaking from a sort of conscious sleep, and gazing wildly round the bed, as if the fiends were anywhere but in your haunted mind." You try to think of pleasanter subjects. You search for anything that will remind you that life is as real as death, innocence as real as guilt. Having done so more or less successfully, "With an involuntary start you seize hold on consciousness, and prove yourself but half awake, by running a doubtful parallel between human life and the hour which has now elapsed. In both you emerge from mystery, pass through a vicissitude that you can but imperfectly control, and are borne onward to another mystery."

Most of what is best in the later works is already suggested here. I shall not now elaborate the parallels between this and the best tales and sketches, but we shall certainly see again many of these visions that come to the haunted mind.

3

Judgment of Hawthorne's relation to the public questions that occupied his contemporaries has moved in the last quarter century through a ninety-degree arc, from the opinion that he was totally unconcerned with and uninformed about social problems to the more recently conventional one that he was both well informed and vitally concerned, even when, as usually was the case, he could not agree with the popular "liberal" solutions. Admirable monographs and papers have been written on his attitudes toward reform, his political opinions, his views on society in general. What has emerged from the conflicting judgments and corrections of judgments is a paradox much like that of the "lonely yet sociable" Hawthorne that emerges from the biographies. There is too much evidence for each of the two most opposed views for the paradox to be resolved, but it may be kept from appearing to be a complete antinomy if we take the trouble to understand not only Hawthorne's particular opinions on such things as politics and reform but the larger views of which these were but special applications. And the best way to do this is to read the Notebooks and the sketches, particularly the sketches. A glance at "Fancy's Show Box," "The Celestial Railroad," and "Earth's Holocaust" will take us quickly to the center of those aspects of his views on religion and ethics, politics and reform which are of primary importance to those who are interested in his work as artist.

Hawthorne subtitles "Fancy's Show Box" "A Morality," and the choice is happily descriptive, for the piece is closely akin to medieval allegory in its form and to orthodox Christianity in its content. He begins by asking the question "What is Guilt?"—a question that his contemporary and sometime neighbor Emerson would have found, had he read the sketch, both unnecessary and essentially meaningless. He answers the question with "A stain upon the soul," thus beginning his sketch with two assumptions: first, that there is a real difference between right and wrong, making it worth while to ask the question "What is guilt?" and not just "What makes me feel guilty?"; and second, that there is an immortal soul which can receive "stains." The question that then follows is "Must the fleshly hand and visible frame of man sets its seal to the evil designs of the soul, in order to give them their entire validity against the sinner?" For it is quite clear that all of us have wished more evil than we have wrought: "In the solitude of a midnight chamber or in a desert, afar from men or in a church, while the body is kneeling, the soul may pollute itself even with those crimes which we are accustomed to deem altogether carnal. If this be true, it is a fearful truth."

Then, with a "Let us illustrate the subject by an imaginary example," Hawthorne describes certain scenes from the past life of an old man, scenes that show how often he was prevented from sin by mere accidents. Part of the point he wishes to make is that Mr. Smith's "innocence" is the product not of blamelessness of intention but of fortunate circumstances; under slightly different circumstances he might have been a thief or a murderer. But another part of the point qualifies this. It is not only that we cannot take much credit for the evil that we have not done, but that we cannot even know, until after the fact, what our "intentions" really were: "In truth, there is no such thing in man's nature as a settled and full resolve, either for good or evil, except at the very moment of execution." Hawthorne knows that the qualifications made by "settled and full" must be made if he is to avoid a fatalism that will link him more closely with his

predestinarian Puritan forebears than he wishes to be linked.
He makes the qualifying statement. But the implications of
the sketch contain a suggestion of that feeling for the power
of fate and the relative impotence of the will which we shall
find in many of his later works.

Hawthorne ends his sketch with a paragraph brief enough
to be quoted entire, and significant enough for all his works
to deserve to be remembered:

Yet, with the slight fancy work which we have framed, some
sad and awful truths are interwoven. Man must not disclaim
his brotherhood, even with the guiltiest, since, though his hand
be clean, his heart has surely been polluted by the flitting phantoms of iniquity. He must feel that, when he shall knock at the
gate of heaven, no semblance of an unspotted life can entitle
him to entrance there. Penitence must kneel, and Mercy come
from the footstool of the throne, or that golden gate will never
open!

Repent and ask God's mercy: if this is "Puritan," it is also
Pauline, and orthodox. Certain monks of Eastern Orthodoxy
center their conscious lives on the repetition of a single short
prayer, the "Jesus Prayer": "Lord Jesus Christ, have mercy
upon me, a sinner." One would like to know what Hawthorne's comment would have been if he had known about
the practice of making this prayer the central act of worship.
Surely it would have been sympathetic. The implications
of "Fancy's Show Box" are perfectly consistent with those
of "Night Sketches: Beneath an Umbrella" and "My Kinsman, Major Molineux." All three works suggest that Hawthorne inclined toward the orthodox formulation derived
from St. Paul, "justification by grace through faith."

Was Hawthorne then a "Puritan," as some scholars have
said? Or was he a Transcendentalist, as others, aware of the
distortion involved in calling him a Puritan, have replied?
I would suggest that the truth about Hawthorne's religious
views cannot be found if we formulate our guiding questions
in this fashion. The answer would have to be that he was
both and neither Puritan and Transcendentalist, but such

an answer would omit most of the distinctiveness of his position.

He was a nineteenth century New England liberal Protestant of a rather special sort. He had no church, though his family had been Unitarian, and he never formulated his religious thought in precise doctrines. Indeed, as an antirationalist he resisted, for reasons both temperamental and principled, the theologian's efforts to achieve clarity in such matters. Nevertheless, Hubert Hoeltje is undoubtedly right so far as he goes in his summary of the religious beliefs that Hawthorne consciously held: "His . . . religious beliefs were limited to a few points, never systematically stated. He had a sure faith in Providence . . . He thought of Jesus as the Redeemer of mankind, though in what sense explicitly he seems not to have recorded . . . He had, finally, an unwavering belief in the immortality of the soul."*

This is what Hawthorne "believed," and all that he "believed," so far as he ever recorded his beliefs. It does not take us very far toward an understanding of the works he wrote. It would be hard to find a better illustration of the fact that art has other sources besides conscious belief. Why would a man who believed just this, and nothing more, write "Fancy's Show Box" at all?

Despite his long absorption in Puritan writings, it is pretty clear that Hawthorne had a typical nineteenth century view of his ancestors. He exaggerated their gloominess and their intolerance and probably attributed their persecution of sexual offenses to ideas other than those they actually held. He made them the villains in *The Scarlet Letter* and created in Hester a somewhat Transcendental heroine. It is very clear, though he apparently never said so in precise terms, that he did not share their Biblical literalism. What he thought of the exclusive emphasis they placed on man's depravity is clear in "Young Goodman Brown": they were just wrong. The revelations that came to Brown in the forest were more the Devil's doing than God's.

* *Inward Sky: The Mind and Heart of Nathaniel Hawthorne* (Durham, N.C., Duke University Press, 1962), pp. 460-461.

Even the very intensity of their faith, so admirable in a way, made them, he thought, liable to bigotry. "The Man of Adamant" has among its other meanings the suggestion that the Puritans did not read their Bible aright despite their devotion to it, and so they missed the point of St. Paul's "faith, hope, and love, and the greatest of these is love." Richard Digby spurned not only the sacrament offered him by Mary Goffe but her plea that he return to those who needed him. The parallels between Hawthorne's description of this Puritan bigot and his remarks elsewhere on the Puritans in general leave no doubt about the matter: this is the way he saw them. He was no Puritan. He would have been amazed as well as unhappy at being described as one by some modern scholars. But he was temperamentally attuned to their meanings, and he generally felt himself closer to their view of life than he did to the views of his most liberal contemporaries, who did not, he felt, take the facts of moral experience seriously. The strongest way of putting the case for Hawthorne's "Puritanism" is to say that he thought there were truths at the center of the Puritan faith that, when suitably translated, were still viable.

A somewhat stronger case can be made for the idea that Hawthorne was a Transcendentalist—stronger at least if we concentrate on Hawthorne's ideas and ignore the feelings that so largely shaped his art. In certain of his moods, his attitude toward nature was similar to theirs, particularly his sense of the continuity of nature and supernature. For him as for Emerson, the natural is more mysterious and the supernatural more natural than had been thought. Both, again, are religious but antidogmatic and individualistic—but not only the Transcendentalists exhibited this nineteenth century tendency. In his criticisms of the Puritans, Hawthorne was nearly as antinomian in his sympathies as Emerson. Both were idealists in metaphysics and based their aesthetics on their idealism, as is very clear in Hawthorne's case in "The Artist of the Beautiful." Both thought of nature as a symbolic language. Emerson's "Pure intellect is pure devil" could have served as Hawthorne's inspiration for his heartless scientific villains if he had needed any outside source of inspiration. He didn't, for his antirationalism was as thoroughgoing as Emerson's. Even his brief stay at Brook Farm, which both he and his biographers later found puzzling, may be interpreted as evidence of his partial kinship with the Transcendentalists.

Why then are his works at their best generally so very un-Transcendental? If he was not a Puritan, why have his readers so often felt that he was? Why did he write so much more often about the dangers of pride (making oneself the center of things) than about the virtues of self-reliance? Why did Emerson once record that he found Hawthorne's works not worth reading, and why did Hawthorne feel he had no questions to ask of Emerson the philosopher?

The passage in which Hawthorne says this tells us why. There were secrets of the heart, he felt, that Emerson could not read. Hawthorne felt that the Transcendentalists did not take evil seriously enough. He might also have felt, though he did not go on record on this matter, that the attitude of those Transcendentalists who define the movement for us, particularly Emerson and Thoreau, was very different from his on the crucial matter of their common religious past. Emerson was in conscious revolt against the Christian past as he understood it. An argument could of course be made that he was in fact salvaging the viable part and preparing the way for Tillichian neo-orthodoxy in our day; but that surely is not the way *he* saw the matter. "God is, not was."

Hawthorne was not in revolt against his religious heritage. Once, when revising a magazine piece for book publication, he deleted two phrases that together negatively define his position. In a derogatory passage he kept the general intent but removed both "Unitarian infidelity" and "Roman credulity." He deplored them equally. Though he had no church at all, so that in one sense he was even more "liberal" than the Unitarians, he was much closer in most of his thinking to Bushnell, the Congregationalist, than to Unitarianism as we are likely to think of it today. His Unitarianism was like that of the elder Channing, who wanted to break with Calvinism, not with Christianity.

This is clear everywhere in Hawthorne's works, even though he seldom speaks out on religious matters to tell us just what he believed. In "The Celestial Railroad," for instance, his sympathies were with Bunyan, not with the modernists, and his characterization of Transcendentalism in that piece is certainly hostile as well as unfair. He agreed with Emerson and the other Transcendentalists on many matters, but he also disagreed with them on a few matters so important that they made all the difference. Much of his work could be described as a translation into romantic and psychological terms of those very parts of Spenser and Bunyan that Emerson was busy rejecting. "Fancy's Show Box" would have seemed only silly to Emerson if he had read it.

"The Celestial Railroad" and "Earth's Holocaust" are sketches of a very different order from "Fancy's Show Box." Whether better or not, they are at least much more substantial, and both are explicit criticisms of his age, so that a complete comment on them would require a good deal of historical scholarship exercised in a long essay. If he is to get the full impact of "The Celestial Railroad," for example, the modern reader should have a first-hand knowledge of *Pilgrim's Progress* and a grasp of religious history, particularly of the way in which New England Puritanism changed into Unitarianism, and of what that change amounted to in doctrine and practice. For "Earth's Holocaust" he should have some knowledge of the reform movements of the 1830's and 1840's, including not only the specific reforms advocated—teetotalism, women's rights, vegetarianism, and abolition of capital punishment, for instance—but the assumptions of the reformers about human nature. As we shall see, Hawthorne's tales and novels do not make nearly so strong a demand for this kind of special knowledge as these sketches do; but that is not surprising, since one of the permanent and fundamental distinctions between art and social criticism is here involved.

Yet without the sort of historical documentation that they invite, the sketches can still tell us something of the directions of Hawthorne's thinking. "The Celestial Railroad" is a pastiche on *Pilgrim's Progress*, with the satire aimed not at Bunyan but at religious modernists of Hawthorne's day. The modern pilgrim has, in his own opinion, inestimable advantages over Bunyan's old-fashioned Everyman. The latest triumphs of applied science have made everything so much easier and quicker—including salvation. Nowadays the pilgrim rides on a railroad instead of journeying laboriously and perilously on foot. He checks his load of sins with the baggage man and is so much freer to enjoy himself on the way. He need no longer be disturbed by certain unpleasant facts, for the Slough of Despond has been filled in by the cheerful books of modern clergymen, philosophers convinced of the natural goodness of man, and Transcendental optimists. The Wicket Gate has been torn down and the Interpreter's House by-passed; the Valley of the Shadow of Death has been lighted by gas lamps and the mouth of Hell has been identified as merely the crater of an extinct volcano. "Giant Transcendentalist," with outlines so indistinct that no one has ever been able to describe him, has taken the place once occupied by Bunyan's very concrete and dangerous enemies, Pope and Pagan. Vanity Fair still continues, but its dangers have been done away with as it has been taken over by the Church. Here machines have been devised to manufacture individual morality, thus disposing of a vexatious problem; and though the occupants of the city have a habit of suddenly vanishing like soap bubbles, no one takes any notice of their disappearance.

The ending is hard on the religious liberals of Hawthorne's day. Mr. Smooth-it-away, the modernist preacher who serves as the speaker's guide and who believes that Hell "has not even a metaphorical existence," refuses at the last moment to enter the Celestial City:

And then did my excellent friend Mr. Smooth-it-away laugh outright, in the midst of which cachinnation a smoke-wreath issued from his mouth and nostrils, while a twinkle of lurid

flame darted out of either eye, proving indubitably that his heart
was all of a red blaze. The impudent fiend! To deny the existence
of Tophet, when he felt its fiery tortures raging within his
breast. I rushed to the side of the boat, intending to fling myself
on shore; but the wheels, as they began their revolutions, threw
a dash of spray over me so cold—so deadly cold, with the chill
that will never leave those waters until Death be drowned in his
own river—that with a shiver and a heartquake I awoke. Thank
Heaven it was a Dream!

If this was a dream, it was a dream from the horned gate,
true to the outlines of Hawthorne's most lasting convictions.
The fundamental assumptions behind it were expressed in
another "dream" that is also one of Hawthorne's major
sketches, "Earth's Holocaust." This too is a sketch which invites, indeed almost demands, the kind of explication best
afforded by historical scholarship, for it is a satirical comment
on many of the most important trends and historical events of
Hawthorne's age. The immediate inspiration for it may very
likely have been Carlyle's *French Revolution*, with its frequent fire imagery and its underlying concept of the revolution as a consuming fire. Other sources have been suggested
for the episode of the burning of the books, and Thoreau's
talk of an Indian custom of annually burning all property pre-
paratory to making a fresh start in life may have contributed
its bit. But whatever the sources, the sketch has implications
that reach out to touch the central problems of Hawthorne's
and of any age—the nature and source of evil, the necessity
and the failure of reform, the meaning of war, tradition, and
the romantic concept of nature and man. The sketch is
dense with allusions to particular men and events, so much
so that full explanatory notes would bulk as large as the piece
itself, but it is also timeless in the way in which it raises
the particular to the universal. Hawthorne's contemporaries,
from Emerson and Ellery Channing to Mrs. Bloomer, and
the chief reforming movements of his time, from the French
Revolution to feminism and the Oneida Colony, enter the
picture; but the central concern remains with the permanent
nature of man and of history.

"Once upon a time—but whether in the time past or time
to come is a matter of little or no moment—this wide world
had become so overburdened with an accumulation of wornout trumpery that the inhabitants determined to rid themselves of it by a general bonfire." Hawthorne's guide to the
site of the fire, on a prairie in the West, who interprets the
events witnessed there, is another Virgil guiding Dante. And
Hawthorne, like Dante, represents himself as bewildered,
naïve, rather uncomprehending. The meaning of the sketch,
then, is not to be found in the reactions of the narrator—
Hawthorne—so much as in the comments of the "thoughtful
observer" who guided him, and not so much in either as in
the implications of the events themselves, partially summarized in the last paragraph by the narrator, who has
profited by prolonged meditation on the events he witnessed
so naïvely.

Neither the observer nor the narrator makes explicit some
of the most important implications of the structure of the
events they observe. The things that are burned in the fire
as "wornout trumpery" range from the obviously vestigial remains of dead institutions and ideas to elements of tradition
about which, in Hawthorne's opinion, there can be the sharp-
est debate. The principle of organization is to be found in
his judgment of the universality of agreement; no reader,
presumably, would agree with all the reformers, and each
would draw at a different place the line between that which
ought to be burned and that which ought to be saved. Thus
the first thing the narrator sees being thrown in the flames
is "the rubbish of the herald's office," which only the avowed
monarchist, favoring return to the medieval system of a fixed
social hierarchy, would want to save.

But if the need for this reform, and the benefits to be attained by it, are all but obvious, the reforms that follow are
such as to command more and more qualified assent. The
temperance reformers, for example, throw all alcoholic bev-
erages on the flames, remarking correctly that drunkenness
is an age-old evil. But it is at least questionable whether
Prohibition is a good way to encourage temperance. The

property of the privileged classes is destroyed by those eager
to promote justice through economic equality. But the pre-
Marxist socialism here alluded to does not seem as undebat-
able today as it did a generation ago: it becomes increasingly
doubtful whether justice will result from the organized
avarice of class warfare.

Again, the restraining and stabilizing force of tradition
is gladly burned while an Emersonian philosopher exclaims,
"Now we shall get rid of the weight of dead men's thought,
which has hitherto pressed so heavily on the living intellect
that it has been incompetent to any effectual self-exertion."
In later years in England Hawthorne sometimes resented
the weight of tradition, but here the tone of the sketch suggests that he found this effort at reform mildly amusing.

The burning of worthless works of literature follows, with
some of the most pointed comments Hawthorne ever made
on his own productions and those of his contemporaries. An
allusion to Emerson's advice to young men in "The American
Scholar" not to be bookworms produced the comment from
the narrator, "My dear sir, is not Nature better than a book?"
in which the fallacies of uncreative "scholarship" and romantic "spontaneity" and nature-worship are equally balanced—
and rejected. But the most debatable reform of all—in terms
of the system of values implicit in the sketch—is yet to
come. Religious reformers begin by burning the trappings
of Popery and proceed to destroy the churches themselves.
The narrator, taking the position that institutional religion
is bad but "personal" religion is good, is still not disturbed,
for, remembering perhaps Bryant's "Inscription for the Entrance to a Wood" and Emerson's constant advice, he believes
that all that is being destroyed is finally unessential: "'All is
well,' said I, cheerfully. 'The woodpaths shall be the aisles
of our cathedral,—the firmament itself shall be its ceiling.
What needs an earthy roof between the Deity and his wor-
shippers?'" When his guide remarks, "True, . . . but will
they pause here?" the narrator is disturbed. He wonders
whether it is an unmixed advantage that "The inhabitants
of the earth had grown too enlightened to define their faith

within a form of words, or to limit the spiritual by any analogy to our material existence. Truths which the heavens trembled at were now but a fable of the world's infancy."

When therefore the reformers finally burn all the religious literature of the past and a mighty wind comes roaring across the plain with a "desolate howl," the narrator grows pale and wonders whether the rage for reform will leave any value undestroyed. But he is comforted by his friend, who assures him that the truths which the enlightened reformers would destroy are too permanent to suffer destruction. "This," the narrator reflected,

was a strange assurance. Yet I felt inclined to credit it, the more especially as I beheld among the wallowing flames a copy of the Holy Scriptures, the pages of which, instead of being blackened into tinder, only assumed a more dazzling whiteness as the finger marks of human imperfection were purified away. Certain marginal notes and commentaries, it is true, yielded to the intensity of the fiery test, but without detriment to the smallest syllable that had flamed from the pen of inspiration.

Here then at last is a clear truth. Here is where Hawthorne drew the line between the probably justified and the dubiously worthwhile reforms on the one side and the plainly mistaken on the other. But we note that the crucial distinction is to be found in the description of an event witnessed, not in the interpretations offered by either the unwise narrator or the wise guide. Facts "speak for themselves," but what they say is always open to interpretation; and here the interpretation is left up to the reader.

The sketch ends with a passage which should serve as a key to the way we must read all of Hawthorne's writing:

"Poh, poh, my good fellows!" said a dark-complexioned personage, who now joined the group,—his complexion was indeed fearfully dark, and his eyes glowed with a redder light than that of the bonfire; "be not so cast down, my dear friends; you shall see good days yet. There's one thing that these wiseacres have forgotten to throw into the fire, and without which all the rest of the conflagration is just nothing at all; yes, though they had burned the earth itself to a cinder."

"And what may that be?" eagerly demanded the last murderer. "What but the human heart itself?" said the dark-visaged stranger, with a portentous grin. "And, unless they hit upon some method of purifying that foul cavern, forth from it will reissue all the shapes of wrong and misery—the same old shapes or worse ones—which they have taken such a vast deal of trouble to consume to ashes. I have stood by this livelong night and laughed in my sleeve at the whole business. Oh, take my word for it, it will be the old world yet!"

This brief conversation supplied me with a theme for lengthened thought. How sad a truth, if true it were, that man's agelong endeavor for perfection had served only to render him the mockery of the evil principle, from the fatal circumstance of an error at the very root of the matter! The heart, the heart,—there was the little yet boundless sphere wherein existed the original wrong of which the crime and misery of this outward world were merely types. Purify that inward sphere, and the many shapes of evil that haunt the outward, and which now seem almost our only realities, will turn to shadowy phantoms and vanish of their own accord; but if we go no deeper than the intellect, and strive, with merely that feeble instrument, to discern and rectify what is wrong, our whole accomplishment will be a dream, so unsubstantial that it matters little whether the bonfire, which I have so faithfully described, were what we choose to call a real event and a flame that would scorch the finger, or only a phosphoric radiance and a parable of my own brain.

"If we go no deeper than the intellect": if this is "romantic," it is also psychiatric; if it is Christian in its implications about the nature and role of the redemptive process, it is also, I believe most of us will agree, realistic. Here Hawthorne took his stand.

4

Among Hawthorne's notes for stories and sketches he never wrote is one for a piece "on the various kinds of death." Another suggests that "the diary of a coroner" would make a good subject. Still again he planned to write a tale in which "a figure of a gay, laughing, handsome youth, or a young lady, all at once, in a natural, unconcerned way, takes off its face like a mask, and shows the grinning, bare skeleton face beneath." These suggestions never got embodied in tales or sketches, but he did write a piece, not one of his best, on tombstones. And he turned the subject around to study the reverse side in the "elixir of life" theme that he tried repeatedly to treat successfully.

Death haunted Hawthorne, not in quite the same way that it did Poe, in terms of the horror of physical decay, but as it did Samuel Johnson and John Donne, as the most striking evidence of evanescence in a world where all was slipping and sliding into ruin. Hawthorne's love of Johnson was a love primarily of the man, not of the works. As he said in *Our Old Home* in connection with his pilgrimage to Lichfield to visit Johnson's birthplace, he did not remember "ever caring much about any of the stalwart Doctor's grandiloquent productions, except his two stern and masculine poems, 'London,' and 'The Vanity of Human Wishes.'" Like attracted like: he visited the spots where Johnson had walked and touched a balustrade that Johnson's hand must have touched. This act of devotion he could really *feel*. The Gothic cathedral, though surely "the most wonderful work which mortal man has yet achieved," left him uneasy: he could not "elevate" himself to its "spirited height." Yet, very typically, he deplored Johnson's "awful dread of death," which showed, he thought, "how much muddy imperfection was to be cleansed out of him, before he was capable of spiritual existence."

Like Johnson, who clung fiercely to classic stabilities in the face of literary and political revolutions which he understood better than some of his vehemently prejudiced utterances on them might lead us to believe, Hawthorne valued and tried to protect whatever elements of stability he could find in a world where all seemed subject to the Heraclitian flux. Like Johnson, he was a conservative and a traditionalist in this, and not in any lesser, sense. He was thoroughly aware of the danger of clinging to false stabilities, of valuing the form from which the inward meaning has gone. In *Our Old*

Home—which is surely in competition only with Emerson's *English Traits* for the honor of being considered the greatest book ever written by an American on England—his remarks on English architectural and social evidences of antiquity make clear his resolute refusal to confuse the mask with the reality. But the deep longing was there, however much he wavered between patriotic praise of America as the land of the future and attraction to England and Italy, where the past was visibly present. His conservatism was a function of his sense of the pressure of time and death. It went deeper than his politics or his patriotism.

Even in his first, totally unsuccessful and immature published piece of fiction, *Fanshawe*, which he recognized almost immediately as bad and tried to destroy, Hawthorne struck the note which he never ceased for long to sound and which he returned to compulsively in the abortive romances of the last years. Fanshawe is a young scholar-recluse doomed to early death. He is able to sacrifice the girl to his rival without being unusually generous because death is more real, more present to him than life. He is of course a stereotype from the Gothic novels that Hawthorne had been reading. But he is more than that, for with some remodeling, of which the most important change was the dropping of the admiration with which he was portrayed, he served Hawthorne all through his career, sometimes as "villain," sometimes as objective self-portrait, but never again as "hero."

For Hawthorne did not admire morbidity, in himself or in others, though some of his contemporaries must have found him morbid, if we may judge anything from his family's repeated attempts to convince us that he was not. The man who saw the skeleton beneath the skin did not, like Poe and Whitman, enjoy self-dramatization. There is a world of difference between the portrayals of Roderick Usher and Coverdale or Young Goodman Brown, the difference between real morbidity and real health. Hawthorne had too much insight, too much capacity for self-criticism, to enjoy the posture of the young man in love with, or terrified by, death. If he himself felt its presence rather more strongly and frequently than he felt the reality of life, he knew that it was but one of several fundamental perceptions that man could lose sight of only at his peril. When he had occasion to, Hawthorne explained why this was so, as he had the wise guide explain in "Earth's Holocaust": "Death . . . is an idea that cannot easily be dispensed with in any condition between the primal innocence and that other purity and perfection which perchance we are destined to attain after travelling round the full circle."

5

Since Melville first detected the darkness in Hawthorne's work and praised him for saying No in thunder, a great many sensitive readers have found the dark Hawthorne more impressive than the light. But this is not the way Hawthorne wanted to be, these not the meanings he intended.

The problem is a complex one, but in part it may be somewhat simplified by making two distinctions, the first between the artist and the man, the second between two types of meaning in the art. Hawthorne the artist often did his best writing when he wrote not of what he "believed," or wanted to believe, or thought he should believe, but of the "phantoms" that came unsought and "haunted" him. "The Haunted Mind" can give us the clue here. To the "passive sensibility" halfway between sleep and waking the spectral shapes of shame and death appear; when we get fully awake and the conscious mind takes control, they vanish. Much of Hawthorne's best writing comes out of the haunted mind.

But it is not pleasant or comfortable to be visited by such specters. Hawthorne had to live as a man as well as survive as an artist, and it may well be that one of the reasons he gave up writing short fiction after he had established himself as a writer is that so many of his best early tales *had* come from the depths of the mind—by a process he had no wish to repeat. Hawthorne's desire to be a well-adjusted "man of society" and his disinclination to reveal his inner

life in public were in some degree in conflict with his desire
to be an artist.

The distinction between the two types of meaning in his
art takes us into an area somewhat less conjectural. The
distinction I have in mind is that between intended and
achieved meaning. Hawthorne hoped that *The Scarlet Letter*
might have a happy ending, but the hope he expressed in
his first chapter in connection with the rose blooming on the
bush beside the prison—that it might lighten his dark tale—
did not materialize, even for him. He resolved that his next
novel would be a happier one.

The conflict here is only between the hope (or intention?
—how consciously had Hawthorne thought out *The Scarlet
Letter* before writing it?) of the man and the achievement
of the artist. There is no conflict in the novel, of the type
that weakens a work, between intended and achieved meanings. The novel is all of a piece, with a magnificent unity of
meaning that emerges equally from what it says and what
it shows. But *The House of the Seven Gables* is perhaps not
so perfect, for this reason among others. It is almost equally
difficult to suppose that the ending was intended to be
ironic and for the modern reader to take it any other way.
And *The Blithedale Romance* was probably intended to
mean only that utopian communities will not succeed unless
their members have a change of heart and that frosty old
bachelors like Coverdale need girls like Priscilla (or Sophia)
to warm their hearts and give them hope. But what it
actually means as a work of art is not so simply said, or so
hopeful.

We may often, as we have seen, go to the sketches to find
out the meanings Hawthorne *intended* to express in the fiction. In the sketches *belief* is generally in control, the phantoms that haunt the mind mostly absent; and Hawthorne's
belief maintains a nice balance between the light and the
dark. "Earth's Holocaust," for instance, tells us what Hawthorne must have intended to say on his theme of social reform in *Blithedale*. The source of evil is in the heart of man,
not primarily in institutions. The devil laughs when man

supposes that lasting progress toward the good can be brought about by merely external and social changes. But the "dazzling whiteness" of the purified Scripture offers reason for hope that man's efforts are not without guidance and support.

"Sunday at Home" maintains the same kind of balance between the light and the dark, negation and affirmation, that we find in "Earth's Holocaust." But since the language in which Hawthorne defines himself in the sketch as at once gentle skeptic and firm believer seems more dated than the language of the greater sketch, and since the meanings are less solidly embodied in dramatic images, "Sunday at Home" may reveal the balance Hawthorne intended to express better than the greater works do. It is more interesting as a piece of self-revelation than as a work of art.

Hawthorne begins by dissociating himself from the committed believers among his fellow townsmen. While they go to church, he stays at home and peeps at them through the window. He hears the bells but misses the sermon—and feels no loss. He finds aids to faith everywhere, not only in the sound of the bells. Even the sunshine seems to have a special "sabbath" quality about it. This last is no doubt an illusion, but such illusions, he believes, are often "shadows of great truths": "Doubts may flit around me, or seem to close their evil wings, and settle down; but, so long as I imagine that the earth is hallowed, and the light of heaven retains its sanctity, on the Sabbath—while that blessed sunshine lives within me —never can my soul have lost the instinct of its faith. If it have gone astray, it will return again."

The ideas being expressed here may strike us at first as just as archaic as the language. Nineteenth-century "religion of the heart" offers as little appeal today to the neo-orthodox as to the skeptical. But if we look again and note the meaning in the idea of a "hallowed" earth, we may find the notion not simply sentimental. To find the earth itself holy is to find the sources of religious faith in experience. The General Revelation—Nature—will then complement and reinforce the special, unique Revelation of Scripture. The idea is, we are likely to say too quickly, a romantic one; too quickly, because it is not only romantic but Scriptural, as we may see in the Psalms.

The sketch is light in tone and does not pretend to any profundity, but it seems fair to say that Hawthorne is groping here toward a sacramental view of nature. He is no primitivist. He does not suppose that going "back to nature" will cure man's ills or automatically dispel all "evil" doubts. But he does think nature, as the handiwork of God, contains a general revelation of God's purposes and life's meaning, if we will only read it aright.

But not only "nature" in the usual restricted sense common in his period. All experience, all the "not-me," as Emerson called it, including people the world would classify as nonentities, could reveal the wonder and mystery of the divine when properly seen. Over and over again Hawthorne expressed this thought, which we have all tended to pay too little attention to. In "A Virtuoso's Collection," for instance, the narrator is shown a magic glass capable of forming any sort of image. He declines to look at it:

"It is enough if I can picture it within my mind," answered I. "Why should I wish it to be repeated in the mirror? But, indeed, these works of magic have grown wearisome to me. There are so many greater wonders in the world, to those who keep their eyes open and their sight undimmed by custom, that all the delusions of the old sorcerers seem flat and stale."

Religious faith, then, in "Sunday at Home," rests on our ability to experience the world in a certain way. And that way of experiencing is dependent on the imagination. When Hawthorne says "so long as I *imagine* that the earth is hallowed," he does not mean "so long as I *pretend*" or "so long as I *make believe*." He means that religion, like art, is visionary. This is the complement to his acknowledgment, in "Earth's Holocaust" and elsewhere, of the authority of a "purified" Scriptural revelation.

"Sunday at Home" maintains the kind of balance Hawthorne always wanted to keep and affirms the light in a way quite typical of him. It reveals a side of Hawthorne that Melville missed—or was not interested in—when he hailed the nay-sayer.

6

Writing in 1842 to the editor of *Sargent's New Monthly Magazine* about a sketch he hoped to place there, Hawthorne made a statement that, while it applies directly to the piece he had in mind, applies also, less directly and not intentionally, to all his fiction. "Whether it have any interest," he wrote, "must depend entirely on the sort of view taken by the writer, and the mode of execution."

As an artist, Hawthorne knew that in art the question is less *what* than *how*, that in a very important, though probably not absolute and exclusive sense, manner is more important than matter, the "fact" unimportant until transformed by "vision." Though he did not normally choose to exercise his talent or test his vision on trifles, he always insisted that the artist's *way of seeing* his subject was the important thing.

This insistence was, of course, both a permanent truth in art and a reflection of the romantic aesthetic, in which the artist is always peculiarly central. Just as clearly, it reflects an idealistic metaphysic. Not the thing known but the knowing, not matter but mind, is the locus of reality for idealism. Here Hawthorne and Emerson agreed. Whether or not Hawthorne should be called a "transcendentalist" depends on how one uses the term—broadly, to point to all varieties of transcendental philosophy, or narrowly, to designate the Concord New Thought. If broadly, then Plato was one of the first transcendentalists, and perhaps the most important; and Hawthorne was a somewhat uneasy and qualified one too. If narrowly, then Hawthorne was still in many respects a transcendentalist *malgré lui*, but it is important to remember that he thought of himself as not "tinged" with that radicalism.

In any case, however much he may have minimized, or been unaware of, his agreements with his neighbor Emerson,

Hawthorne believed that not only the finished work of art but reality itself depended on "the sort of view taken" by artist or man. The best sort of view would, he thought, be that which provided *distance*—in time or space—so that the raw fact as such could not dominate, so that irrelevant multiplicity would be dimmed and softened by distance to allow the pattern, the meaning, to emerge. Long views were best, just *because* the viewer could not see the details so well.

In view of this conviction, it is not hard to see why the past was so useful to him. The past was not only his South Seas, where romance was, but his relevant truth. We may see the consequences of such an aesthetic credo clearly enough in *The Scarlet Letter*. It is not the fact of adultery itself that engages Hawthorne's interest. Adultery might mean anything or nothing. Let it occur before the novel opens and explore its consequences. In Hawthorne's view it was personal guilt, not sin abstractly defined, that was interesting. This was one of the differences between him and his Puritan ancestors.

Writing the novel, Hawthorne took pains to supply just enough verisimilitude to make it credible. But for the most part he was simply not deeply concerned with merely external reality—except as that reality, perceived as symbol, could take us into the interiors of hearts and minds. That is why writing that must be classified as expository and descriptive (as compared with narrative) bulks so large in the work.

"The Old Apple Dealer" does not have even *The Scarlet Letter*'s minimum of action, but it illuminates what Hawthorne was about in his greatest novel. As a sketch rather than a tale, it is purely descriptive and expository: in it nothing happens except to the speaker, who gains a recognition which alters his point of view. There is even a sense in which the sketch is not "about" anything—or rather, in which it is about "nothing." It is for this reason that any interest it may have must come, as Hawthorne explained to the editor of *Sargent's*, from something other than the intrinsic interest of the subject itself.

For the old apple dealer who will be described is, Hawthorne says in the sketch, a purely negative character, featureless, colorless, inactive, hardly alive apparently. He seems an embodiment of torpor, an instance of nonentity. Such a subject is a challenge to the artist, and Hawthorne opens his sketch with a confession of his difficulty. How could one make interesting, or even imaginatively real, a subject intrinsically colorless and featureless? Hawthorne is not sure he can succeed, but he will try, for the very insignificance of the old man gives him a special kind of interest. "The lover of the moral picturesque may sometimes find what he seeks in a character which is nevertheless of too negative a description to be seized upon and represented to the imaginative vision by word painting."

That Hawthorne had indeed found in the old apple dealer what he sought as a lover of the "moral picturesque" is attested by the success of the sketch. For the subject allows Hawthorne to do several things at once. From one point of view, the sketch is about man's nothingness, and the significant qualification of that nothingness. From another, it is about the difficulties, opportunities, and dangers of the artist.

By the end, the difficulties have become opportunities—though Hawthorne does not claim so much—but the dangers remain. Against them Hawthorne issues a final warning that unites the two "subjects" of the sketch, art and life—issues it to himself most clearly, but to all artists by implication. The language of the ending is explicitly religious, but the aesthetic implications of it are clear enough.

Hawthorne had begun his sketch by telling us that without his subject's being aware of his scrutiny, he has "studied the old apple dealer until he has become a naturalized citizen of my inner world." Since what interests one in this "featureless" man is the perfection of his insignificance, if he is to come alive for readers, the artist will have to give him life. By what James would later call "the alchemy of art" he will be brought into being.

Power so great as this brings with it great danger. Hawthorne's metaphor for art in the sketch is witchcraft. Was art a kind of black magic? If the artist can legitimately claim his literary creations as entirely his own, may he not as man similarly conceive of other people as created—and perhaps controlled—by his knowing them? But if we think of other people as objects to be studied and manipulated, as Chillingworth thought of Dimmesdale and Ethan Brand thought of the subjects of his moral experiment, we shall be totally shut out from the saving realities of life. The fate to which the artist, like the scientist, Hawthorne felt, was peculiarly liable was alienation.

The assumption of Godlike knowledge could destroy artist and man equally. Knowledge brings with it the possibility of control, and the artist must achieve control of his subject by controlling his medium; but he will falsify reality if he omits the element of mystery and assumes that he knows the unknowable. One error, then, to which the artist is peculiarly liable, threatens both artist and man. But to see how Hawthorne prepares us to accept his conclusion, which tests art by life's standards and sees life through the eyes of the artist, we must return to Hawthorne's way of bringing the old apple dealer to life in his pages.

Early in the sketch Hawthorne decides that with so negative a subject the only way to describe him is to use negative comparisons, to tell us what he is *not* like. Perhaps in this way he will be able to get at the paradox of a man who seemed completely inactive and stationary, yet whose immobility was composed of continuous minor, almost undetectable, movements. (So "stationary" a man will never "go ahead," never join in "the world's exulting progress.") Then the inspiration comes: what he is most of all *not* like is the steam engine that roars at intervals through the station where the old man sits so quietly. "I have him now. He and the steam fiend are each other's antipodes . . ."

"I have him now." By using contrast the artist has succeeded in conveying to us what he had almost despaired of conveying, the reality of a person who is almost nothing. But as soon as it is made, the claim seems excessive: Hawthorne does not finally "know" the old man at all, nor do we.

For he has omitted something from his description, something all-important that he has no way of getting at—the soul. In a superficial sense he has succeeded: insofar as the old man is merely viewed, merely scrutinized, he is a torpid machine in perfect contrast to the active, "progressive" machine. But there is a deeper contrast involved than mere activity or lack of it, and here the artist must confess the limits of his art. "Could I read but a tithe of what is written ... [in the old man's "mind and heart"] it would be a volume of deeper and more comprehensive import than all that the wisest mortals have given to the world; for the soundless depths of the human soul and of eternity have an opening through your breast. God be praised . . ."

So in the end Hawthorne makes his last confession: whatever his success in describing the old man behavioristically, he did *not* "have" him when he compared him, the stationary machine, to the steam engine, the active machine. Man cannot be fully known in the way we know a machine. This is the deeper sense in which the old man is the antipodes of the engine. To confuse the two is the ultimate error, for both artist and man.

7

"The Old Apple Dealer" emphasizes the creativity of the artist and the danger such creativity brings with it. The danger is partly that the artist will suppose that he *knows* more than he can possibly know. "Night Sketches: Beneath an Umbrella" dramatizes the danger of the artist's becoming so isolated from reality that his art will be a sort of daydream. Considered together, the two pieces imply that art is both a kind of knowledge—which must never pretend to finality, never lose its sense of mystery—and a kind of dream —which must keep in touch with reality. Art is more like myth than like document, but there are true myths and false myths, and art had better be true.

"Beneath an Umbrella" opens with a long paragraph devoted to describing the pleasures of the unrestricted imagination as it takes one on imaginary travels to exotic lands.

"Pleasant is a rainy winter's day, within doors!" the speaker exclaims at the beginning, going on to explain that the "sombre" condition of the world outside the chamber window makes the exercise of unrestrained fancy all the more delightful by contrast. The warm, well-lighted chamber contains the whole world, so long as imagination is active.

Nevertheless, pleasant as daydreaming is, reality *will* break in: "the rain-drops will occasionally be heard to patter against my window panes . . ." As nightfall approaches, "the visions vanish, and will not appear again at my bidding." Irresponsible dreaming, it would seem, finally ceases to be even pleasurable: "Then, it being nightfall, a gloomy sense of unreality depresses my spirits, and impels me to venture out, before the clock shall strike bedtime, to satisfy myself that the world is not entirely made up of such shadowy materials as have busied me throughout the day. A dreamer may dwell so long among fantasies, that the things without him will seem as unreal as those within."

About to step outside, the speaker pauses to "contrast the warmth and cheerfulness of my deserted fireside with the drear obscurity and chill discomfort" into which he is about to "plunge." The contrast contains, it becomes clear as the sketch goes on, nearly all of Hawthorne's favorite antinomies: the light and the dark; warmth and coldness, in the human heart as well as externally; faith and doubt; even, implicitly, the heart and the head, if we see here the meanings Hawthorne constantly implies elsewhere when he uses hearth and chamber as heart images. The sketch is rich in meaning. It contains, indeed, in epitome nearly all the central issues of Hawthorne's moral and religious thought, and it significantly illuminates a side of his aesthetic thinking it is easy to overlook.

On the doorstep now, the speaker asks the reader to pardon him if he has "a few misgivings." He is, he thinks, entitled to them, our "poor human nature" being what it is. And in view of what is about to be revealed about reality outside the chamber, the world of fact, as contrasted with the world of feeling and dream he is leaving, we find the misgivings justified. For once he is really outside, he finds himself confronted by "a black, impenetrable nothingness, as though heaven and all its lights were blotted from the system of the universe. It is as if Nature were dead . . ."

A "dead" Nature was of course the specter conjured up by nineteenth-century naturalism, the conception of a purposeless, valueless, colorless world, a "charnel house" world, faced by Ishmael at the end of the chapter on the whiteness of the whale in *Moby Dick*. Melville, we have long known, stared in fascinated horror at this vision of an "alien universe," stared at it more fixedly and with greater philosophic rigor than Hawthorne did. But one of the uses of this sketch is to remind us that Hawthorne was very much aware of what Melville was looking at, even though both his way of looking and what he finally saw were different from Melville's.

Here, for instance, the speaker, though at first plunged into a Slough of Despond, soon finds that there are various kinds of lights in what had at first seemed an unbroken darkness. Some of the lights are deceptive or illusory, especially if they are so bright that they seem utterly to dispel the darkness, but others are real and trustworthy. As the speaker continues his "plunge into the night," he discovers a way of distinguishing the false lights from the true: any light which makes men "forget the impenetrable obscurity that hems them in, and that can be dispelled only by radiance from above," is certain to be illusory.

Like Wallace Stevens a century later, who proposed to create a "skeptical music," Hawthorne is talking here at once about art and about life. He is proposing a life test for art's truth, without at all suggesting that the artist should abdicate, leaving "fact" and Nature in control. The internal world, the chamber of the heart where imagination operates freely, the world of dream, is the peculiar realm of the artist, and Hawthorne returns to it after his excursion into an apparently meaningless external reality has served its purpose. But the internal world is embedded in an external world, which it may ignore only at its peril. The imagination must remain responsible, even while it guards its freedom. No mere daydreaming will do. The romancer, Hawthorne wrote of himself elsewhere, need not aim at "a very minute fidelity" to history and nature, but he "sins unpardonably" if he violates "the truth of the human heart."

Irresponsible daydream, responsible imagination, fact without meaning, or even destructive of meaning—all are present and played against each other in this sketch. The center of Hawthorne's interest is, to be sure, elsewhere, in the moral and religious meanings which, with his usual emphasis, he makes explicit at the end. (Having encountered a figure with a lantern that casts its light in a "circular pattern," Hawthorne concludes, "This figure shall supply me with a moral . . . thus we, night wanderers through a stormy and dismal world, if we bear the lamp of Faith, enkindled at a celestial fire, it will surely lead us home to that heaven whence its radiance was borrowed.")

But the aesthetic meanings are here too, implicitly. No overreading is required to see them. It was as a "dreamer," with insufficient experience of the world, Hawthorne says several times elsewhere, that he produced his tales and sketches during his apprentice years. But even while he dreamed and created, he was dissatisfied with dreaming. He wanted to test his dreams against a reality he could not control, to determine their truth. As he has the narrator say in "A Virtuoso's Collection" when he is shown Aladdin's lamp and it is explained that "the man who rubs Aladdin's lamp has but to desire either a palace or a cottage," "I might desire a cottage . . . but I would have it founded on sure and stable truth, not on dreams and fantasies. I have learned to look for the real and the true."

When, in the Preface to *The House of the Seven Gables*, Hawthorne made his famous distinction between the novel and the romance, he was not at all intending to assign "truth" to the novel and mere "fantasy," or escapist dreaming, to the romance. He was distinguishing between "fact" (which the novel deals with) and "truth" (which is the province of the romance), and at the same time suggesting an orientation in which "fact" is external and "truth" internal. So far as he was defending, implicitly, the validity of his own practice as a romancer, he was implying a "mere" before "fact." (He was ambivalent about this, as he so often was on other matters, to be sure. He thought Emerson *too* idealistic, and he greatly admired the "beef and ale" realism of Trollope.)

The romantic artist creates, Hawthorne thought, by transforming fact into symbol, that is, into *meaningful* fact. Facts that he cannot see as meaningful may be disregarded. He is at liberty to manipulate his materials, to shape them freely into meaningful patterns, so long as he does not violate the truth of the human heart. Hawthorne felt that he himself could pursue his desired truth best by a combination of looking within and exercising the kind of imaginative sympathy that had been both his subject and his method in "The Old Apple Dealer." In a very suggestive metaphor in the Preface to *The Snow Image and Other Twice-Told Tales* in 1851, he defined his role as artist as that of "a person, who has been burrowing, to his utmost ability, into the depths of our common nature, for the purposes of psychological romance—and who pursues his researches in that dusky region, as he needs must, as well by the tact of sympathy as by the light of observation . . ."

8

As Hawthorne himself was well aware, evidences of the operation of "the tact of sympathy" and of "the light of observation" were not so nicely balanced in his work as he would have liked them to be. "Blasted allegories" he once called his tales, looking back upon them with a sense of dissatisfaction with his achievement. They were like flowers that had blossomed, he thought, "in too retired a shade"; their tints were pale and ghostly. They would have been more impressive if there had been more evidence in them of "the light of observation." When he wrote them he had known too little of the world.

This desire of Hawthorne's to make his works more realistic suggests another paradox of man and writer. He was a keen and accurate observer of men and events, but he seldom made any direct and extensive use of his observations in his best writing. And not because he did not care to: all of his life, and not simply in his years in England, Hawthorne filled his Notebooks with observations he hoped to use in stories. He made trips in the summers to what were then distant parts of New England, visited unusual spots, noted down the details of much that he saw. But he could usually find no way to use what he had gathered.

The often remarked barrenness of the English Notebooks when compared with the earlier American ones is related to the fact that in Hawthorne's new situation the temptation to observation was very great—or, as Hawthorne thought of it, the opportunities for gathering material were almost unlimited—while the stimulus to the functioning of his unique gift, his special kind of creative imagination, diminished. A chance like this was what he had always longed for as he sat in his little third-floor room in Salem, forced, as he thought, by the scantiness of his experience to fall back on his reading and his imagination for material for stories. There were so many castles and ruins in England, so much to see and inquire into and record. Surely what would come out of this would be a story far finer than those he had spun out of an early experience so limited that he had had little but the visions of the haunted mind to write about. But nothing came out of it, nothing at all in the way of even one completed novel or tale, nothing but frustration. Though he was in many ways an acute self-critic, especially of the limitations of his stories, Hawthorne did not fully understand the nature of his gift. He knew his weaknesses well enough but not his strength.

His sketchlike story "The Canterbury Pilgrims," on which I shall comment later in another connection, will illustrate the point. In 1831 Hawthorne took a trip with his uncle to Canterbury, New Hampshire, to visit a large Shaker community in that town. The existing American Notebooks do not begin until 1837, but C. P. Lathrop's study includes a part of a letter written in 1831 recording Hawthorne's impressions of this visit.

I walked to the Shaker village yesterday [he says], and was shown over the establishment, and dined there with a squire and a doctor, also of the world's people. On my arrival, the first thing I saw was a jolly old Shaker carrying an immense decanter of their superb cider; and as soon as I told him my business, he turned out a tumblerful and gave me. It was as much as a common head could clearly carry. Our dining-room was well furnished, the dinner excellent, and the table attended by a middle-aged Shaker lady, good looking and cheerful . . . This establishment is immensely rich. Their land extends two or three miles along the road, and there are streets of great houses painted yellow and tipt with red . . . On the whole, they lead a good and comfortable life, and, if it were not for their ridiculous ceremonies, a man could not do a wiser thing than to join them. Those whom I conversed with were intelligent, and appeared happy. I spoke to them about becoming a member of their society, but have come to no decision on that point.

We have had a pleasant journey enough . . . I make innumerable acquaintances, and sit down on the doorsteps with judges, generals, and all the potentates of the land, discoursing about the Salem murder [that of Mr. White], the cow-skinning of Isaac Hill, the price of hay, and the value of horse-flesh. The country is very uneven, and your Uncle Sam groans bitterly whenever we come to the foot of a low hill; though this ought to make me groan rather than him, as I have to get out and trudge every one of them.

When we have noted the tone of this letter, and the sorts of things Hawthorne observed and remembered—the cider, the well-furnished dining room, the rich land, the yellow and red houses—and then when we have gone back to "The Canterbury Pilgrims" to see what sort of story he made of this experience, we shall be in a position to begin to understand something of the relation of "experience" and art in Hawthorne, or, better, of the *kinds* of experiences in Hawthorne's life and the creative uses he was able to make of them. "The Canterbury Pilgrims" uses precisely three elements from this whole complex experience, and only two of them were matters of observation. Not mentioned in the letter quoted by Lathrop but undoubtedly impressive to Hawthorne after his five-mile trip from Canterbury village, was the granite watering trough, or "fountain," described in the opening of the tale and still to be seen today, though the spring which kept it full no longer flows into it. Then there was the fact, not only mentioned in the tale but used there symbolically, that the community is at the top of a hill above the spring. Finally, there is in the tale the *idea* of a Shaker settlement as a place of retreat from the world, an ascetic, an "other-worldly" community, a sort of Protestant monastery.

This is all. These are the elements of his visit to Canterbury that Hawthorne was able to use, the residuum amenable to his kind of creative shaping. The symbolic significance he attaches to the Shaker community in the tale—renunciation, asceticism, "other-worldliness"—is quite out of keeping with the impression we receive of *his* impression from his words about the cider, the jolly companions, and the excellent food, all of which tend to suggest that the Shakers have certainly not renounced the good things of the world in any very extreme way. There would seem, in short, to be a rather radical discontinuity between the impressions Hawthorne thought worth recording in his letter and the use made of the experience in the tale. If the suspicion arises that this degree of discontinuity is unusual in Hawthorne— we may think, after all, of the use of his notes on his trip to the Berkshires made in "Ethan Brand"—then we might check "The Canterbury Pilgrims" against the Notebook account of the later visit, with Melville and others, to another Shaker community. Here the divergence between the copious Notebook entry and the tale is even more striking. When toward the end of his life he tried hard to use his English and Italian notebook material in romances—and partially succeeded in *The Marble Faun*—he became involved, as we shall see, in creative problems which he never was able completely to solve. The relation between "experience" and art to be ob-

served in a study of the genesis of "The Canterbury
Pilgrims" was typical of the first two-thirds of Hawthorne's
writing career, a period which saw nearly all of his greatest
work produced.

Sometimes he tried so hard to write an imaginative piece
based on observation that he almost succeeded. His "Buds
and Bird Voices," the only "nature essay" he ever wrote, is a
charming thing of its kind. It records the pleasure he and
Sophia felt when spring came to the Old Manse, records it
with attention to details like the lilac bushes under his study
window and the litter on the lawn as the snow receded—
"Nature is not cleanly, according to our prejudices." It is
completely lacking in the gush and the attitudinizing so
common in "nature appreciations." It is honest, cool,
thoughtful. Yet its very virtues are the measure of its defects:
it is so cool, so detached, so passionless that it is pretty clear
that Hawthorne did not really care very much about the
subject. Put beside one of the many passages from Thoreau's
pen on similar subjects, it suffers greatly from the comparison. It seems to be, as Hawthorne said of all his works in
"Earth's Holocaust," made entirely out of ice. The very
diction is icy in its impersonality and abstractness: the bird
"voices" are never particularized, the "songsters" merely
create a welcome "melody."

Only once does the sketch rise to Hawthorne's best level.
The paragraph beginning "One of the first things that strikes
the attention when the white sheet of winter is withdrawn is
the neglect and disarray that lay hidden beneath it" moves
from the litter beneath the snow to the litter the past has
left in our own springtime, from this actual spring to springtime in Eden when the world was fresh and not littered with
evidences of death and decay. On past and present, fatality
and freedom, death and rebirth Hawthorne could really feel
and write. He is removed from any comparison with
Thoreau here, for he is writing from the center of a very
different sensibility. The conscientious effort to describe is
forgotten, and he is off on the track of meaning. But then
the passage ends and the interest declines. Only in the final

paragraph, when he returns to the experience of spring as "type" or "emblem" of a more general experience, does the essay regain something of the power of that one earlier paragraph.

His strictly autobiographical and journalistic sketches illustrate the same point. Reflections of his early experiences like the "Sketches from Memory" and "My Visit to Niagara" make interesting reading. Their veracity is so transparent, their descriptions of objects and events so patently to be trusted, that one has the sensation of being not in the presence of literature at all but of "sheer fact." And this is perhaps very nearly the case. Hawthorne's imagination was sluggish in the presence of Niagara Falls, as he himself was the first to insist. What distinguishes these descriptive pieces indeed is chiefly the amazing honesty with which they reflect not simply the thing seen—that is not after all so very rare an achievement—but the emotion with which it was seen, the aura and quality and meaning and value—or lack of it—of the seeing. Hawthorne in these pieces achieved nearly a hundred years earlier what Hemingway has said he tried to learn in the twenties: how to be true not simply to the fact but to the feeling about the fact. The other thing that distinguishes these pieces is the style, which was amazingly mature, controlled, and pure even in Hawthorne's earliest published writing.

Here then is the last paradox that I wish to underscore and that we shall have to try to understand: that the man who could observe so keenly, with so much detachment, and more than this, could note his feelings about what he saw with such perfect candor, could not do his best creative work when writing directly of his actual present experience of things and external events. This is a paradox not to be explained away by saying that Hawthorne wrote in the "romantic tradition," for his own tradition, the tradition which he accepted and felt, was compounded partly, to be sure, of the Gothic novel and Scott—himself not lacking in the ability to use the results of observation—but even more of Dante and Spenser and Bunyan and Johnson. Hawthorne, as has often been remarked, was in many respects more a man of the seventeenth and eighteenth centuries than of his own. Bunyan was more of a formative influence on him even than Scott, who was his favorite nineteenth-century writer. Surely "romanticism" did not prevent him from using the material in his Notebooks that he could not use.

If, with "Ethan Brand" as the chief exception, he could ordinarily use only the moral conceits, the snake in the stomach, the laugh which is misplaced and sinister, the man who searches around the world for the unpardonable sin, only to find it at last in himself, we must find some other explanation. Hawthorne's sensibility, I think we shall have to decide, could respond fully only to moral values. When he could see no moral significance in a fact, he could not ordinarily use the fact creatively. It followed that he could do his best work only when he was far enough from his subject so that the aspects of it to which he could not respond were not distracting. This would seem to be one of the chief reasons why his more personal sketches are generally the least satisfactory, and why in his fiction the past was so useful to him.

CHAPTER TWO

THE TALES: *The Use of the Past*

Hawthorne published *Fanshawe* in 1828 and attempted to destroy all copies of it soon afterward, convinced that it was too imperfect a work to deserve circulation. But even before *Fanshawe* was published he had begun to experiment with rather different materials from those which he had attempted unsuccessfully in *Fanshawe* to anneal into art. The two bodies of knowledge and experience that Hawthorne tried to work with when he started the novel were his experience at Bowdoin and the convention of the Gothic romance. But deeper than these in the novel, and the source of those elements which make it possible for us to recognize even in it, conventional claptrap though it mostly is, certain ties with Hawthorne's greatest works, we find such abiding feelings and attitudes as the premonition of early death felt by the hero and the concern with the problem of isolation from normal life. Yet in writing *Fanshawe* Hawthorne could discover no adequate images for his feelings. His emotions, his experiences in college, and the Gothic formula for the novel could not be fused.

Meanwhile, in the earliest of the short tales, probably written in his senior year in college,* Hawthorne was already beginning to find his way. Anticipating by a decade

* See Hubert H. Hoeltje, "Hawthorne as a Senior at Bowdoin," *Essex Institute Historical Collections,* 94:205-228 (July 1958).

Emerson's call in "The American Scholar" for a native literature based on native materials, he turned to the past of his region and his family, and first of all to a subject in the past that had a special importance both for Salem and for Salem's Hathornes.* It had the advantage, moreover, of inviting treatment in the currently fashionable Gothic manner.

Witchcraft is the subject of both of the two earliest surviving tales, "Alice Doane's Appeal" and "The Hollow of the Three Hills." Now that witchcraft was no longer believed in, this "picturesque wrong" of old New England, as Hawthorne calls it, offered a naturally romantic subject to a young writer of sensibility beginning his work in the middle of the 1820's. Poe might prefer to explore the terrors not of Germany but of the soul, but for Hawthorne witchcraft had the advantage of being not just weird and picturesque but historically located on American soil, on his soil indeed and in his own history. Had not his own ancestor persecuted the witches? Here was something that would do in place of those "storied and poetical associations" that he and James both were to deplore the lack of in the American scene. Years later when he came to write the preface to *The Marble Faun* he would complain that "No author, without a trial, can conceive of the difficulty of writing a romance about a country where there is no shadow, no antiquity, no mystery, no picturesque and gloomy wrong, nor anything but a commonplace prosperity, in broad and simple daylight, as is happily the case with my dear native land." But being as yet neither weary nor sophisticated, he was more easily satisfied. Witchcraft in seventeenth century Salem seemed gloomy and picturesque enough.

Witchcraft was history already become legend, fact that had gathered to itself feeling and meaning. The *fact* was important: Hawthorne was never one to be satisfied with mere dreaming. Witches had been persecuted in this very town, by one whose blood flowed in his own veins. Irving

* Hawthorne added the "w" to the family name when he began to publish his stories.

several years before had had to import from Germany most of his Hudson valley folklore, or at least had thought he had to. Hawthorne in Salem found materials for mythopoetic fiction closer at hand.

Anyway, he had a stronger sense of fact than Irving. His feeling for the New England past was more like Whittier's, as Whittier expressed it in his *Legends of New England in Prose and Verse*, published some half-dozen years after Hawthorne began his own explorations of the subject. He knew, years before Whittier expressed it in his preface, just how "rich" New England was in "traditionary lore" that cried out for literary treatment. The trouble with Whittier's treatment of his legends, as Hawthorne implied in his review of Whittier's later *Supernaturalism of New England*, was that it lacked imagination: the "traditionary lore" remained inert, preserved just as Whittier had found it. Hawthorne wanted to treat New England history, but to raise history to poetry and myth. With witchcraft as his subject, it seemed possible to do so.

It was the right subject for him for more personal reasons as well. For Hawthorne it evoked feelings and meanings he would explore over and over again for a lifetime. "The Hollow of the Three Hills" introduces at the very beginning of his career the themes of guilt, isolation, compulsion, and death that would never be dropped. The "hollow basin" between the hills is the first of the heart images that would be constant thereafter. The water of the pool is another image that will recur over and over, in various forms and with various meanings. Later these images would often get explicit interpretation in Hawthorne's comments. Here everything is implicit, yet there can be no mistaking what they "mean," whether Hawthorne was conscious of their meaning yet or not. At its deeper level what happens here happens in the secret places of the heart, where "no mortal could observe" the workings of evil. Years later in *The Marble Faun* Hawthorne would suggest that the darkness of the catacombs of Rome was like the darkness of dream, in which guilt was incurred. Both the hollow in the hills and the labyrinthine underground passages of the catacombs are heart images.

Hawthorne has found himself as an artist by turning to what he calls, in his opening sentence, "those strange old times, when fantastic dreams and madmen's reveries were realized among the actual circumstances of life." "Fantastic," "actual": if we change "actual" to "real" we have the key words in Hawthorne's explanation of his purpose in *The Marble Faun*, with which his career effectively closed. And just as he had trouble dealing with his current experience in *Fanshawe*, so in his last completed romance he had trouble integrating and making meaningful the experiences in Rome that he had written up so painstakingly in the Notebooks. But in "The Hollow of the Three Hills" he has no such difficulty. Contemplating this picturesque and gloomy wrong of the past, he could find ways of making outward and inward reality, history and dream, coalesce and reinforce each other. Here head and heart could come together and his imagination could move freely. Meditating on "those strange old times," he could make sense of his feelings and reveries, project them, scrutinize them, criticize them, in a sense master them. This is why, it seems to me, "The Hollow of the Three Hills" is so much better a work of art than *Fanshawe*.

The past supplied Hawthorne the distance he needed to do his best work, but it did not guarantee it. How even the past could come too close may be seen in "Alice Doane's Appeal." How it could supply just the right amount of distance may be seen in "My Kinsman, Major Molineux," one of the greatest tales in the language. Between the two of them, these stories will reveal all that is really essential about Hawthorne's use of the past.

2

Some years after Hawthorne's death his surviving sister, Elizabeth, recalled that in 1825, the year of his graduation from college, Hawthorne had shown her his first work,

"Seven Tales of My Native Land," later destroyed after it had been refused by publishers, and that among the tales was one called "Alice Doane." Hawthorne himself refers, in the frame of "Alice Doane's Appeal," to the fact that the tale he read to his listeners was one of "a series written years ago," most of which had "fed the flames." If his sister's memory was accurate and this internal reference can be depended upon, the inner tale must indeed be among the first that Hawthorne wrote. What we have in the present "Alice Doane's Appeal," then, is some fragments of an earlier tale incorporated in a sketch written probably not long before its publication in 1833.

If, as has been said, the late romances should have been short stories, it may with equal justice be said of this sketch that it contains material for a novel. It opens with Hawthorne describing a walk he once took with two female companions to Gallows Hill. Impressed by the tragic and terrible history of the spot, where now "everything that should nourish man or beast has been destroyed" by woodwax, as though a physical curse had blasted the place, he decided to try to make his companions as aware of the past of the ground on which they stood as he himself was. Accordingly, he read to them a tale he had once written about murder and witchcraft in seventeenth-century Salem. Certain portions of the tale which he read are quoted in the sketch; the rest is incompletely summarized, with the transitions between the quoted fragments managed by such expressions as "I read on, and . . . described"; "By this fantastic piece of description . . . I intended to throw a ghostly glimmer round the reader"; and "I dare not give the remainder of the scene."

The tale thus partly quoted and partly summarized is highly complex. In main outline it runs like this: Leonard Doane, living alone with his sister since their parents were killed by Indians, and possessed by what Hawthorne calls a "morbid" affection for her, in a jealous rage kills a young stranger who has made love to her. Then he confesses his crime to a wizard, who by his sinister chuckles and smiles makes it clear that he already knows all about it and must indeed, through witchcraft, have had a hand in contriving it. Finally the brother and sister walk to the graveyard and there witness the multitude of the dead rising from their graves and going through the actions habitual to them in life. The fragments of the tale included in the sketch do not justify the emphasis given by the title to Alice, who exists in the fragments merely as a name, while the characters of her brother and his victim are at least lightly sketched in.

Nevertheless, nearly all of Hawthorne's later themes are implicit in the work: the secret guilt, the haunted mind, fate, the universal sin, the curse from the past. Leonard Doane is said to be conscious of a guilt deeper and more terrible even than that for the murder he has committed. He is haunted by an obscure shame and an obscure dread, so that the world seems cold and unreal, frozen and lifeless. He has a feeling of being *compelled* by some nameless force, of being bewitched. There are the strands from which many of Hawthorne's finest and most typical tales were later woven.

But the strands are not woven in this tale, they are loosely tangled. I have the impression as I read the tale that there is a significant revelation of Hawthorne here, that Hawthorne has not achieved the distance between himself and his symbols necessary for a good story, and that the tale is curiously like the late unfinished romances. Two or three scenes are particularly significant. First, there is that part of the interview between Doane and the wizard in which Doane describes the events leading up to his murder of Walter Brome. Brome is, as Randall Stewart has pointed out, an early and rather mechanically contrived sketch of the typical Hawthorne villain—hard, cold, egotistical, mocking, educated "in the cities of the old world." But the significant fact is not his villainy but his likeness, very strongly emphasized, to Doane, who, like that other early morbid protagonist, Fanshawe, is a sympathetic character. He was, Doane finally realizes after he has killed him, the very "counterpart" of Doane himself.

And the likeness is not simply or even chiefly physical. Doane recognizes in his enemy the traits and potentialities, both good and bad, which he knows to exist in himself: "my soul had been conscious of the germ of all the fierce and deep passions, and of all the many varieties of wickedness, which accident had brought to their full maturity in him. Nor will I deny that, in the accursed one, I could see the withered blossom of every virtue, which, by a happier culture, had been made to bring forth fruit in me." If in the other passages describing him Brome is a sort of stage villain, as Professor Stewart says, he is saved from being a mere contrivance by this. In him the adequate symbol is not achieved, but the Hawthorne sensibility may be seen at work.

Hawthorne's sympathy for the darker sides of life, his intuitive knowledge of the springs and conditions of human action, his sense of what E. A. Robinson later expressed as "how little we have to do with what we are," a sense which he made the central theme of "Wakefield," prevented him from sentimentalizing his protagonists as it did from caricaturing his "villains." It was moreover an aspect of his sense of brotherhood, for he saw as a significant part of our shared fate the fact that we are all liable to the influence of conditions beyond our control. Thus though he exercised moral judgment, he condemned actions and attitudes rather than people. Hawthorne's villains are usually convincing precisely because Hawthorne understands the reasons for their villainy and distinguishes between actor and action. Thus Wakefield was not an evil man, Rappaccini loved his daughter, Chillingworth was at first a mild and unworldly scientist who had led a blameless life. We recall that Hawthorne said in "Fancy's Show Box" that "Man must not disclaim his brotherhood, even with the guiltiest, since, though his hand be clean, his heart has surely been polluted by the flitting phantoms of iniquity."

But there is another passage even more revealing than this. Doane continues to tell the wizard his tale. He tells how he met Brome on a lonely road, how he was maddened by

Brome's revelation that Alice loved him, how he struck him down and was terrified by what he had done and horrified by the expression on the dead man's face, where death looked "so life-like and so terrible." Then, as he looked at the man he had just killed, he had a "vision." The passage that follows is so suggestive, so revealing in its combination of power in itself and irrelevance to the rest of the fragments, that it must be quoted entire. If ever a competent psychoanalytic study of Hawthorne is done, surely this will come under consideration.* Remembering the death of Hawthorne's own father when Hawthorne was four, the neuroticism of his mother and his elder sister, his own years of unhappy seclusion, his feeling that he had been "saved" by his marriage, his lifelong restlessness which, after the first year or so, not even his marriage, happy though it was, could cure, one can make what he wishes out of this hallucination in which there is lacking only the explicit transference of the guilt:

I know not what space of time I had thus stood, nor how the vision came. But it seemed to me that the irrevocable years since childhood had rolled back, and a scene, that had long been confused and broken in my memory, arrayed itself with all its first distinctness. Methought I stood a weeping infant by my father's hearth; by the cold and bloodstained hearth where he lay dead. I heard the childish wail of Alice, and my own cry arose with hers, as we beheld the features of our parent, fierce with the strife and distorted with the pain, in which his spirit had passed away. As I gazed, a cold wind whistled by, and waved my father's hair. Immediately I stood again in the lonesome road, no more a sinless child, but a man of blood, whose tears were falling fast

---

* Since this sentence was first published, in the first edition of this book, such a study has been done, though it is limited to the reasons for the failure of the last romances. Dr. John H. Lamont's paper "Hawthorne's Last Novels" won the Deutsch Prize given by the Boston Psychoanalytic Society; in shortened form it was published under the title "Hawthorne's Unfinished Works" in the *Harvard Medical Alumni Bulletin,* 36:12-20 (Summer, 1962). The longer version of the paper makes considerable use of "Alice Doane's Appeal" as evidence in support of the analysis of the failure of the late romances. It is pleasant to receive professional support for the validity of one's unprofessional surmises.

over the face of this dead enemy. But the delusion was not wholly gone; that face still wore a likeness of my father; and because my soul shrank from the fixed glare of the eyes, I bore the body to the lake, and would have buried it there. But before his icy sepulchre was hewn, I heard the voices of two travellers and fled.

Still another scene demands special attention. Like the brother-sister relation and the remarkable vision of the dead father who is also an enemy, it invites reading in psycho-analytic terms. But unlike them it is a persistent explicit symbol in Hawthorne's works. It is a picture of a *frozen* world. In an effort, as he says, to throw a "ghostly glimmer round the reader," Hawthorne describes Salem during an ice storm. Ice glittered everywhere in the cold darkness, and "One looked to behold inhabitants suited to such a town, glittering in icy garments, with motionless features, cold, sparkling eyes, and just sensation enough in their frozen hearts to shiver at each other's presence." Now this description of a frozen world is quite unnecessary for the fragmentary "plot" of the inner tale. It is, in fact, not even satisfactorily linked with the other fragments. Like so much of the material in *Fanshawe*, it is the projection of the experience of an immature writer who has not yet achieved impersonality. As in *Fanshawe*, Hawthorne here "worked in" something he had known just because it had been important to him. In *Fanshawe* it was the countryside around Bowdoin where he had rambled and been comparatively happy; in "Alice Doane's Appeal" it was the Salem in which he had shivered and longed to "open an intercourse with the world."

It is perhaps unnecessary to remark that this scene suggests some of Hawthorne's most persistent themes and character types in one powerful omnibus image that is more expressive than the phantoms in "Fancy's Show Box." Here we are close to the deep channel of the current of Hawthorne's imagination. In *Fanshawe* Hawthorne had portrayed a young man estranged from normal human relations, but in that work the strength of the Gothic tradition which he was uncritically following in an effort to write something salable had tinged his portrait of the scholar-recluse with admiration. In "Alice Doane's Appeal" the isolation is more impersonal: there is less of Gothic tradition and of conscious self-portraiture to complicate and confuse the projection. In later works he was to become more critical of the self-image, picturing isolation as the evil most to be avoided, the frozen heart as the origin of sin.

Finally, there is the climactic scene of the dead arising from their graves as Leonard and Alice Doane watch, certainly entranced, possibly bewitched, compelled in horror and fascination. When brother and sister arrive at the graveyard, graves open and the past inhabitants of the town appear. Our first impression on beginning to read the passage is that *all* the dead are here; at the end, we feel confused: are these all the dead, or merely the damned among the dead? Finally we decide that there is certainly a crucial confusion here, but that it is not in the mind of the reader.

The opening is clear enough:

Each family tomb had given up its inhabitants . . . There was the gray ancestor, the aged mother, and all their descendants . . . There, too, were the children who went prattling to their tomb, and there the maiden who yielded her early beauty to death's embrace . . . old defenders of the infant colony . . . pastors of the church . . . ready to call the congregation to prayer . . . *All, in short, were there; the dead of other generations.* [Italics are mine.]

It comes, then, as a shock to read in the final sentence of the long paragraph that "none but souls accursed were there, and fiends counterfeiting the likeness of departed saints." Why this confusion of the damned with the dead? Is Hawthorne being, for the moment, more Calvinistic than the Puritans themselves and condemning to perdition not only the unregenerate but all the former inhabitants of Salem? The paragraph comes close to being incoherent.

Yet the confusion is significant. In the hideousness, the agony, the torment ascribed to all the dead, a part of Hawthorne's deepest experience is speaking, as it is in the picture of the icy world. Only in the last, anticlimactic, and unconvincing sentence does he criticize and rationalize his feeling. In a vivid page he projects his image; in a sentence he guards himself against the accusation that he has been guilty of an error of judgment. None but the damned were here, but all were damned! Such a statement could not be allowed to stand, must be modified by the addition of "counterfeiting" fiends. In just the same way the strongly felt description of the frozen world had to be called, in the first sentence of the following paragraph, a "fantastic piece of description." Just so the whole tale must be framed in comments calculated to remove it to a safe distance.

There is a sense in which we may say that there is more revelation here than is intended. Hawthorne wanted to open an intercourse with the world, but he had no desire to lay bare his mind and heart to the casual reader. Of course it depends on what we mean by "expression" whether this tale is deeply expressive or not. On the psychological level I think it expresses a great deal. Artistically it expresses only certain blocks of feeling which Hawthorne afterwards learned to build together into unified structures. The later great tales are both more impersonal and finally more expressive, for in them fantasy has been transmuted into art. Not until he had achieved his full artistic stature could he, in "Young Goodman Brown," deal in universal, permanent, and fully meaningful terms with this sense of the omnipresence of guilt.

The sketch ends with a frame paragraph which serves as a key to Hawthorne's use of the past in all his works. The reading of the manuscript story had produced the desired effect; it had made the past come alive for the listeners. "I had reached the seldom trodden places of their hearts, and found the wellspring of their tears." Hawthorne had achieved the effect which any young writer in 1830 who was uncertain of his powers might be expected to desire. But the emphasis in the end is not on what Hawthorne as artist has achieved but on what his re-creation of the past has done and should do. "And now the past had done all it could." And what was that?

It was, as Hawthorne put it, "to assist the imagination in

appealing to the heart." And *the heart* in Hawthorne's usage suggests both emotions and will. Perhaps in most general terms we could say that the vision of the past was intended to arouse the emotions of pity and terror, pity for the unfortunate dead and terror because they were so like ourselves. The emphasis throughout the tale is on the continuity of past and present, and the final sentence reëmphasizes the point which has been made both implicitly and explicitly throughout: "And here, in dark, funereal stone, should rise another monument, sadly commemorative of the errors of an earlier race, and not to be cast down, while the human heart has one infirmity that may result in crime."

The belief in witchcraft, and the judicial murders that it led to, Hawthorne has said in symbol and statement, are fortunately things of the past, but our kinship with the persecutors and the persecuted remains and will remain. We too know the evil passions of the wizard, the emotions of the murderer and the murdered, the fear of the victims. We too tread the streets of an icy and still bewitched village. Death so terrible and so lifelike and life so helpless, so frozen, so deathlike, have appeared before us to be recognized for what they are. The past has illuminated the present and thus has helped to educate the will, which is concerned with the future.

3

On the surface, "My Kinsman, Major Molineux" is a historical tale of the disturbances occasioned by the conflict of crown and people in Massachusetts Colony. Young Robin, looking in the city for his wealthy kinsman, who will, he hopes, help him to rise in the world, finds at last, at the end of a mysteriously frustrating search, that Major Molineux is an unpopular Tory and is indeed being ridden out of town by an angry mob, whose leaders are disguised so that they may not be recognized by the authorities. With no help to be expected from this quarter, Robin is encouraged by a friendly stranger to hope that he may rise in the world without the help of his kinsman.

This historical level of the tale is not merely started and then dropped, as the corresponding level is in some of the later tales. It is carried through from beginning to end with fullness and consistency. The opening paragraph is devoted entirely to establishing the historicity of the story, even mentioning the sources on which Hawthorne has drawn. And after this historical "preface," as Hawthorne calls it, we are never allowed to forget that this is a piece of historical fiction. We see aspects of the clothing and manners of the age; we see the aroused populace preparing its triumph over the aristocracy and laughing at Robin for his innocence; we meet, with Robin, a prostitute in a back street, vivid with laughter and beckoning and scarlet petticoat. When we see the marching crowd, we understand, as at first Robin does not, the nature of the proceedings, the reasons for the disguises, and the political significance of this "democratic" mob action. The whole story may in fact be read as a political fable, as Mrs. Leavis was the first to do. Read this way, the story would seem to express both "the psychological and cultural burdens . . . of national independence" and "a qualified, half-skeptical hope that when the town wakes up from its collective nightmare, tradition will be re-established in accordance with the new dispensation of absolute liberty which the Devil's league had won in the darkness."[*]

But about three pages along in the story we become aware of another set of meanings at work. When Robin is "pursued by an ill-mannered roar of laughter from the barber's shop," we begin to feel the tale taking on the texture of a dream. And this feeling continues and grows, until at last Robin falls asleep and is left wondering how much of the night's adventure he has dreamed and how much experienced waking. Laughter echoes through the tale as a dominant motive, cruel, mocking laughter, like the laughter of the wizard in "Alice Doane," laughter that bewilders and shames Robin as it pursues him through "a succession of crooked and nar-

---

[*] Daniel G. Hoffman, *Form and Fable in American Fiction* (New York, Oxford University Press, 1961), p. 124. Mrs. Leavis's political reading is in the *Sewanee Review*, Spring and Summer issues, 1951.

row streets" in which he becomes "entangled." Caught in a
maze from which there seems no escape, searching for something forever eluding him, innocent yet somehow obscurely
in the wrong, Robin experiences complete frustration before
sleep and the friendly stranger come to his aid and restore
the sanity that had seemed to be slipping away in the ambiguity of evil and innocence.

When Robin meets the mysteriously sinister person with
the twin bulges on his forehead he is simply frightened and
bewildered. But the reader understands the reasons for the
terror: for this leader of the mob, disguised for safety's
sake, is in some sense the Devil himself, complete with
scarcely concealed horns, eyes that glow "like fire in a cave,"
and a complexion appropriate to the lord of sin and death—
"One side of the face blazed an intense red, while the other
was black as midnight . . ." No wonder that "the effect was as
if two individual devils, a fiend of fire and a fiend of darkness, had united themselves to form this infernal visage."

Here then are all the ingredients of an adventure with
good and evil going on beneath the surface of an apparently
simple historical tale. Stretched on the frame of the archetypal journey-search plot, the dream material takes on more
and more connotations as "that evening of ambiguity and
weariness" proceeds. I have called attention to the laughter,
but only a very close reading of the tale will disclose with
what subtle and complex effects it is used. From the first roar
of mirth coming from the barber's shop, to the laughter of all
those in the tavern, "in which the innkeeper's voice might be
distinguished, like the dropping of small stones into a
kettle," to the "drowsy laughter—stealing along the solitary
street," following and shaming Robin after his encounter
with the woman in the scarlet petticoat, to the "sluggish
merriment" of the beadle and the "peal of laughter like the
ringing of silvery bells" of the saucy maid in scarlet, the
laughter builds up in intensity until at the climax the
laughing voices blend in one ugly roar and Robin himself,
bewitched, joins in. "The contagion was spreading among
the multitude, when all at once, it seized upon Robin, and

he sent forth a shout of laughter that echoed through the street,—every man shook his sides, every man emptied his lungs, but Robin's shout was the loudest there." Then, after a pause when there seemed nothing left in the world but that hideous laughter, the mob moved on, "like fiends that throng in mockery around some dead potentate, mighty no more, but majestic still in his agony."

No wonder Robin felt that his mind was "vibrating between fancy and reality." No wonder he was "almost ready to believe that a spell was on him." For the laughter that never ceases throughout the tale, yet never for a moment remains the same or is without realistic justification, is as sinister as the laughter of any of Hawthorne's men of evil in any of his works: as hysterically compulsive as the laughter in "Alice Doane's Appeal," which is heard even in the voice of the wind and seen frozen on the face of the "dead enemy" that "still wore the likeness of my father"; as cold as the smiles of Chillingworth and Rappaccini; as contaminating as the laughter of Westervelt, in which Coverdale, like Robin before him, joins against his will. Hawthorne made much of laughter as a mask of evil in all his works, but nowhere did he use it with more powerful effect and more subtle and far-reaching meaning than here, where it is the dominant image throughout.

But all the while that the laughter is echoing and re-echoing as through the labyrinths of an endless cavern of the mind, other images are contributing their implications to make this the journey of Everyman. Like the "enemy" in "Alice Doane" who is recognized in dream as the father, Major Molineux embodies paternal kinship, here removed to the safer distance of father's cousin. Again, the feeling of compulsion that is given historical justification in "Alice Doane" and "Young Goodman Brown" by being externalized in "witchcraft," is here too, but less disguised, appearing as various levels of consciousness, or "degrees" of dream, from the mere feeling of "strangeness" that first overcomes Robin, to the suspicion that he has been bewitched, to the apparently waking nightmare of his laughter as the procession goes by, to the actual sleep that steals over him at some point undiscoverable either by him or by the reader, leaving in final doubtfulness the question of how much has been "real" and how much "dream," how much externally suggested and how much internally projected.

As the waking and the dream worlds become more and more confused, all distinctions lose their clarity, all certainty slips and slides into ambiguity. Robin's simple, straightforward questions become occasions for obscene mirth. The woman in scarlet, with her face "oval and pretty, her hair dark beneath the little cap," and her eyes bright, speaks so winningly that Robin "could not help doubting whether that sweet voice spoke Gospel truth." A dreadful uncertainty disturbs Robin: "What if the object of his search, which had been so often and so strangely thwarted, were all the time mouldering in his shroud?" Utterly alone despite the many he had met and been unable really to communicate with, Robin longs for the companionship of "any breathing thing" to break his terrible isolation. But when he recalls the happy domestic scenes of his childhood, he feels more desolate than ever, for now "he was excluded from his home."

Bewildered by the shifting appearances of the leader in evil, by the laughter and the shouting, Robin is enlightened by the friendly stranger whom he has encountered beside the church and who asks, "May not a man have several voices, Robin, as well as two complexions?" But the enlightenment does not go deep enough to prepare him for what happens as "the double-faced fellow" fixes his hypnotic gaze on Robin. For when Robin finally sees his kinsman, "large and majestic" but with a face as "pale as death" with the shame of his situation, his knees shake and his hair bristles with the depths of his emotion, compounded, as Hawthorne says, of "pity and terror." A "bewildering excitement began to seize upon his mind," he joins the evil throng in laughter at his kinsman's expense, and his innocence is lost.

" 'Well, Robin, are you dreaming?' inquired the gentleman, laying his hand on the youth's shoulder." Was Goodman Brown dreaming all those terrible revelations of his night in the forest? Does it matter? Truth, as Hawthorne believed, may sometimes come more clearly to the haunted mind hovering between sleep and waking than to the mind fully awake. As all the separate peals of laughter join in the mighty shout that awakens Robin at the point when his dream would have become intolerable, they reveal more about man's image of himself as the destroyer of the father —because he has wished the destruction—a destroyer bathed in guilt yet somehow justified, than do any stories in American literature in the nineteenth century, with the exception perhaps of some of Melville's. And the art here is more perfect, because less compulsive, than Melville usually achieved.

Everything in the story contributes to this perfection of embodiment. I have stressed the dominant image of laughter, but color too plays its part, from the black and red of the projected and personified evil in the leader of the mob to the scarlet seductiveness of the sweet-voiced girl who whispers of sin, from the blackness of the night in which Robin wanders to the "radiance" in the church and "golden light" in which he visualizes his father holding the Scriptures. Shapes, too, and distortions of shape, play their part in the revelation: the stone pillar to which Robin clings, the horseman with the sword, the phantasmagoria of figures half-seen before and behind but unapproachable. "Next he endeavored to define the forms of distant objects, starting away, with almost ghostly indistinctness, just as his eye appeared to grasp them." Two objects most engage his attention toward the end, the church where he takes refuge and the mansion with the pillars and the Gothic window. But nothing, not even the seemingly solid mansion, is what it seems, or remains for long what it was in this world of shifting values: "by turns, the pillars of the balcony lengthened into the tall, bare stems of pines, dwindled down to human figures, settled again into their true shape and size, and then commenced a new succession of changes." Out of such bewildering fluidity could come no hope of finding what he sought, until the words of the friendly stranger suggest that he accept the revealed reality and learn to do without the "kinsman."

On the personal level, the story is one of moral initiation. Robin comes from the country armored in innocence and armed with a club and his native shrewdness. But one does not force one's way through moral initiations with a club nor attain moral maturity by intelligence alone. As for his innocence, it must be lost before maturity can be gained. As Daniel Hoffman has said, this self-reliant "shrewd youth from the backwoods proves to be the Great American Boob, the naïf whose odyssey leads him, all uncomprehending, into the dark center of experience." Like Giovanni in "Rappaccini's Daughter," Robin was unprepared for the ambiguities and complexities of the moral world. His shrewdness, on which Hawthorne keeps up a constant ironic play, is as inadequate to save him as Giovanni's simple empiricism is in the later story. Both young men find evil all around them but fail to understand it and deny that it has any relevance to them. Insofar as the ending of "My Kinsman" is a hopeful one, the hope rests on our having been made to feel that Robin has finally come to understand something of the moral complexity of the world and to accept his own complicity in the universal guilt.

But he has not been unaided in his journey to maturity. Religiously, he has been saved by grace through faith, not by works. When he comes to the church beside which he rests, he thinks, "Perhaps this is the very house I have been seeking," suggesting at once his own unawareness and Hawthorne's awareness of the mythic dimensions of his search for the father figure. Looking inside, he sees "an awful radiance" around the pulpit and one ray of moonlight resting "upon the open page of the great Bible." The narrator speculates, "Had nature, in that deep hour, become a worshipper in the house that man had builded?" Clearly, something is going on here that Robin does not understand. The scene arouses in him only a feeling of loneliness, of the distance he has come from home and family. He thinks of his father, at home, "holding the Scriptures in the golden light that fell from the western clouds . . ." He may be, as he realizes in his dream, "excluded from his home," but he is not excluded from the sources of revelation. The Bible both at home and in the church is illuminated by light from the heavens: nature and Scripture agree, as always in Hawthorne, in suggesting a graceful reason and a reasonable faith. The General Revelation and the Special Revelation are in harmony, though only the kindly stranger seems to understand what they have to say.

The religious implications here are similar to those in "Night Sketches." The moonlit Bible appearing at the end of Robin's evening of ambiguity and weariness is not unlike the light of faith that shone from the tin lantern of the traveler met at the edge of town, where the darkness was deepest. As Hawthorne had said in the sketch that such a light, kindled at the hearth, would surely lead us home, so the sight of the Bible in the church leads Robin home, in dream, to see his father holding a Bible similarly illuminated. By contrast, the reason why the man of adamant cannot profit by reading his Bible is that he tries to read it in a cave, from which the light of nature is excluded. We recall that in "Sunday at Home" Hawthorne had said that properly apprehended, nature is "hallowed." Between a "hallowed" nature and a purified Scripture there could be no real conflict. The light that falls on the Bible in "My Kinsman" falls equally and simultaneously from "heaven" and "the heavens."

But it will not do to elaborate the theological implications too much, for Hawthorne suggests them as delicately as he does the political and the moral meanings. Any criticism is likely to seem heavy-handed when dealing with this story. Hawthorne here has found a way of using the past to discover meanings at once personal and universal. He is writing neither compulsively nor from the top of his head, but from the depths of his sensibility. The tale is as true to New England's past as any of Whittier's legends, even if we define "true" in a quite literal and unimaginative sense, but unlike the tales that Whittier told, it has the reverberations of myth and dream and the past perceived in depth.

4

"My Kinsman, Major Molineux" was published in 1832, a year before the portions of the tale of Alice Doane and her brother that Hawthorne had managed to salvage came into print, a year after the publication of "The Wives of the Dead" and two years after "The Hollow of the Three Hills." It belongs with the stories written during the first half-dozen years of the apprenticeship, and its greatness partially justifies Hawthorne's discouraged remark made in a preface nearly a quarter of a century later that he could see little improvement in the late tales over the early ones. Yet if it is as good as the best that he could produce twenty years later, it is just as clearly in a very different category from what he was producing only a few years before. Hawthorne achieved aesthetic control of his materials in the years between 1825 and about 1831. In the twenty-year period that followed, all of his greatest work was published.

What he learned between 1825 and 1831 can be stated in many ways, in many different terms suggested by different, and valid, approaches. But I suggest that the formulation which most needs to be made at the present stage of Hawthorne criticism and scholarship will take its direction from the visible changes to be studied in Hawthorne's use of the past in his early tales. Hawthorne learned his craft as he learned what to do with the past. His often remarked transformation of the Gothic tale into the moral tale was a transformation of the terms in which he treated his material. The material itself did not change: there are as many Gothic elements in "Young Goodman Brown," published in 1835, as in "The Hollow of the Three Hills," as many in *The Scarlet Letter* and "Ethan Brand" in 1850 as in "Major Molineux," and considerably more in *Blithedale* and *The Marble Faun* and the late unfinished romances than in "Roger Malvin's Burial" or "The Wives of the Dead," both published in 1832. The material, again, does not notably change; the terms change. Hawthorne's "creativeness" lay in his invention, or discovery, of the terms in which he could treat the past in his own way.

To treat it in this way was to master it. To "master" it as an artist it was necessary for Hawthorne to accept it as a man. The whole body of his work implies that we must accept the past, and the guilt it entails, before we can move with maturity into the future. This is one of the meanings into which Hawthorne's naïve young men must always be initiated. It is presumably a meaning that sprang from Hawthorne's personal experience. To investigate it with any authority one would, I should suppose, have to be a psychoanalyst with a knowledge of literary criticism. Literary criticism as such, apart from the psychological perspectives that some critics incorporate into their method, would seem to have no special wisdom on the subject.

Nevertheless, I shall offer a single instance of the kind of difference that might be looked for if one were pursuing the subject psychologically. One difference between "Alice Doane's Appeal" and "My Kinsman" that appears to be significant is that the father figure in the tale that Hawthorne could not finish is single, while in "My Kinsman" he is split up into three figures, the paternal kinsman toward whom Robin entertains mixed feelings, the Devil figure, and the kindly stranger. It may be that this difference has something to do with the fact that the writing in the earlier tale is compulsive and chaotic and in the latter tale firmly controlled and meaningful.

But the subject may be approached philosophically as well as psychologically. To the literary critic this approach offers the advantage of permitting him to talk about the works rather than about their genesis. When it is necessary or desirable to go outside the works, one may still feel that he is on firmer ground. Consciously held beliefs have their psychological dimensions, of course, and may sometimes conflict with feeling, as seems often to have been the case with Hawthorne. But the record of belief, as stated outside the works and implied in the works, is fixed, there to be inter-

preted. At least to the critic not professionally trained in
psychoanalysis, dealing with the subject philosophically
would seem to require dealing with fewer unknowns. Modern literary criticism is deeply indebted to psychoanalysis,
but it need not be specifically psychoanalytic in method.
What then can a more generalized critical approach say
about Hawthorne's use of the past in his work?

One half of Hawthorne the man felt that, as he said in
The Scarlet Letter, "the stern and sad truth" was that "the
breach which guilt has once made into the human soul is
never, in this mortal state, repaired." The other half believed, or believed he believed, that there was freedom as
well as fate in life, so that a fresh start was possible, choice
was real, the past not completely determinative of the future. I suspect that Hawthorne the man never resolved this
crucial uncertainty. But Hawthorne the artist resolved it in
his stories, in many different ways. The hope of "Major
Molineux," the triumph of "Egotism, or the Bosom Serpent,"
the quiet confidence of "Young Goodman Brown," the ambiguity of *The Scarlet Letter*, the somewhat forced confidence of *The House of the Seven Gables*, the questioning
of *The Marble Faun*, are some of Hawthorne's ways of resolving the question of the nature and meaning of the past.

"The past" for Hawthorne extended unbroken through his
own past and the past of his race and place, with no artificial
boundary between what was "his own" and what was
"merely history." For Hawthorne both consciously and unconsciously—as indeed for all of us, though we do not often
recognize it and may even deny it—the past was living in
him, so that any boundary at all would be artificial. Hence
the earliest tales in which he achieved mastery of his art
are both "personal"—in that they objectify aspects of his
personal past which we are likely today to read in Freudian
terms—and "historical"—in that they treat old New England. A useful approach to the problem of what Hawthorne
learned between 1825 and 1831 is suggested by saying that
he found in the past of New England a way of projecting
and objectifying the concerns, the tensions, and the deep

feelings that haunted him from the personal past of his childhood.

In "Alice Doane's Appeal" he had tried to bring to expression some of the feelings of "our secret souls." He had "rolled back," as he said, the "irrevocable years since childhood" and written compulsively of fantasies that could not be criticized in that form. The "blood-stained hearth," the guilt of the protagonist, "no more a sinless child, but a man of blood," the dead enemy-father who was yet also obscurely the self, the "unutterable crime, perpetrated . . . in madness or a dream," these images had to be further impersonalized before they could be treated rationally and artfully. (Not that art is necessarily perfectly rational, but in all but "automatic writing" and certain types of surrealism, the conscious mind operates, I assume, as critic and judge.) In "Major Molineux" and in many stories written in the same period and later, he achieved the necessary distance, found the way to the necessary impersonality, discovered the terms which enabled him to treat the themes that he had to treat if he was to do his best work. For Hawthorne as for James—and perhaps for any artist in proportion to his greatness—his art was his life and his life his art.

That he could not ordinarily, despite lifelong efforts to do so, treat "contemporary" experience successfully does not contradict this. For Hawthorne, as for all of us, "experience" existed at different levels and had different degrees of relevance and urgency. When company called, Hawthorne was often absent, even when he did not disappear out the back door on their arrival. It is certainly no exaggeration, though it may invite misinterpretation, to say that Hawthorne did not understand his current external experience as he understood his experience, through reading and memory and thought, of the past. "Sublime and beautiful facts," Hawthorne wrote in his volume of English sketches entitled *Our Old Home*—and he might have said all the facts in which he was most interested as an artist, had not the context demanded the narrowed statement—"sublime and beautiful facts are best understood when etherealized by distance."

Distance was necessary that facts might be steeped long in a "powerful menstruum of thought."

The past provided the distance necessary if the imagination was to work with the freedom it needed, but it did not leave the imagination wholly free; it did not license unrestrained fancy. If it offered freedom, it also offered the discipline of fact. The frequency with which Hawthorne prefaced his tales with remarks on their historical background, insisting that the reader grant their historicity before exploring, with him, their imaginative dimensions, is significant. If no factual basis were at hand he would even make one up out of unrelated bits of history, as he did in the preface to *The Scarlet Letter*. But generally he worked close to his documents. Sometimes indeed he even did what we should call "research," as he seems also to have done for *The Scarlet Letter*, so that, if there were no Hester to be found in history, at least the details of the setting might be authentic.

But the distance provided by history was even more important to him than the restraint it offered in the way of fact. Distance was perspective, and only from perspective could meaning emerge in an idealistic metaphysic. If perceived reality is a function of the perceiving process, then the position of the perceiver—his "perspective," his point of view—is all-important. Hawthorne was of course no systematic philosopher, and he had not thought this all out clearly. But a passage in the French and Italian Note-Books for 1859 suggests the degree to which he was conscious of the principles underlying both his art and his faith.

He is thinking here in moral and religious terms, but it would take a minimum of translation to make the aesthetic relevance of the experience clear. The family had journeyed to Geneva through mountains that now lay at some distance. Hawthorne looks back at them, remembering how they appeared when he was surrounded by them:

Some of these mountains, that looked at no such mighty distance, were at least forty or fifty miles off, and appeared as if they were near neighbors and friends of other mountains, from which they were really still farther removed. The relations into which distant points are brought, in a view of mountain scenery, symbolize the truth, which we can never judge within our partial scope of vision, of the relations which we bear to our fellow-creatures and human circumstances. These mighty mountains think that they have nothing to do with one another, each seems itself its own centre, and existing for itself alone; and yet, to an eye that can take them all in, they are evidently portions of one grand and beautiful idea, which could not be consummated without the lowest and the loftiest of them. I do not express this satisfactorily, but have a genuine meaning in it nevertheless.

He did indeed have a "genuine meaning," and not only a genuine one but a persistent and fundamental one. There is a sense in which it may be said that both his thinking and his art depended upon this idea throughout his life. Pondering it, we are in a better position to understand why he usually wrote more successfully of the past than of the present.

It is in no way surprising therefore that the voluminous notes intended to provide authentic backgrounds for projected romances which fill his English and Italian journals were useless to him, as he suspected with increasing distinctness that they would be even while he gathered them and as proved to be the fact when he returned to America and tried to use them. "I once hoped, indeed," he wrote in 1863 in the preface to *Our Old Home*, to which he had turned after realizing that it would be impossible for him ever to complete his English romance,

that so slight a volume would not be all that I might write. These and other sketches, with which in a somewhat rougher form than I have given them here, my journal was copiously filled, were intended for the side-scenes and backgrounds and exterior adornment of a work of fiction of which the plan had imperfectly developed itself in my mind, and into which I ambitiously proposed to convey more of various modes of truth than I could have grasped by a direct effort. Of course, I should not mention this abortive project, only that it has been utterly thrown aside and will never now be accomplished. The Present, the Immediate, the Actual, has proved too potent for me. It takes away not only my scanty faculty, but even my desire for imaginative composition . . .

Though he was probably thinking in part of the Civil War and other current distractions when he blamed the Present for his failure of creative imagination, the facts of his whole career as a writer justify our assuming a far broader referent for "the Present, the Immediate, the Actual": not just the Civil War, but any experience present, immediate and actual had generally, in greater or less degree, proved "too potent" for him. He should have known when he was compiling them, as he realized later, what must happen to his notes before he could use them creatively. When he had attempted earlier to use current material in his romance about Brook Farm, the place had turned out to be not Brook Farm at all but a false Paradise, a delusive Arcadia, or the mythical Happy Valley of Imlac and Rasselas. Hawthorne's contemplation of his most recent external—and superficial—experience usually produced sketches, not tales; and when it was used in tales and romances it almost never produced his best and most typical work.

So we may say that when Hawthorne learned how to use the past, he learned how to treat the present and the future in the only way possible to him. Seeing the reflections mirrored in the well of the past, he could, in the fullest sense, understand them, and so deal with them.

CHAPTER THREE

THE TALES: *The Discovery of Meaning*

We have no proper term for the type of story Hawthorne created. The best of his tales are not quite what we usually mean by allegories, though some of them come rather close to fitting the ordinary meaning of that term. Neither are they symbolic stories of the type exemplified by "Flowering Judas," though again a few of them approach quite closely the sort of thing Miss Porter did in her famous story. At their most typical they lack something of the "illusion of reality" that characterizes the stories of Kafka, though they resemble them in the possibilities for allegorical interpretation they contain. Most obviously of all, they are not fiction of the type that fills the popular magazines today—or any day—with imaginary people and events designed to take our minds off our problems, help us to escape our boredom and our pain, or amuse us with "harmless" daydreams; in short, fiction with only one controlled level of meaning, and that the simplest, based on the most primitive of the many appeals fiction makes to us. Most of Hawthorne's best tales exist, like the stories of Conrad Aiken, in a realm somewhere between symbolism and allegory, as those terms generally are used today. If we are to arrive at a more precise statement than this, we shall have to analyze Hawthorne's usual procedure, and then look closely at several of his stories.

One of the most valuable of Hawthorne's commentators,

F. O. Matthiessen, put the matter in a way that may be taken to represent the usual opinion. Hawthorne started, he tells us, "with a dominant moral idea, for which [the scene he was describing], like Spenser's, was to be an illustration." Thus Pearl, in *The Scarlet Letter*, should be studied "as the purest type of Spenserian characterization, which starts with abstract qualities and hunts for their proper embodiment."* Hawthorne, according to this way of thinking, was an allegorist and his tales are allegories.

But there are several reasons why such a classification is inadequate. In the first place, Hawthorne's practice in his tales is not always the same kind of practice. "The Great Carbuncle" may profitably be studied in terms of Spenserian allegory, but "The Wives of the Dead" bears no discernible relation to that traditional form. In between these two extremes lies Hawthorne's normal practice. Though Hawthorne's debt to Spenser was very great, we should not fall into the error of trying to make a discovered relationship account for too much.

In the second place, it is significant that Matthiessen selected Pearl to illustrate Hawthorne's dependence on the Spenserian mode of creation in *The Scarlet Letter*, for though she is not his only illustration, she is certainly his best. Pearl has always struck readers as one-dimensional. Drawn "from life," from Hawthorne's memories of his daughter Una as she had been a few years before, Pearl is still for most readers the least convincing character in the book. Compared with his failure with her, Hawthorne's too early and too obvious revelation of Chillingworth's villainy is a minor flaw. But is Hester Spenserian in conception? Or Dimmesdale? Or even Chillingworth as initially presented, before he becomes a "fiend"?

The same questions may be raised about the other novels. Phoebe in *The House of the Seven Gables* is perhaps only a "type" of maidenly health and purity, but are Hepzibah and Clifford essentially Spenserian, or allegorical, in con-

* *American Renaissance* (New York: Oxford University Press, 1941), pp. 301, 278.

ception? Hilda in *The Marble Faun* is an "emblematic" character in something like the Spenserian mode, but is Miriam? Hawthorne's range of character types is as wide as his range of stories. His practice cannot be so simply categorized. What we must recognize is that he wrote different kinds of stories, and created different kinds of characters, often in the same story. Recognizing the range of variation, we may then try to decide what is the typical or normal procedure.

The way Hawthorne normally proceeded in his writing may be suggested in a preliminary sort of way by the phrase, *thinking in terms of image and situation, character and action.* Adding "feeling" after "thinking," with a hyphen between the two, would make the phrase more accurately suggestive, but only at the cost of complicating an already complicated matter. Short of adding some such descriptive word as "feeling," I do not see how the awkwardness of the phrase may be kept within bounds without increasing the element of inaccuracy. The tales are not *thoughts fictionized,* but *thinking:* for *thoughts fictionized,* though perhaps a less cumbersome phrase, implies that the thought preexists in the absence of the tale, which later is "made up" to express it; or that a "thought" may be detached from the tale and leave nothing essential behind, as we take the meat from a nut after cracking the shell.

Neither of these latter ways of conceiving Hawthorne's tales is finally rewarding. For the ideas for stories which are so frequent in the Notebooks are not the "meanings" of the tales any more than the morals that Hawthorne sometimes appended are. They are simply the starting points, in situation, image, or concept, the opportunities, sometimes developed, sometimes not, for tales that had to get written for the "meanings" to exist. "A snake taken into a man's stomach and nourished there from fifteen years to thirty-five, tormenting him most horribly. A type of envy or some other evil passion." This is the Notebook idea which later developed into "Egotism, or the Bosom Serpent." But "Egotism" does not mean that Roderick Elliston has a snake in his stomach, nor is its meaning equivalent to "envy or some other evil passion," of which the snake, or the snake in the stomach, is a "type." What it does mean we can find out only by reading the story.

But if a change of "thinking" to "thoughts" would tend to imply an abstract and static and inorganic set of meanings, and particularly that the idea exists complete before the tale expresses it, neither will it do to say something like *tales with emphatic themes*. For this suggests that the tale preëxists and the theme is an additional, perhaps an optional, attachment, like the frosting that can be added only after the cake is baked. Hawthorne's tales were not conceived first and then found to have meaning later. Rather, they grew out of the work his mind, consciously and unconsciously, did on material which only he would have found promising.

Of these two approaches to an understanding of Hawthorne's procedure in his tales, the temptation is greater, perhaps, because of the existence of the suggestions for stories in the Notebooks, to say that he found his moral first and invented his story later to fit it. And if this description is used only to point the contrast between Hawthorne's way of working and that of many other writers of fiction, the distortion involved is probably justifiable. For Hawthorne's stories were relatively abstract in conception, just as they lend themselves with relative ease often to paraphrase in abstract terms. But one must not overlook the word "relatively" in this proposition. It is truer to say that Hawthorne's stories are fictional thinking—or processes of insight conceived and structured in narrative terms—than it is to say that the narratives *originate* in thoughts, ideas, or insights. The Notebooks have misled many into conceiving of the tales as though they were clothes draped loosely over already created skeletons of abstract thought. But of all the Notebooks jottings that Hawthorne used in existing stories, I know of none that can serve as an even approximately adequate statement of the meaning of the story to which it finally led, or in which it got embodied.

If this were not so, we should be able to measure the conceptual value of Hawthorne's tales by applying a yardstick—subjective, presumably—to the value of his "philosophy," his ideas as he expressed them outside his tales, for example in his Notebooks. But when we do so, we find—by my yardstick, at least, and it is applied sympathetically—that Hawthorne's thinking outside his tales is much less impressive than his thinking in his tales. It is, to be sure, instinct with the realism that made him unable to read Emerson or Emerson him. It is attractive in the quality of absolute honesty that shines through it, and the shrewdness that so often deflated the pompous and redefined the stereotyped. But still I suppose the most sympathetic commentator would not claim for Hawthorne a place among the world's—or even America's—great philosophers or "thinkers." Yet his tales are generally held to be among America's great short stories, and their greatness has been conceived by nearly all critics to be a product of their depth and complexity of meaning.

One way of resolving this seeming paradox is to recall Hawthorne's words, already quoted, on what he had hoped to accomplish in his English romance. In his fiction, he said, he could apprehend "more of various modes of truth" than he could grasp by "direct effort." What we have to recognize is that in some sense the story *is* the meaning, and the meaning the story. Sometimes this is very clear, indeed almost obvious when we stop to think of it. "Wakefield," for example, which is in some of the most important respects typical of Hawthorne's procedure (though a failure of development, a failure of creative energy, keeps it from being one of the great tales) begins like this:

In some old magazine or newspaper I recollect a story, told as truth, of a man—let us call him Wakefield—who absented himself for a long time from his wife. The fact, thus abstractly stated, is not very uncommon, nor—without a proper distinction of circumstances—to be condemned either as naughty or nonsensical.

The fact "thus abstractly stated" is not meaningful, though it is the starting point of the story, the stimulus, in contact with Hawthorne's sensibility, to meaning. But the tale that Hawthorne developed from it has all kinds of meanings, including some that Hawthorne tried to state for us. It means, among other things, what Hawthorne said abstractly in his final sentences, though we shall not fully understand these words unless we know their context:

Amid the seeming confusion of our mysterious world, individuals are so nicely adjusted to a system, and systems to one another and to a whole, that, by stepping aside for a moment, a man exposes himself to a fearful risk of losing his place forever. Like Wakefield, he may become, as it were, the Outcast of the Universe.

It means, then, that we must not break what Hawthorne called in "Ethan Brand" the "magnetic chain" of organic relationships that bind us to society. Or it means that individualistic isolation, complete independence if you will, is possible only at the price of death. Or it means that our lives are only partially under our control, so that we are not the masters of our fate, the captains of our souls. Hawthorne interrupts his tale at one point to express his wish that he might "exemplify how an influence beyond our control lays its strong hand on every deed which we do, and weaves its consequences into an iron tissue of necessity." The tale "means" all these things, and more.

And these meanings which it has are discovered, as Hawthorne makes clear in his introductory paragraphs, in the course and structure of the tale itself—discovered by Hawthorne as well as by the reader. Hawthorne's own words should be quoted at this point:

This outline is all that I remember. But the incident, though of the purest originality, unexampled, and probably never to be repeated, is one, I think, which appeals to the generous sympathies of mankind. We know, each for himself, that none of us would perpetrate such a folly, yet feel as if some other might. To my own contemplations, at least, it has often recurred, always exciting wonder, but with a sense that the story must be true, and a conception of its hero's character. Whenever any subject so forcibly affects the mind, time is well spent in thinking of it. If the reader choose, let him do his own meditation; or if he prefer to ramble with me through the twenty years of Wakefield's vagary, I bid him welcome; trusting that there will be a pervading spirit and a moral, even should we fail to find them, done up neatly, and condensed into the final sentence. Thought has always its efficacy, and every striking incident its moral.

Nature then is a symbolic language: the incident has its moral meaning, if only we have the wit to see it. This would imply that the proper order of the artist's creation is not, first, abstraction, then the concrete embodiment (made up to illustrate it); but the "incident," then the artist's discernment of its meaning. But Hawthorne also knew that nature, the incident, had to be *seen* in a certain way before it would yield its meaning: thought has its efficacy only when the imagination properly fulfills its role. And at least once Hawthorne suggested that we should not think of *any* temporal order in the artistic process at all but rather of the simultaneous and inseparable co-existence of fact and meaning. In "The Antique Ring" Hawthorne's story-teller is asked, "What thought did you embody in the ring?" Both the manner of the reply and the reply itself suggest the naïveté of the question: "You know that I can never separate the idea from the symbol in which it manifests itself."

Of course Hawthorne thought it quite proper for him to try to state abstractly, if he could, the meanings his incidents had conveyed to him. Sometimes he tried, and confessed failure. In other stories he did not try. In "The Canterbury Pilgrims" and "Roger Malvin's Burial" he made no attempt to abstract and condense the moral "neatly" in the final sentences, but they are stories in which everything is dominated by what we may call their "moral meaning." They will serve better than some of the more famous tales —partly because we can approach them with fewer preconceptions—to illustrate the kind of "efficacy" which "thought" has in Hawthorne, and the way in which the "moral" is discovered through the "incident."

2

"The Canterbury Pilgrims" is one of the less well-known tales, and there is a sense in which its obscurity is justified: it is surely not among the greatest tales by any standard. It is quite abstract, its characters are types, there is almost no action in it, and when the characters speak they tend to speak in artificial "set speeches." It is more like a pageant than a story, a *tableau vivant* with actors posed in emblematic attitudes against a picturesque and expressive backdrop. Yet all this does not mean that the tale is without value, however far it may be from the sort of thing we naturally tend to like today.

We have seen something of the nature of Hawthorne's actual experience in his first visit to a Shaker village. But when he came to write the tale prompted by the visit, he ignored the cider and the good food and jolly company: these did not fit into any meaning that he could grasp. He began instead with the settlement as viewed from a distance: from a distance great enough to enable him to see its whole outline, its significance, its meaning. He began with the *Gestalt* of the Canterbury Shakers.

Reading the accounts of the actual visit and then reading the story, it is easy enough to see the kinds of questions prompted by this *Gestalt*. The Shaker community was a form of Protestant monasticism. Though it might serve excellent food, it was essentially ascetic in its orientation, as was evidenced by its vow of chastity. It believed in giving up the world. Was its otherworldly ideal of renunciation justified by the nature of experience? Quite apart from theological problems, was the possibility of fulfillment in life so slight as to justify, on what we may call pragmatic grounds, the Shaker preference for security, both here and hereafter, at the price of experience?

But before these questions could be meaningfully asked they had to be conceived in dramatic terms. If a young Shaker couple leaving the establishment to marry and try life together in "the world" were to meet a group of the world's embittered failures on their way into this retreat, what would the effect be on the lovers? Would this sight of the frustration and disillusionment that come with experience make them want to turn back? What should their attitude be toward the suffering and evil in the world? So the story which grew out of Hawthorne's pleasant visit with the Shakers has nothing to do with any of the details he recorded in his letter. It is built instead around the dramatic meeting on a moonlit night of two groups traveling together in opposite directions, Josiah and Miriam leaving the community and a group of converts on their way in to this refuge from the world. The painting of this emblematic scene, and the stories told by the incoming travelers, make up the substance of the tale. Almost the only action is the arrival and final departure of the two groups, and the characters are too lightly sketched in to develop as characters. But the theme develops, and meanings that arise from and are discovered in the technique are many and far from obvious.

The first sentence introduces a note of ironic blending of romance and reality, wish and fact, which is to be one of the main motives. "The summer moon, which shines in so many a tale, was beaming over a broad extent of uneven country." The summer moon, romance, is immediately qualified by the memory of the false moonshine of the popular romantic tale. The statement without the qualification would be, as Hawthorne recognizes, flat and banal: "The summer moon . . . beams." But the qualification is not an apology for an inept sentence, for the rest of the tale develops, qualifies, and enlarges the tension developed by the incongruity of the statement and modifier of the opening sentence: dreams exist (though they are moonshine without the facts) and facts exist (though they do not fully exist without the dreams that complete them and give them meaning). And the relation between them is not disjunctive but inclusive. Or again, from a different point of view, the first sentence tells us that this tale will be written within the popular romantic tradition, but its attitudes will be partly antiromantic. All the commonplaces of romantic fiction will be here—summer moonlight, a rural setting full of "the beauty of nature," a modest young couple very much in love, a final decision to dare all for love—yet used with a difference.

The opening statement is expanded, the ironical qualification dropped, in the remainder of the first paragraph. Hawthorne describes, in a more intimate and personal tone than he ordinarily adopted, a spring that has been made to flow into a hand-hewn granite trough placed beside the road leading up the hill to the Shaker settlement. Now the spring in its primary aspect, the sparkling water itself, is natural and beautiful; it reinforces the primary, or unqualified, meaning of the moon symbol. We have then a moon–water combination, of which the paraphrasable content might perhaps be inadequately stated as *the beauty, innocence, and purity of nature*; or, simply, *romance*. (When the romantic poet takes a drink of the water, he is moved to compose an "effusion.") But this meaning, already challenged by the irony attached to "moon," and later to be further modified by being associated with the complementary beauty, innocence, and purity of ascetic renunciation, is immediately qualified by being juxtaposed with the value achieved not by nature but by man, particularly by man as artist. The narrator is pleased to note that here nature has been modified by man's hand in the shaping of the granite receptacle for the water: "The work of neat hands and considerate art was visible about this blessed fountain."

The paragraph ends on what appears to be a note of whimsy. The spring seemed not to overflow, yet the water bubbled up into the basin continuously. Could this mean that nature could not afford "to lavish so pure a liquid, as she does the waters of all meaner fountains"? Here we have, I think, the key to the chief symbolic significance of the "fountain," as Hawthorne calls it—a man-made arrangement for containing the water provided by nature in the form of a spring—which is so strongly emphasized that it would be surprising to find it not wholly functional. Here "nature" and "art" are nicely balanced, held in equilibrium, like the water which maintained its constant level. (A glance at the now dry granite basin today will show how the Shakers contrived this: the intake and outlet pipes were close together at the bottom of the "fountain," where they would be difficult to see.) If we keep in mind the distinction thus suggested between the natural and the artful or human, we shall see at the end of the story that it parallels other contrasts set up and explored. And if we remember the unqualified approval with which Hawthorne describes this "blessed fountain" which so nicely unites such contrasts as nature and art and the eternal and the temporal, achieving what seems if not a miraculous unity at least an ideal equilibrium, we shall, I think, come to realize that the paragraph Hawthorne devotes to this spring or fountain is not a wasteful bit of added "nature description."

Now two lovers come down the road from the buildings on the hill. They stop at the spring to drink and rest before continuing their "flight"—for, Shakers from early childhood, they dare not face the elders of the community, avow their "carnal" passion, and announce their intention of leaving, even though Shaker rules did not forbid a member's leaving at any time. Though they are breaking no law, they have feelings of guilt and anxiety mingled with their yearning for each other and their dreams of happiness together. And not only guilt and anxiety but reluctance to leave a familiar and dear spot—"and this may be the last time we shall ever taste of this water." (Before his own marriage, Hawthorne sometimes wondered whether love could survive marriage.) Their decision has already been a difficult one, and its reaffirmation will be made yet more difficult.

For now some travelers come toiling up the road and stop at the spring to rest. Worn and dirty from their journey afoot and with an as yet mysterious gloom in their aspect, they are depressing even before they begin to talk. Here is an inauspicious beginning for an elopement. And the tales they tell are calculated to disillusion the young couple if anything could. They confront romance with the hard facts of life.

The first of the travelers to tell his story is a disappointed poet. " 'In me,' said he, with a certain majesty of utterance,—

'in me, you behold a poet.'" Now the burden of the poet's story is that the world does not reward true merit, that the bad and the vulgar in art are more widely praised than the fine; that, in short, the world is gross, practical, and insensitive: it positively prefers the second-rate. We remember Hawthorne's impatience with that "damned mob of scribbling women" who, in his day, were so popular, while his own earlier works went comparatively unread. We think of the aging Melville collecting customs duties and of Poe in his barren cottage and we think we know what Hawthorne means: genius must starve in a garret or enter a Shaker community while mediocrity rules the day.

But such a reading is closer to being the opposite of the meaning intended than to representing it. The poet speaks "with a certain majesty," and there is much truth in what he says of the public; but as he continues to talk, his words make him a ridiculous as well as a pitiable character. He is a caricature of a romantic poet. Conceiving himself as a brave, lofty, and suffering soul, he wears his hair long and arranged to emphasize the height of his forehead. With "an intelligent eye" and striking features, he enjoys his role of nobility in exile, genius unappreciated. He revels in self-pity. He dwells upon the loftiness of his gifts—he is a poet of the soul, not a mere versifier—and upon his suffering. A *poseur* enjoying martyrdom, he is sensitive to the moonlight, likes the word "ethereal," and, after drinking the water, composes "effusions." The one prominent item in the setting to which he does not respond is the one that Hawthorne has most emphasized, the fountain, the elaborately contrived container of nature's pure water. He is a type for which Hawthorne evidently had little sympathy. Little—but some; for though it is strikingly apparent that the poet is treated with less sympathy than the other pilgrims receive, it is also apparent that he is more like Hawthorne himself than are the others—a merchant, a farmer, and a farmer's wife—for he too is, or wants to be, "an artist of the beautiful." Hawthorne's most cutting irony is reserved for the type most like himself— the dreamer, the artist, the seeker after significance, the writer who believes he has great gifts, but who is unappreciated by the public.

The second refugee from the world's ills to tell his story is a merchant who has failed in business and lost his fortune. Too old and too discouraged to begin again, he joins the poet in seeking haven from a world which has frustrated his ambitions. Like the poet, too, he is vain. Like the poet, finally, he is embittered by experience. But he is unlike the poet in all other respects. The poet was a misfit from the beginning. The merchant is practical and worldly; he has always accepted the world's standards and lived by them. By them he became a great success, and by them he now knows himself a failure. There was a touch of nobility, however pitiable, in the vain and deluded poet; there is nothing but ignobility in the merchant. "A small man, of quick and unquiet gestures, about fifty years old, with a narrow forehead, all wrinkled and drawn together," he hopes to find a place for himself in the Shaker community by becoming their business manager and increasing their wealth through shrewd management. The only questions he addresses to the lovers concern the extent of the community's holdings.

Yet the merchant is treated with less irony than the poet. Why? Partly, perhaps, as I have already suggested, because Hawthorne's strongest irony was usually reserved for himself. But for another reason too, certainly: as the merchant is less vain than the poet, less consumed and dominated by pride, so he is more nearly "true." With lower standards and potentialities than those of the poet, he is yet less of the dissimulator, less the fraud. The tone of the passage that presents him is serious and unambiguous for the most part. The only notes of irony are reserved for the emphasis on his worldly motives for entering an ascetic religious society and on the absurd pride that coexists with evident failure as he comforts himself and attempts to impress others with the memory of his former great riches.

Since Josiah and Miriam have no wish either to be poets or to gain riches, they are not discouraged by these reports of the vicissitudes to which those who live "in the world's way" are liable:

> "I will not turn back for this," replied Josiah, calmly, "any more than for the advice of the varse-maker, between whom and thee, friend, I see a sort of likeness, though I can't justly say where it lies."

But the confidence which has not yet been shaken is about to receive a jolt, for now the farmer speaks. From the first sentence introducing him, it is evident that he is more worthy of our respect than the poet or the merchant. He is no fop, like the poet, nor is there any apparent vanity in his behavior. He is not pinched, nervous, and mean, like the merchant. All he has asked has been a simple livelihood, earned with his own hands, and a chance to rear his family in peace and love. He has asked, that is, what Josiah and Miriam hope for. But he has been crushed by repeated failures brought on by no fault of his own, neither by vain and inordinate ambition nor by a too mercenary view of what constitutes success and failure. Now, sullen and despondent, he tells how years ago he married "just such a neat and pretty young woman as Miriam," and how he has failed.

> "I have labored hard for years; and my means have been growing narrower, and my living poorer, and my heart colder and heavier, all the time; till at last I could bear it no longer. I set myself down to calculate whether I had best go on the Oregon expedition, or come here to the Shaker village; but I had not hope enough left in me to begin the world over again; and, to make my story short, here I am. And now, youngster, take my advice, and turn back; or else, some few years hence, you'll have to climb this hill, with as heavy a heart as mine."

This story, unlike the other two, affects the young couple deeply. Here, after all, is a simple person like themselves, a person who has asked for little and received nothing, who has had no delusions, unless justice be a delusion. ("I thought it a matter of course that the Lord would help me, because I was willing to help myself.") But their greatest shock is

yet to come. The farmer had referred to his bride at the beginning of his story but has made no further reference to her
as his story has progressed. Miriam thinks that both the wife
and the children must be dead. Now we learn that the tired,
dispirited, unhappy woman in the party is the farmer's wife,
and that the two children asleep on the ground are theirs,
two others having died. The wife's expression and tone of
voice mingle "fretfulness," "irritability," and "sadness." It is
she who tells that part of the tale that "makes all the rest
so hard to bear":

"If you and your sweetheart marry, you'll be kind and pleasant
to each other for a year or two, and while that's the case, you
never will repent; but, by and by, he'll grow gloomy, rough, and
hard to please, and you'll be peevish, and full of little angry fits,
and apt to be complaining by the fireside, when he comes to rest
himself from his troubles out of doors; so your love will wear
away by little and little, and leave you miserable at last."

This last revelation of the nature of experience shakes the
lovers profoundly. Their experience has given them no basis
for judging whether the experience of the unhappy couple
is rare, typical, or inevitable. But Hawthorne makes sure that
the reader knows more than Josiah and Miriam. The tone in
which these last two tales, especially the wife's, is told is one
of utter seriousness: there is real pathos in their story, more
moving than the frustration of the poet or the failure of the
merchant. If this be true of the world, then it may well be
given up.

Still Hawthorne is not through with his unhappy couple.
There is more to their stories than can be revealed simply by
a tone which implies that tragedy is real. Action, and an
author's comment (the only intrusion of the author after the
introductory paragraph) are needed for the final revelation:

As she ceased, the yeoman and his wife exchanged a glance,
in which there was more and warmer affection than they had
supposed to have escaped the frost of a wintry fate, in either of
their breasts. At that moment, when they stood on the utmost
verge of married life, one word fitly spoken, or perhaps one

peculiar look, had they had mutual confidence enough to recipro-
cate it, might have renewed all their old feelings, and sent them
back, resolved to sustain each other amid the struggles of the
world. But the crisis passed and never came again. Just then,
also, the children, roused by their mother's voice, looked up, and
added their wailing accents to the testimony borne by all the
Canterbury pilgrims against the world from which they fled.

Now that the last of the pilgrims has told her tale, Hawthorne returns our attention to the young lovers. Each succeeding story has affected them more than the preceding
one, and now they are deeply disturbed. These tales have
come to seem "omens" of the "disappointed hope, and unavailing toil, domestic grief, and estranged affection" which
they too may well expect. But they do not hesitate for long.
Embracing, they declare that they will not go back. "The
world can never be dark for us, for we will always love one
another."

This statement of the lovers, which is also the last bit of
dialogue in the story, must seem, in the context of the summary that I have given thus far, to be quite unjustified by
the revelations of the nature of the world that have preceded
it. The story, which has opened with moonlight and the
beauty of nature, closes with young love reaffirmed. More
moonlight? Has the tension between the irony and the "romance" disappeared, to leave this just another romantic tale
after all, despite the qualifications? Before we attempt to
decide, we must turn back to look more closely at certain
implications of the nature of the travelers and of the arrangement of the tales they tell.

First, we remember that the pilgrims are presented in a
climactic order of increasing sympathy for them on the part
of the author and the reader, of increasing pathos, and of increasing relevance to the situation of the lovers. Second, we
recall that Josiah sees something in common between the
poet and the merchant. What the two have in common is
plainly vanity or pride and the false values that spring from
that vice. The poet lives for fame, the merchant for wealth
and power; each has striven in vain for a vain end, an end

calculated, if achieved, to magnify the self in the way peculiar to that self. But is there any relationship between these two and the farmer and his wife? That there is Hawthorne has suggested in his presentation of the death of their love and of their missed opportunity for the beginning of a renewal of it. The farm couple have once felt the "romantic love" which Josiah and Miriam now feel, but worry, disappointment, hardships, and the natural lessening of desire with the years have destroyed that romantic love. Their troubles, as they have hardened and embittered the couple, have driven both man and wife into self-absorption, so that finally the two are isolated from each other and from the world. They too, like the poet and the merchant, are victims of pride.

The story, then, indirectly suggests the theme of pride that is so often present in Hawthorne's work. For the opposite of the pride of poet, merchant, and the farm couple is love. But *love* is a peculiarly ambiguous word. The Shaker couple are already "in love," but the implication of the story is that "the world" generally deals harshly with this sort of love. Unless their love survives the attrition or death of desire, unless to some degree *eros* changes to *agape*, they will surely not "always love one another."* Whether they will continue to love after they have ceased to be "in love" we cannot know, and fortunately for the effect of the story, Hawthorne does not try to tell us. If their love does survive it will become more conspicuously an aspect and a manifestation of Christian *caritas*. This too is a part of the meaning of the tale.

But this question of the meaning of the climactic state-

---

* That Hawthorne was a realist about the normal course of married love is just what we should expect, unless our views of him have been formed not from his works but from Mrs. Hawthorne's re-creation of her husband in her *Passages from the American Note-Books*. Once, after describing a display of affection by a newly wed couple whom he had observed in a stage-coach, Hawthorne added the comment, "It would be pleasant to meet them again next summer, and note the change." See Randall Stewart, ed., *The American Notebooks* (New Haven, Yale University Press, 1932), pp. 33-34.

ment has led us away from the broader theme, which, as we have seen, is whether the nature of life is such as to justify, or even to require, extreme renunciation. In "The Shaker Bridal" and elsewhere Hawthorne expressed himself on the Shakers, and his attitude was one of disapproval.* Like Melville, he was much interested in this remnant of an earlier day lingering on in bustling, secular nineteenth-century America. But his religious outlook was not ascetic. Interested in the fulfillment rather than the extinction of the human creature, with completion rather than substitution as the goal, he was willing to follow reason as far as reason would carry him and to explore the full implications of the concept of incarnation. He decided that asceticism was more of a distortion than a fulfillment. When the "world's people" continued up the hill at the close of the story to enter the Shaker society, they "sought a home where all former ties of nature or society would be sundered, and all old distinctions leveled, and a cold and passionless security be substituted for mortal hope and fear, as in that other refuge of the world's weary outcasts, the grave." Hawthorne's sympathies went with the lovers as, "with chastened hopes, but more confiding affections, [they] went on to mingle in an untried life."

They went down the road, *down* from the pure and noble but inhumanly lofty Shaker community to the middle world. Both the Shaker ideal and the world of nature, the story suggests, have a beauty and a purity not exhibited in man's experience. As the Shaker community is the symbol of all religious renunciation, here defined as a too romantic or idealistic response to life, so the water and the moon are symbols of romance and of that morally neutral beauty of nature which often seemed to Thoreau a more than adequate substitute for human companionship. And since the two "escapes" from man's humanity, the one above, the other

---

* See *The American Notebooks*, pp. 229-230. On the occasion of his visit with Melville to a Shaker community in the Berkshires, Hawthorne wrote of "these foolish Shakers" that "the sooner the sect is extinct the better."

below, have much in common, it is interesting that they should be linked together at the beginning of the tale, and then that the one should be rejected and the other left behind as the tale proceeds.

So the tale that begins in light and develops in darkness emerges at last into the light again. But the shadows have not been totally dispelled at the end. Ominous destructive agents at first, they have become the accepted circumference of the shrunken but clearer core of light. The summer moon, which opens the tale like the statement of the theme in the first bars of a quartet, is immediately so qualified that as a symbol it points both to lasting value and to delusive hopes. Perhaps the only unambiguous symbol in the whole tale is the fountain. Young love, introduced, like the moonlight, at first idyllically, is quickly confronted by the harsh reality that would destroy it. Even the hill, with its religious ideal at the top and the world of sordid experience below, is an ambiguous symbol.

But the story does not end in unresolved antinomy. Moonlight and moonshine, romance and fact, noble ideal and ignoble reality, each has been modified by the presence of its opposite. So that when the young couple decide to go on into "untried life" they embody an idea which is significantly different from that which they suggested at the beginning. Something has been achieved, some new meaning created, by the antinomies that have been explored. Out of the contrasts of the height of the hill and the depth of the world below, the excessive romanticism of the poet and the base realism of the merchant, the naïve idealism of the lovers and the hopeless frustration of the married couple, a meaning has emerged which we now recognize as faintly foreshadowed at the very beginning in the "blessed fountain." For here too "opposites" were brought together and reconciled by some "secret charm," so that the narrator was struck by the fancy that here was some almost impossible ideal actually achieved. Nature and "the work of neat hands and considerate art" had coöperated to achieve this ideal: nature and human craft, or art, together had made it possible. The fountain, both natural and artful, suggests, as we now are in a position to see, a middle ground between the merely "natural" lives of "the world's people," lives ultimately defeated by the world's contingencies, and the unnatural, "ideal" renunciations of the Shakers.

"The Canterbury Pilgrims" is, then, a tale literally built out of progressively complex explorations of contrasted themes. The whole meaning and value of the tale are products of the tension thus produced. And when hindsight enables us to see that the resolution achieved out of discord at the end was already foreshadowed in the opening paragraph, we realize that Hawthorne has here written a tale very like a beautifully constructed piece of music. If nevertheless it is not one of the really great tales, it is easy to see why. It is intricately balanced and harmonious in structure but relatively thin in texture. It has, at best perhaps, only half the value of "My Kinsman, Major Molineux," for its values remain, comparatively, mere ideas—musical ideas of the highest order, but only lightly sketched in, as in a preliminary plan rather than in a developed work. The characters are very nearly allegorical figures, their tales little more than summaries of significant action. The value that the story has—and it has considerable value in my judgment—is a function very largely of what we may call its structure. And its structure is a structure of meanings fictionally, or dramatically and pictorially, discovered and conceived.

3

If "The Canterbury Pilgrims" suggests a scale up and down which the meaning moves like a melody stated and elaborated with classic artistry, "Roger Malvin's Burial" is more likely to suggest to most readers a dream, with more than the usual dream's depths visible beneath the limpid surface. The immense difference between these two tales suggests the range of Hawthorne's artistry, but the two are alike in one respect: in both, the burden of meaning carried by structure is relatively greater than it is in some of the better-known later tales such as "Rappaccini's Daughter." (By "structure" I mean the shape of the action and the relations of its parts, in contrast with style, the *manner* in which the action is presented, which I call "texture.")

Like "My Kinsman, Major Molineux," "Roger Malvin's Burial" opens with a paragraph of historical background, not properly a part of the tale itself but a preparation for it. "The fate of the few combatants who were in a condition to retreat after 'Lovell's Fight' " in the border wars of 1725 will provide the subject for a tale which will play "the moonlight of romance" over a page of Colonial history. The tale that follows provides further evidence of what Hawthorne meant by "romance" and of the use to which he put history, but what chiefly concerns us now is the way in which the structure of the tale expresses the meaning.

In summary, the situation is this. Two of Lovell's men, one old and the other young, have escaped the destruction of their force and are making their way back to the settlements. The older of the two, however, has been severely wounded in the fight, and as the story opens he is resting beneath a rock in a forest glade, unable to go farther. He urges the young man to go on and save himself if possible, pointing out that staying with him will mean that two lives will be lost instead of one. Finally the younger man decides to do so, comforting himself with the thought that he may thus be able to send back help for the older. Later as he is about to die of his own severe wounds he is found near the edge of the settlement and nursed back to health by the girl whom he later marries, the daughter of the friend he left to die in the forest. Although he intends to tell of the circumstances of the older man's death, he never actually does so. He marries the daughter of his friend, keeps his secret to himself, and rears a son who grows to adolescence. But a feeling of guilt increases within him until he can bear it no longer, and he sets out with his family for new land to the west. Journeying through the forest, he finds himself drawn continually away from the planned course and in the direction of the place where years before he had left his friend to die alone.

Arrived at the spot without the man's recognizing it at first, the family makes camp, and father and son go into the woods separately. Hearing a sound near him, the father fires blindly, killing his son, who has been his only comfort in the unhappy isolation that has grown on him through the years.

Even a bare summary of this sort suffices to suggest some of the overtones of the tale. Here, most clearly, is the usual preoccupation with secret guilt, with the resulting isolation, and with a sense of compulsion. The young man who grows old in bitterness is another Goodman Brown, introduced to the evil in the world by his own participation in it. He is Robin of "My Kinsman, Major Molineux," in later years compelled to return to the spot where he had joined in laughter at his kinsman's expense. He is Abraham sacrificing Isaac: compelled as it seemed to him by a "supernatural power," he kills his son. The plot of the tale is as elemental and suggestive as any that Hawthorne ever wrote.

The deepening and strengthening of the suggestions implicit in the basic situation are accomplished with great economy, without the profusion of imagery common in the later tales. The rock against which the dying old man leaned and beneath which the child is later killed is explicitly a gravestone and implicitly an altar like those in the Old Testament on which sacrifice was offered. The two key scenes of the story take place deep in the *heart* of the dark forest, in a glade which Reuben is unable to forget as he is unable to cast out the secret that lies in "the sepulchre of his heart." The branch around which he had tied his handkerchief upon leaving his older friend so that he might find the spot again has been withered by time ("Whose guilt had blasted it?") and falls in "soft light fragments upon the rock, upon the leaves, upon Reuben, upon his wife and child, and upon Roger Malvin's bones" after the son has been sacrificed. These few are the outstanding symbolic devices in this tale rich in its depths and deceptively plain on its surface.

For the rest, the implications are developed in the contours of the situations. Did Reuben do wrong in leaving the dying man? He himself was gravely wounded, and staying, though it could be conceived as a religious duty, could certainly have no practical benefits. Where would the right lie in a situation like this? Surely one's duty to others should not require self-sacrifice when the sacrifice would almost certainly be useless to the other person. It is not at all certain that Reuben did any wrong in leaving the dying man.

Why then was he consumed by a sense of guilt thereafter until he had killed what was most dear to him? Hawthorne suggests that, in the first place, it was not so much the overt act of desertion as the conditions under which it took place that justified the feeling of guilt. When Roger Malvin urges his "son" to leave him, he plays shrewdly upon the capacity of man to rationalize his interests. He points out that if Reuben leaves he will be able to look after the daughter he is to marry, he may get help to come, and that at any rate it is his duty to obey the one who has loved him like a father and who "should have something of a father's authority." Thus in the conflict between the claims of opposed duties it is possible for Reuben to follow self-interest without admitting to himself that he has done so. Malvin's words

reminded him that there were other and less questionable duties than that of sharing the fate of a man whom his death could not benefit. Nor can it be affirmed that no selfish feeling strove to enter Reuben's heart, though the consciousness made him more earnestly resist his companion's entreaties . . . No merely selfish motive, nor even the desolate condition of Dorcas, could have induced him to desert his companion at such a moment—but his wishes seized on the thought that Malvin's life might be preserved, and his sanguine nature heightened almost to certainty the remote possibility of procuring human aid.

The moral complexity of the original situation, in short, amounts to almost complete ambiguity. In a situation so opaque with conflicting rights, no clear judgment can be brought against Reuben for his action. But the state of mind and heart which permitted and prompted the action is another matter. Reuben was not honest with himself about his motives. Here was a clear reason for the feeling of guilt that came to torment him.

And this original failure of honesty was compounded by another act of rationalization that was likewise almost, if not entirely, justifiable: he did not tell Dorcas and the others that he had left her father to die alone. Circumstances conspired to make it easy for him to keep this to himself. He was near death when he was discovered near the settlement. He found that everyone assumed that he had heroically remained with the dying man, to do what he could for him at the end and to bury his body. When, once, he tried to tell the truth he found that his words were interpreted according to the preconceptions of his hearers. The thought occurred to him that to tell the truth would inflict upon his wife useless suffering which he would like to spare her. So he allowed the untruth to be believed. Again, whose motives are so perfect that he can safely, as Hawthorne puts it, "impute blame"?

But the actions which thus far had seemed so natural, so justifiable, involved a consequence which Reuben could not escape or justify to himself. When he had left Roger Malvin to die, he had promised that he would return to give the bones of his friend Christian burial. Now he was unable to keep that vow without revealing that he had permitted a lie to be believed. But not to keep his vow was not only to break a promise but to fail to carry out a specifically *religious* duty. That the man to whom the promise was made is dead, and so cannot benefit by its being kept, and that the performance of the duty will presumably do no one else any good—these are precisely the lines of reasoning followed by Reuben in his attempts at self-justification, but such pragmatic considerations do not lessen his sense of guilt.

The story then is concerned not with the obvious guilt of recognized sinners but with the complex and obscure guilt in which one who "means well" and is as good as the next man gets involved. Like Original Sin, Reuben's guilt is at once, and paradoxically, the result of a chain of previous wrong choices and the consequence of a "fatal necessity." Like Original Sin too, it required a dramatic and extraordinary sacrifice for the undoing of its consequences.

Nothing in the tale clarifies the "simple" and "obvious" question of how much if any wrong Reuben did in leaving the dying man. Indeed the answer to the abstract ethical question of the degree of self-sacrifice demanded by Christian ethics is deliberately obscured. In terms of purely rational ethics the only implication of the surface level of the story would be the same as the explicit moral of *The Scarlet Letter*, "Be true! Be true! Show freely to the world, if not your worst, yet some trait whereby the worst may be inferred." Reuben was not true. From one point of view not sin but refusal to acknowledge sin drove him to his doom.

Although this theme of the effects of concealment—so common in Hawthorne that there is a temptation to call it *the* meaning once we have discovered it—is surely developed, the central meaning of the story is not to be found here either, but equally, and alternatively, on the levels of myth and of the unconscious. In our day, when readings of stories in these terms are being overdone with the enthusiasm of fresh discovery, it may be natural to suspect that at this point we are overreading, seeing too much in a simple tale. But Hawthorne himself has answered this objection: he has made it impossible to disregard the mythical and the unconscious in reading the story.

In the first place, his emphasis on Reuben's motives in his two "guilty" acts prepares us for what is to follow. Hawthorne understood consciously and thoroughly the process we now call rationalization, and he described the process as it took place in Reuben's mind. To discern the motives of thinking is to penetrate some little way below the level of what is normally in the consciousness. But more significantly, he makes Reuben's return to the place of his first "guilt" compulsive. From the route which had been consciously selected to take them to their new home Reuben continually strays, though he is an excellent woodsman, and his straying takes always the same direction. Corrected by his son, who notices the strange "mistake," Reuben agrees and changes his direction, only to turn again and again in the way he was obscurely compelled to take. "Cyrus, perceiving that his father gradually resumed the old direction, forebore to interfere; nor, though something began to weigh upon his heart, did his adventurous nature permit him to regret the increased length and mystery of their way."

And it is indeed a mysterious journey which they are undertaking. After they arrive near the place of Roger Malvin's death, Reuben leaves Dorcas at the fire to follow Cyrus into the woods in search of game. I have said that Hawthorne underscores the "mystery" here, but the precise emphasis he gives to the mystery deserves to be noted. Reuben, wholly preoccupied with the "strange reflections" arising from his feeling of guilt, which has lately come so much to the foreground as to destroy the man Dorcas had loved and married, "strays" through the woods "rather like a sleepwalker than a hunter," circling the camp and approaching without realizing it the nearby great rock in the glade.

He was musing on the strange influence that had led him away from his premeditated course, and so far into the depths of the wilderness. Unable to penetrate to the secret place of his soul where his motives lay hidden, he believed that a supernatural voice had called him onward, and that a supernatural power had obstructed his retreat. He trusted that it was Heaven's intent to afford him an opportunity of expiating his sin; he hoped that he might find the bones so long unburied; and that, having laid the earth over them, peace would throw its sunlight into the sepulchre of his heart. From these thoughts he was aroused by a rustling in the forest at some distance from the spot to which he had wandered. Perceiving the motion of some object behind a thick veil of undergrowth, he fired, with the instinct of a hunter and the aim of a practiced marksman. A low moan, which told of his success, and by which even animals can express their dying agony, was unheeded by Reuben Bourne. What were the recollections now breaking upon him?

I suppose Hawthorne could not have made the element of unconscious compulsion in the return to the spot and the shooting of the son more explicit than he has without dropping entirely the surface level of the story. But there is another aspect of the situation that Hawthorne merely hints. As he has been ridden by his feeling of guilt through the years, Reuben has grown away from Dorcas until there is a wall of separation between them. But he does not lose his love for his son. "The boy was loved by his father with a deep and silent strength, as if whatever was good and happy in his own nature had been transferred to his child, carrying his affections with it." When he kills the child, then, he is killing what he most loved, but he is doing more than that: he is killing the symbolic extension of himself. A feeling of guilt arising out of one's relation to the father may lead, the psychologist might say, to the need to destroy or mutilate the guilty self. What the psychologist would know and document systematically, Hawthorne knew in his creative mind in this story and wrought into a structure of relationships that involve archetypal patterns.

The relation between this tale and the stories of Leonard Doane, who suffered from the fantasy that he had killed his father, and Robin, who laughed cruelly at the man he hoped would be like a father to him, should by now be clear enough. But there are other aspects of the story that deserve mention. In all of Hawthorne's tales there is perhaps no subtler presentation of certain aspects of the nature of secret guilt—its springs, its nature, and its effects. Reuben Bourne is guilty, in so far as his guilt can be related to the objective moral world and is not merely "psychological," of what Hawthorne calls "moral cowardice": he cannot bring himself first to face the truth about himself and then to share it with others, even those he loves. "Unable to penetrate to the secret place of his soul where his motives lay hidden," he is prevented from knowing himself, and so from changing himself constructively. A psychologist might say that he lacked "insight." A theologian might say that his blindness and cowardice spring, like Dimmesdale's, from a very subtle, quite unconscious, pride. He is unable to humble himself to the extent that would be required by a recognition of his true motives and nature and by subsequent confession of sin. He suffers but, like Dimmesdale again, does not really repent until he is driven by his suffering to the self-sacrificial act which brings his release. Then "His sin was expiated,—the curse was gone from him; and in the hour when he had shed blood dearer to him than his own, a prayer, the first for years, went up to Heaven from the lips of Reuben Bourne."

These closing words of the story, like the Biblical allusions throughout, make it clear that a reading of the tale in terms of both primitive religious myth and the historical and theological aspects of creedal Christianity are as clearly justified as the psychological reading is. Oedipus and the sacrificial savior loom in the background of this tale whose foreground is fashioned out of Colonial history and the nature and effects of concealed guilt. Original Sin and the Atonement are as clearly involved in Reuben Bourne's story as are the psychology of guilt and the demands of the unconscious.

And all these meanings are embodied in structure—in situation and character and action, in motive to action and result of action. The tale is not as rich in texture as the greatest of Hawthorne's later stories; not so much of the meaning is carried by style, including imagery. But it is one of Hawthorne's greatest tales nevertheless, for there is no part of its structure which is not instinct with meaning, and no meaning in the tale which is not embodied in its structure. In it we see exemplified the structure of meaning as Hawthorne created it.

4

Hawthorne's weaker tales make it clear that the danger he constantly faced was that he would overintellectualize his material. "Wakefield" carries too great a burden of thought for so slight a framework. What stimulated Hawthorne here was the initial situation of a man who willfully isolates himself. Between Wakefield's departure from his wife and his return, Hawthorne merely summarizes the actions of twenty years. The story never expands much beyond anecdote.

"The Canterbury Pilgrims" is stronger, I think—though

that has not been the usual opinion, if we may judge by frequency of inclusion in the anthologies. In it we have more immediacy, more life, more concreteness. Even so the characters are rather abstractly conceived: the romantic young couple, the vain little poet, the embittered merchant, the defeated farm couple. These are descendants of the Virtues and the Vices of the medieval morality plays. Josiah is Everyman, young and in love and wondering whether his dreams will be fulfilled. With "The Christmas Banquet," "The Man of Adamant," "The Great Carbuncle," "Lady Eleanor's Mantle," and a half dozen or so others, "The Canterbury Pilgrims" seems almost to justify the description of Hawthorne as simply an allegorist.

Yet even in these tales there is a significant difference between Hawthorne's practice and allegory as we see it in Spenser and Bunyan. Hawthorne does not start with a wholly preconceived, an abstract and external, set of meanings and then embody them, even in his most allegorical tales. We may say that a system of values and beliefs such as Bunyan knew was not available to him; or at any rate, that he could not accept whatever was available. But whatever explanation we may give of the fact, the fact remains that Hawthorne's "allegories" are more subjective, more complex, and more ambiguous than anything in *Pilgrim's Progress* or *The Faerie Queene*. If these tales are allegory, they are allegory in a new mode, a mode which it might be less misleading to call a highly intellectualized form of symbolism.

Hawthorne's besetting danger of overintellectualization was only the misuse of his greatest strength. "Roger Malvin's Burial" is certainly one of his best tales, but it too has very little action and its characters are only sufficiently sketched in to make them credible. Its illusion of reality is slight by comparison with contemporary practice, and its burden of meaning great by any standard. Any reader wholly insensitive to its meanings as they develop would surely find it something less than compelling. It does not invite us so much to share Reuben Bourne's experience as to contemplate it.

The experience it affords is highly intellectual, but it is experience conceived in aesthetic, not in philosophic, terms.

Like "Wakefield," "The Canterbury Pilgrims," and "Roger Malvin's Burial," most of Hawthorne's tales contain very little overt action, but what action there is, is symbolic. In the greater tales this economy helps to produce the effect of concentrated brilliance. In the weaker ones, it contributes to our impression that the tales are not fiction at all, but sketches. Lack of action is characteristic of both the weaker sketchlike tales and the very best among both the tales and the novels. It has often been noted that *The Scarlet Letter* begins after the actions that would provide the plot of most novels; and the subsequent "actions" it does treat take place largely within the minds and hearts of the characters. *The Marble Faun*, in contrast, which has a great deal more overt action, is clearly an inferior novel. "Young Goodman Brown," one of the very finest of the tales, contains so little and such simple overt action that a summary concerned with its plot alone could be adequately given in an uncrowded sentence. "Mr. Higginbotham's Catastrophe," on the other hand, has a rather full and complicated plot, but it is surely not one of Hawthorne's best works.

The action is not only relatively little in proportion to the length of the tales but is usually of the simplest character. One form that plot commonly takes is the journey. "My Kinsman, Major Molineux" is built around Robin's trip to and through, and implied later departure from, Boston. We see him arrive and wander through the streets, receiving the revelations that lead to his departure. The physical action in "Roger Malvin's Burial" is limited to Reuben's preparing to leave his friend and his later return to the same spot, the events of the intervening years being chiefly summarized rather than presented as they happen. In "The Canterbury Pilgrims" travelers going in opposite direction meet, talk, and depart on their different ways; that is all the action there is. Wakefield leaves his home and later returns. The searchers for the great carbuncle, once they have been introduced in their camp, set out on their quest; what they discover on the way is the essence of the story. The man of adamant journeys to his cave and there receives a visitor from across the sea; since he does not depart with her, he is lost. Ethan Brand searches far and wide for the Unpardonable Sin, returns to his lime kiln, and throws himself into the flames because he has at last found, in an unexpected place, what he has been seeking. Goodman Brown journeys into and returns from the forest, bringing back with him the revelations he has gained there. This journey-plot is so frequent in Hawthorne that sketches like "The Procession of Life" and "Main Street" differ from the tales not so much in "lacking plot" as in failing to develop character: the casual reflections of the narrator, clearly in these pieces Hawthorne himself, are not an adequate substitute for the creation of a Goodman Brown, or even of a Reverend Mr. Hooper with his veil.

From these very simple patterns of action Hawthorne developed designs of great complexity. Once he had seen the general meanings implicit in his basic situation, he saw reflections and qualifications of them everywhere. The *Gestalt* once perceived came to dominate everything, even the style, so that what I have called "texture" gets assimilated to "structure" and the basis of any distinction disappears. Actions, characters, and scenes fell naturally into pairs, or into groups of three or four. He liked to bring balance out of apparently random arrangements, or to experiment with unbalance when balance was too strongly expected.

"The Canterbury Pilgrims" is wrought in terms of duality. Everything comes in pairs. The incoming travelers balance the outgoing pair—in circumstances as well as in the direction and intent of their journey. The community on the hill balances the world in the valley—in its nature as well as in its location. The incoming group of six travelers may be divided into two groups of two and four persons, with the four divisible into two and two: the poet and the merchant who speak first and are united by the "likeness" Josiah sees between them; the farmer and his wife, whose tales follow and complement each other, and their two sleeping children.

At the end of the story, when the two contrasting groups prepare to continue each in its own direction, even the style is affected by the strength of the controlling pattern. "The Shaker youth and maiden," Hawthorne writes,

looked mournfully into each other's eyes. They had but stepped across the threshold of their homes, when lo! the dark array of cares and sorrows that rose up to warn them back. The varied narratives of the strangers had arranged themselves into a parable; they seemed not merely instances of woful fate that had befallen others, but shadowy omens of disappointed hope and unavailing toil, domestic grief and estranged affection, that would cloud the onward path of these poor fugitives. But after one instant's hesitation, they opened their arms, and sealed their resolve with as pure and fond an embrace as ever youthful love had hallowed.

Everything here—and on through the next two paragraphs to the final sentence of the tale—is in twos: *youth* and *maiden*; *had but stepped* when *cares and sorrows rose*; not merely *instances* but *shadowy omens*; *disappointed hope* and *unavailing toil*; *domestic grief* and *estranged affection*; they *opened their arms* and *sealed their resolve*; *pure* and *fond*. Even the rhythm is a reminder of the basic dualisms in the tale. Lightly suggested in the passage I have quoted, it comes out more strongly as we move toward the final sentence: "The lovers drank at the Shaker spring, and then, with chastened hopes, but more confiding affections, went on to mingle in an untried life." At the risk of seeming to some overobvious and to others arbitrary, I shall arrange this sentence to emphasize the sound patterns as they appear to me:

The lovers drank	at the Shaker spring,
(and then)	
with chastened hopes,	but more confiding affections,
went on to mingle	in an untried life.

This sort of thing is much too common in Hawthorne to

require extended comment or emphasis.* What needs to be said, and what may be said briefly since it must be obvious, is that the passage I have analyzed for its rhythm is evidence that even the sound of this tale is expressive. Rhythm, sentence structure, image and symbol, structure in its larger aspects as patterns of action and character and situation—all are subdued to the demands of the "subject," with its contrasts of the world and the spirit, pride and love, the life of full experience and the life of renunciation, pessimism and optimism, despair and hope, past and future, death and life.

If the number two permeates "The Canterbury Pilgrims," three is no less prominent in "Roger Malvin's Burial." The action, as we have seen, falls into three parts: Reuben's leaving Roger Malvin, living with the secret guilt, and returning to expiate the sin. (This may of course also be thought of as journeys in opposite directions over the same route, from and then to the place of guilt, with a pause in between, during which the effects of the wrongful departure accumulate to require the expiating return.) The characters, too, are a part of the pattern. For though there are four chief characters in all, they do not exist at the same time, so that effectively there are first one set of three, then another set of three: father-in-law to be, son-in-law to be, and wife to be; then father, wife, and son.

With this triadic design dominant throughout the tale,† as it is, we should not be surprised to find that the last sentence catches up all these suggestions and expresses them in one final pattern in which sound, grammar, and rational

---

* Compare, for example, the ending of "Young Goodman Brown," where rhythm and euphony, including alliteration and assonance, combine to add their emotional intensities to the tale: "And when he had lived long, and was borne to his grave a hoary corpse, followed by Faith, an aged woman, and children and grandchildren, a goodly procession, besides neighbors not a few, they carved no hopeful verse upon his tombstone, for his dying hour was gloom."

† "Egotism, or the Bosom Serpent" is another tale in which everything comes in threes.

content all work together to express what is at once and alternatively the "matter" and the "manner," the subject and the vehicle, the theme and the expression, of one of the great tales in the language:

His sin was expiated,—the curse was gone from him; and in the hour when he had shed blood dearer to him than his own, a prayer, the first for years, went up to Heaven from the lips of Reuben Bourne.

CHAPTER FOUR

THE TALES: *The Texture of Meaning*

One of the most rewarding critical examinations of Hawthorne's work is entitled "Hawthorne as Poet."* Though Mrs. Leavis's title is apt, Hawthorne does not seem to have cared much for the poetry of his own century, or for the work of the lesser poets of any period. Shakespeare, Milton, Spenser, especially Spenser, he loved, but except for these he seems for the most part to have found prose more to his liking. Yet at least once, writing to Longfellow, he called himself a poet, and his own works in prose are a kind of poetry.

Even his pieces that come closest to being pure history or pure allegory are ordinarily enriched by that kind of texture that we have come to expect to find in verse. The usual contrast between "realistic" and "romantic" fiction, in which Hawthorne is assigned a place at the far end of the romantic side of the spectrum, is less useful for an attempt to understand Hawthorne's fiction than has been supposed. His fiction is "romantic" enough, to be sure, whatever meanings such a statement may carry; but it is more significant to note that it is completely *made*, as the poet, the maker, makes his poems. The more helpful contrast is between fiction as report, as a branch of journalism or of the writing of history, and fiction as Hawthorne conceived it, as a formal aesthetic

* Q. D. Leavis, in *Sewanee Review,* Spring and Summer 1951.

structure wrought from whatever materials, whether the visions of the haunted mind or ideas or the data of history or a little of all of these. His fiction at its best is mythopoetic.

Hawthorne, in short, was an artist, not a reporter and not a historian, despite his extensive use of the material of history. He conceived of himself as, and was, "an artist of the beautiful," even when he wrote what he sometimes thought of as his "blasted allegories." His "allegories of the heart" introduce a new element into the traditional mode. Neither Spenser's nor Bunyan's work is in any significant sense allegory of the "heart": Spenser and Bunyan allegorized "Truth," public, accepted, external truth; and the texture they gave it was incidental. In Hawthorne's work the texture is decisive, the "truth" dubious, ambiguous, indecisive. The evidence of this can be found as easily in "The Minister's Black Veil" as in "Roger Malvin's Burial," in "The Man of Adamant" as in "Rappaccini's Daughter." In all of Hawthorne's successful tales the texture is rich. The images become symbols, and the symbols and allusions expand to myth.

2

"The human heart to be allegorized as a cavern," Hawthorne jotted in his Notebook as an idea for a story. "The Man of Adamant" comes as close, I think, to being pure Spenserian allegory as any tale that Hawthorne ever wrote. A comparison of it with "Roger Malvin's Burial" will suggest two of the limits within which the tales exist. Yet even here, where the symbolism is so abstractly clear and the general structure so obviously an embodiment of an abstract judgment, or set of judgments, the texture enriches the theme. Though Hawthorne calls his tale an "apologue" and it is tempting to dismiss it as an allegorized sermon on the dangers of spiritual pride, the piece turns out to be a work of art and not merely a statement of doctrine.

With "The Gentle Boy," "The Maypole of Merrymount," and "Main Street," the "Man of Adamant" is one of the clearest revelations of Hawthorne's attitude toward the Puritanism of his ancestors. Indeed the theme, in all but its largest outlines, is directly concerned with a judgment of the kind of religiousness of which Hawthorne always saw the Puritans as "types," and we shall understand *The Scarlet Letter* more fully if we know the judgments made here. The whole situation is outlined, and the outcome foreshadowed, in the opening paragraph.

In the old times of religious gloom and intolerance lived Richard Digby, the gloomiest and most intolerant of a stern brotherhood. His plan of salvation was so narrow, that, like a plank in a tempestuous sea, it could avail no sinner but himself, who bestrode it triumphantly, and hurled anathemas against the wretches whom he saw struggling with the billows of eternal death. In his view of the matter, it was a most abominable crime —as, indeed, it is a great folly—for men to trust to their own strength, or even to grapple to any other fragment of the wreck, save this narrow plank, which, moreover, he took special care to keep out of their reach. In other words, as his creed was like no man's else, and being well pleased that Providence had intrusted him alone, of mortals, with the treasure of a true faith, Richard Digby determined to seclude himself to the sole and constant enjoyment of his happy fortune.

In his first sentence Hawthorne sets up the historical boundaries of his theme, justifying our seeing this tale as his judgment of the errors not of an individual but of an era. For Richard Digby is unlike his fellow Puritans only in carrying their traits to an extreme: he is "the gloomiest and most intolerant" in a time of "religious gloom and intolerance." The tale anatomizes a "stern brotherhood."

But the negative judgment of the first paragraph is qualified as soon as it is made. If it is uncharitable and intolerant of Richard Digby to consider it "a most abominable crime" for men to "trust to their own strength," it is not doctrinally mistaken or foolish to do so. Hawthorne's "as, indeed, it is a great folly" establishes the limits of Digby's error: not wrong doctrine but hardness of heart, not mistaken faith but a failure of charity. In the same way Hawthorne later characterized the Puritan populace in *The Scarlet Letter*:

not that adultery was not a sin but that condemnation of the
sin must not preclude charity toward the sinner.

The second paragraph of the tale establishes a parallel, at
once historically accurate in its reflections of Puritan thought
and symbolically suggestive in its context, between Digby
and the Chosen People of the Old Testament. To keep his
unique religion uncontaminated, Digby decides not to
"tarry longer in the tents of Kedar." The third paragraph
continues to enforce the parallel as it pictures his departure
from the settlement in order to build himself "a tabernacle
in the wilderness." The Old Testament overtones, suggesting
the Chosen People's devotion to the true God, remind us
that such action may sometimes be necessary. Though the
irony in the suggestion that he will "smite and slay any
intruder upon his hallowed seclusion" is strong, memories
of the righteous smiting and slaying done by the Chosen
People act as counteragents to the negative judgment. In
short, Digby is clearly established as a man like Aylmer in
"The Birthmark," who does the wrong things from a motive
not in itself wrong, indeed in isolation high and noble; like
him also in falling into sin because of too perfect a trust in
his own powers; like him finally in being a paradoxical figure
the depth of whose error is a measure of the strength of his
devotion to what seemed an "ideal" cause.

What follows may be considered a commentary on the
words of St. Paul, "And now abideth faith, hope, charity,
these three, but the greatest of these is charity." Digby's faith
was intense but he had no charity; lacking this, his faith too
became false. (Just so, by implication, Hawthorne had
judged the Puritans in "The Gentle Boy.") Concerned only
to keep his faith pure, he took the steps which inevitably
corrupted it. He who had had no sympathy for the "poor
wretches whom he saw struggling with the billows of eternal
death," when he reaches a cave reminiscent of "Elijah's cave
at Horeb, though perhaps it more resembled Abraham's
sepulchral cave at Machpelah," is unable in its dim light
even to read his Bible correctly. Remembering the way the
Bibles in "My Kinsman" are spotlighted by the shafts of

moonlight and sunlight, we are not surprised here when Digby's faith becomes corrupt. Naturally, when the vision of Mary Goffe appears to him, begging him to return with her to those who need his help, he turns her away. Since it is clear that the vision of Mary Goffe is a heavenly influence offering him a last chance to escape his self-imposed doom ("What else but faith and love united could have sustained so delicate a creature . . .?"), it is likewise clear, as St. Paul said, that "If ye have not charity" ye have nothing, not even faith. Richard Digby is lost in his dark cave, lost from the very thing it had been his supreme purpose to guard and cultivate. The tale expresses the depth and centrality of Hawthorne's understanding of Christianity.*

As in the first paragraph Hawthorne qualified his condemnation of Digby by expressing his own agreement with the doctrine that there is no salvation by good works alone —for if there were, then men might safely "trust to their own strength"—so he uses Biblical allusions throughout to enrich his tale by making Digby's ultimate damnation ironic. The denunciations Digby hurls at those whose faith he judges corrupted are like those of the prophets who recalled their people from worship of false gods. His cave, like Elijah's and Abraham's, is a sacred place in the wilderness. He remembers that strait is the gate and narrow the way that leads to salvation, and few there be that find it: "Of a truth, the only way to heaven leadeth through the narrow entrance of this cave,—and I alone have found it." He shares the conviction and the single-minded dedication of the prophets and saints who have corrected the errors of their times.

* The tale seems to me a little untypical only to the extent to which it may imply a non-Puritan, or Anglican, "orthodoxy" on Hawthorne's part. In "Hawthorne's 'Man of Adamant': A Spenserian Source-Study," *Philological Quarterly*, 41:744-756 (October 1962), John W. Shroeder has shown that the tale not only draws heavily upon Spenser but that in the crucial episode of the birchen cup Hawthorne echoes some of the words of the sacrament of Holy Communion in the Book of Common Prayer. Perhaps Hawthorne's closeness to Spenser here accounts for what would surely be an unusual implication in his work. His religious point of view may be related to classic or historic Christian "orthodoxy" in several ways, but certainly not in being sacramentalist in its emphasis. See his reactions to Anglican services in the English Notebooks.

He forgets that the entrance to heaven is through a gate, not a cave. The cave in which he sits until he is calcified is at once the cavern of the heart's isolation and the entrance to the underworld. If it is like Elijah's retreat, it is even more like Abraham's place of death. The initial tentative suggestion of this is at once a foreshadowing of the outcome of the plot and a suggestion of the way in which the tension between the "hallowed seclusion" and the "dreariest depths of the forest," both initially applied to the place of Digby's retreat, is to be resolved. We have been prepared then for the discovery that the feet of Mary Goffe bear the wounds of thorns. Denying his brotherhood with sinful and wretched mankind, rejecting the sunlight for the darkness of his cave and the pure water of the spring that bubbled near the entrance for the drippings from the roof—that he might not be interrupted in the reading of his Bible, so intense was his devotion—Digby rejects likewise the sacramental cup of "hallowed water" which Mary Goffe offers. A cavern, clearly, is a most unsuitable spot in which to worship God. Refusing to come out of it, Digby rejected what Hawthorne tells us is "pure Religion."

For "pure Religion" not only does not forget that "the greatest of these is charity," it does not reject the natural light of the sun or the pure water of the natural spring in which Mary Goffe dipped her "birchen cup." The imagery of light and water and cave in the apologue of Richard Digby takes us into areas of meaning at once historical, theological, and psychological, though the tale remains an almost pure allegory on the nature and effects of bigotry. The Puritan flight into the wilderness across the sea that they might practice their purified Biblical faith and rear their children in it without danger of corruption, their great emphasis on the Old Testament and their conviction that they were the new Chosen People, their intolerance and their cruelty in persecuting dissenters from what was itself dissent, their rejection of general opinion embodied in tradition—all these aspects of the history of Hawthorne's forebears are here symbolized. The Puritan doctrine of total depravity is likewise a part of the background of this tale of a man who, like Jonathan Edwards in "Sinners in the Hands of an Angry God," predicted "vengeance and unutterable woe" for all but the elect; but so is the sense of isolation from which Hawthorne suffered before his marriage helped him to "open an intercourse with the world"; and so are the dreadful specters that spring from the heart in vision or in dream in "Alice Doane's Appeal" and "My Kinsman, Major Molineux." Digby rejected the corrective influences both of nature—the General Revelation offered by nature to reason in the spring and the sunlight—and of love, and so was lost, as Roderick Elliston, intent upon the serpent in his bosom, would have been if he had not been saved by Rosina and his friend, symbolically by the voices of love and reason.

Abstractly allegorical as it is, then, in comparison with most of Hawthorne's better-known tales, "The Man of Adamant" can take us, through the implications of its imagery and its allusions, into meanings richer than those we should expect in an "apologue." Though its value is largely conceptual, it can tell us much of the nature of imagery and symbolism in the tales, for both its difference from and its similarities to such stories as those of Roger Malvin and Major Molineux are instructive. It defines one end of the scale of Hawthorne's practice, which includes "The Wives of the Dead" and "The Hollow of the Three Hills" at one extreme and "Dr. Heidegger's Experiment," "The Minister's Black Veil," "The Great Carbuncle," and "The Man of Adamant" at the other.

But a tale more centrally located, more nearly in Hawthorne's middle ground between symbolism and allegory, will disclose aspects of his practice which none of the tales we have examined so far has shown us. Such a tale is "Rappaccini's Daughter."

3

The tale opens with Giovanni Guasconti, a student who has come from southern Italy to study in Padua, taking lodgings in an old mansion. He is described as homesick, poor, and well acquainted with "the great poem of his country." Two of these three characterizing traits deserve to be remembered in any analysis of the story: the reference to Dante, to which Hawthorne gives more emphasis than anything else in his opening paragraph, and the young man's nostalgia for the south, where nature is more "cheerful" and "sunnier," turn out to be functional in the development of the tale's meanings.

Now Hawthorne has the caretaker of the mansion point out to Giovanni a remarkable garden that may be viewed from the window of his apartment. This garden, it quickly becomes clear, will be the focal point of the story. Hawthorne devotes more than a page to its description before he introduces further action, and then the action is in the garden. What strange sort of garden is it that merits so much emphasis?

Learning that it belongs to the famous Dr. Rappaccini, Giovanni looks out his window at it with at first only mild curiosity. But his attention is immediately caught by a fountain that has some interesting features. Classical in design and once a thing of beauty, with its details wrought with "rare art," it is now "wofully shattered" into a mere "chaos of remaining fragments." "Serpent-like" vines entangle and partly cover it. A statue of Vertumnus is recognizable, though it too is almost hidden from sight by the creeping vines. But in the midst of all this ruin and decay, the water of the fountain "continued to gush and sparkle into the sunbeams as cheerfully as ever."

In this fountain image Hawthorne has suggested most of the thematic material of the story. The water, making a sound that prompts Giovanni to think of it as an "immortal spirit," is nature in its aspect as revelation, God's pledge that a ruined world is not all, the soul's surmise of the eternal. Like the water of the spring that refreshed the Canterbury pilgrims, it is at once, ambiguously, natural and divine; what it is not, in any sense, is something contrived by man. Neither the ruins of the structure men built to contain it nor the poisonous plants growing beside it, the product of Dr.

Rappaccini's skill, have any effect on its purity. We shall find an analogue of its incorruptible purity later in the heart of Beatrice. Though it has not generally been so recognized, I think we must call the water a heart image, though the heart is not that of the ordinary run of mankind. Rather, it is a heart like those unusually pure and generous ones described in "The Intelligence Office," hearts "which have their well-spring in the infinite," of which Hawthorne writes, "Sometimes . . . the spiritual fountain is kept pure by a wisdom within itself, and sparkles into the light of heaven without a stain from the earthy strata through which it had gushed upward."

The ruined structure of the fountain is all that remains of classical civilization. Now the emphatic reference to Dante in the opening paragraph takes on added meaning: two worlds, the classical and the Christian, are being contrasted. The classical world, Hawthorne thought, was spiritually deficient not only in lacking the light of Revelation but in having an inadequate sense of evil. The snakey vines that almost cover the ruins of antique art here imply a judgment succinctly expressed in "A Virtuoso's Collection." When the narrator inquires about the meaning of a "chafing dish of glowing coals," he is told,

"That . . . is the original fire which Prometheus stole from heaven. Look steadfastly into it, and you will discern another curiosity."

I gazed into that fire,—which, symbolically, was the origin of all that was bright and glorious in the soul of man,—and in the midst of it, behold, a little reptile . . .

Just how we should think of the meaning of the serpent in the garden is suggested by the statue of Vertumnus. In Ovid's story of Vertumnus and Pomona, Pomona, like Beatrice, is secluded in a garden, tending plants. Vertumnus woos her, as Giovanni does Beatrice in this Christian garden. But unlike Giovanni, he is successful: there were no serpent-like vines or poisonous plants in *his* garden. Ovid's myth is essentially naturalistic: nature is all, and enough. No powerful antidote is needed to counteract intrinsic poisons. As we shall see, in Hawthorne's garden there is no redemption in nature alone. The water of the fountain, though natural in contrast with the structure built by man to contain it, still points beyond nature, beyond the ruins of time to the immortal; it sparkles because it catches and reflects the sunlight from above. Vertumnus, as Hawthorne well knew, was the Roman god of change, associated with the changes of the seasons, the cycles of time. It is appropriate that the statue of Vertumnus is the only one recognizable among the ruins.

Now Giovanni's attention turns from the fountain to a striking plant that grows beside it. Bearing a profusion of purple blossoms, its beauty is so resplendent that it seems enough "to illuminate the garden, even had there been no sunshine." We soon learn that it is deadly poison, even though it draws sustenance from the water of the fountain and seems bright enough to replace the sunlight. It is given into Beatrice's special care and she acknowledges her affinity with it, calling it "sister" and her "breath of life." She is perfectly "in communion with nature"—until awakened by love to a deeper insight; but it is a nature quite unlike Giovanni's idea of it. ("The young man rejoiced that, in the heart of the barren city, he had the privilege of overlooking this spot of lovely and luxuriant vegetation. It would serve, he said to himself, as a symbolic language to keep him in communion with Nature.") Giovanni is puzzled by what he sees. He likes to have things brought "within the limits of ordinary experience," but his experience has not prepared him for this.

From the cluster of garden images the tale now shifts to the father in the garden. Giovanni becomes aware of "a tall, emaciated, sallow, and sickly-looking man, dressed in a scholar's garb of black." Old and somewhat infirm, the man is especially distinguished, Giovanni thinks, by "a face singularly marked with intellect and cultivation, but which could never, even in his more youthful days, have expressed much warmth of heart." At this point the temptation is

strong to stop reading, to underline this passage, and to decide that the tale is simply a "companion-piece," as it has
been called, to some other tale, for the portrait is so familiar:
a scientist, coldly intellectual, consumed by the *libido
sciendi*, with a heart as stony as Ethan Brand's. But we
should not go too fast. The portrait of the father in the
garden is not complete.

Giovanni watches the old man inspect his garden and
notes an obscurely frightening aspect of the scene: "the
man's demeanor was that of one walking among malignant
influences, such as savage beasts, or deadly snakes, or evil
spirits." This peculiar behavior of the old man is the strangest
thing in the tale so far. It is the first explicit revelation of the
fact that we have here to do with no ordinary garden and no
ordinary old man pottering around it, that here we shall
encounter magic and myth. "It was strangely frightful,"
Hawthorne tells us, "to the young man's imagination to see
this air of insecurity in a person cultivating a garden, that
most simple and innocent of human toils, and which had
been alike the joy and labor of the unfallen parents of the
race." The words "that most simple and innocent of human
toils" serve, one sees, both to re-emphasize the theme of the
mixture and deceptiveness of good and evil and to prepare
for the striking transposition of the theme into another key
in the clause that follows. It is clear now that we are moving
from a garden in Padua to a mythic garden. "Was this
garden, then, the Eden of the present world? And this man,
with such perception of harm in what his own hands caused
to grow,—was he the Adam?"

This is the end of the first part of the story, the first scene
that prepares for the drama. All but one of the important
symbols and characters have now been presented, and that
one, Beatrice, is the most important of all, the Hamlet who
does not enter until scene two. We do not need to go beyond
this first part to see the direction the story is taking. Though
the familiar Hawthorne theme of the *libido sciendi* has appeared, we should not emphasize it at the expense of what
Hawthorne has himself emphasized. What we have here so

far is an observer, a magic, and mythic, garden, a mythic father, and an obscure evil somehow wrought by him.

The rest of the tale develops the situation which has been created before Beatrice appears—which does not, of course, mean that she is not the main character and the chief symbol, but only that she has been properly prepared for. Rappaccini calls for his daughter. Giovanni, watching from his window, is immediately struck by her beauty as she comes through the garden. Her voice before he sees her ("as rich as a tropical sunset") and her clothes after he sees her ("beautiful as the day") suggest to him the strange luxuriant beauty of the flowers in the garden. "She looked radiant with life, health, and energy." Beatrice seems perfectly a part of the nature which provides her setting.

Thus far we see Beatrice chiefly as an extension of the garden imagery. If this were the complete Beatrice we might be justified in concluding with Austin Warren that the tale is not one of Hawthorne's best because the analogy between the girl and the flower, between human nature and subhuman nature, is false. The physical and the psychic certainly do not perfectly correspond. But the story does not finally suggest that they do. We have not seen Beatrice as a person yet, only as a figure in the garden.

If Beatrice reminds Giovanni of the flowers, and particularly of the shrub with the purple blossoms, and if the flowers seem both beautiful and obscurely evil, then the first paradox associated with Beatrice has already been established. It simply extends and deepens the paradox of the garden itself, the fountain, and the special plant: intermingled beauty and ruin, health and death, good and evil. This correspondence of the several symbols—inorganic, vegetable, and animal—has yet to be further emphasized before there can be any significant modification. For it is so obvious to "common sense" that girl and plant are not the same that Hawthorne must first establish his analogy before he can reveal a further insight by altering it. To do so he is forced again, as in the suggestion of obscure evil in the garden, to turn from the "realistic" to the magical. The father commits the special plant to his daughter's sole charge. She accepts gladly, calls the plant "sister," expresses love of it, and exclaims that its fragrance is to her "as the breath of life." Giovanni watches her as she tends the plant with loving care. Darkness falls and he closes his window. When he goes to bed he dreams "of a rich flower and a beautiful girl. Flower and maiden were different, and yet the same, and fraught with some strange peril in either shape."

By this point in the story the thematic materials that are finally shaped into its largest meanings have all emerged, so economically has Hawthorne worked. Two civilizations with their associated views of nature and man, the classical and the Christian, have been suggested as in conflict—the world of the *Divine Comedy* and the world of the ruined fountain, Adam and Vertumnus, the creeping vines on the shattered marble. Hawthorne tells us that Giovanni has a "Grecian" head and is very handsome: lacking both a vision of evil and a "spiritual sense," as it turns out, he is also naïve as well as classically attractive. This modern Vertumnus is one of Hawthorne's Innocents, about to undergo an initiation. His upbringing in a sunnier land has not prepared him for what he will discover about both nature and man: that no simple naturalism will do to describe the facts of a world at once worse and better than the classical mind conceived it. He has perceived, without yet understanding the fact, that so far as "flower and maiden were . . . the same," they were equally "fraught with some strange peril." But they were also different. What makes the difference remains to be revealed.

The development during the middle portion of the story may be summarized briefly. Giovanni is consumed with curiosity about the garden and its inhabitants. He looks out of his window whenever possible. He rationalizes his interest, explaining to himself his prying curiosity with the thought that in his exile in this strange northern city the garden will keep him close to nature. He learns from Professor Baglioni that Dr. Rappaccini is marvelously skilled in science but that his reputation is bad. When he presses for other details, he learns that the particular evil imputed to Dr. Rappaccini is that he "cares infinitely more for science than for mankind. His patients are interesting to him only as subjects for some new experiment." Giovanni concludes that Rappaccini must be an "awful man indeed."

Now since this *libido sciendi* characterization of Rappaccini has so often been taken to be *the* meaning of the tale, I should like to pause at this point and suggest some of the reasons why it cannot be more than one of several meanings and not the chief of them. First, Beatrice is the chief character, the center of interest, and the primary symbol throughout, from the title to her death at the end. In his playful preface Hawthorne suggests an intention that is clear enough from the work itself. Pretending to be merely editing the works of an obscure French writer, he gives the original title of the tale as *Beatrice; ou la Belle Empoisonneuse.* In his work as "translator" he gives the story an English title which sacrifices the literal to the thematic but still keeps the major emphasis where it was: not Rappaccini but Rappaccini's *daughter* is his subject.

Rappaccini, from the time when we first see him inspecting the garden until, at the end, he steps forward again to join Giovanni and Beatrice, is nearly always in the background, a sinister but shadowy figure. Once Giovanni sees him in a crowd. The doctor seems to be studying the young man with cold curiosity, and Baglioni warns that he may be performing a "new experiment"—that is, planning to let Giovanni come in contact with Beatrice so that he may study the result. But of course this "experiment" would involve no significant new act on the doctor's part: he would simply allow the young people to have their way while he watched the spreading effects of his poison. Neither the significance of Rappaccini as a symbol nor his position in the story as a background character is changed by this or by Giovanni's suspicion that it may have been Rappaccini who prompted Dame Lisabetta to reveal the gate to the garden.

To repeat: Rappaccini with his black magic and his "insane zeal for science," as Baglioni calls it, must be ever present to make the story literally possible and symbolically meaningful, but it is present evil, a woman poisoned, that is the chief subject of the story. Black magic is simply assumed here as witchcraft is in "Young Goodman Brown." It is not the father, whose cold intellectuality has been established before the tale is one-fifth completed, but the evil which he has wrought which here chiefly concerns us.

Returning to the action, we find Giovanni's interest in the garden and its inhabitants becoming fascination and the fascination centering on the person of Beatrice. He is attracted first of all by her physical beauty, but he soon notes also the "sweetness" and "simplicity" of her face. When flowers seem to wilt at her touch, when a lizard dies after the juice of the plant is dropped on him, when a butterfly dies after it comes too close to her, he is forced to think of the apparent affinity between Beatrice and the beautiful but obscurely dangerous plant. He tries to believe that his eyes have deceived him. Surely the garden contains no real evil. Warned by Baglioni against becoming further involved in Rappaccini's experiment, he experiences new doubts and fears but manages to push them into the back of his mind. But when, in the garden at last and alone, he examines the flowers closely, he is further disturbed by noting that "their gorgeousness seemed fierce, passionate, and even unnatural." It begins to seem to him that they are not truly "of God's making, but the monstrous offspring of man's depraved fancy, glowing with only an evil mockery of beauty."

The only new revelations in the remainder of the middle part of the story concern Beatrice. They make her a person, not simply, as she has chiefly been when viewed only from the distance of the window, a symbol of man's involvement in nature. When she first finds Giovanni in the garden she is of course surprised, but the surprise in her face was "brightened by a simple and kind expression of pleasure." We should not expect this of an evil person. Hawthorne's normal practice would lead us to expect some suggestion of cunning, some hint that this "simple and kind expression" is only a mask of evil designs if she were really evil. F. O. Matthiessen has said that Giovanni was wrong in supposing that he could save her, that he was wrong because she has been made really evil. But of course she is evil only in so far as she shares the poison of the plant. She is both a creature of nature and an immortal spirit. Nature cannot wholly contain her. It may turn out that the poison is ineradicable as long as she lives: but she has a spirit which can choose death. Like the rest of mankind, she has a dual nature.

Again, when she becomes aware of Giovanni's doubts and fears concerning her, she protests her innocence and says that she is not, as is reputed, skilled in science, that she knows nothing of the lore of her father. Her appearance is deceptive but her words come from the depths of her heart: "Those you may believe." She seems, Hawthorne tells us, as she says this to be more radiant than ever, to radiate "the light of truth itself." Once more we must say that if Hawthorne meant Beatrice to be wholly evil he has written ineptly. For unlike the many ideas that are the productions of Giovanni's fancy, these suggestions of the purity of Beatrice's intentions are directly stated by Hawthorne: not that it seemed to Giovanni that she was kind and simple but that she *was*. On the other hand, when he looked into her eyes and saw the beauty of her soul, it *seemed* to him that there was no more danger. Hawthorne is distinguishing carefully between conceptions which he presents as justified and those which are the products of poor Giovanni's ability to delude himself. There was danger, more danger than Beatrice herself knew, though everything she said was true. Giovanni's "mistake" reminds us of young Goodman Brown's. He had not the wit to see her as other than simply good or simply bad. He "had not a deep heart," Hawthorne tells us.

Only two more revelations of the nature of Beatrice are needed to complete this central part of the story. First, she falls in love with Giovanni. She watches daily for his appearance and flies to his side "with confidence as unreserved as if they had been playmates from infancy." Second, as her love for Giovanni grows her dependence on the plant lessens.

Even after their first meeting, though she still addresses the plant as before, she notes that "For the first time in my life . . . I had forgotten thee." Now her former "sisterhood" with the plant saddens her. She warns Giovanni not to touch it or to touch her. Her happiness at their meetings is punctuated by an increasingly "desolate" awareness of her "separation." Giovanni's initiation has not been the only one going on here. Beatrice too has been awakened to her true situation. Aware of evil for the first time, she sees it as separating her both from nature and from man, leaving her essentially alone. Communing with nature is no longer able to satisfy her, now that she recognizes nature for what it is; but she is still too much a part of nature to move into a heavenly realm where love would be all and pure motives would ensure beneficent results. Recognizing her poisonousness, she joins that "brotherhood of guilt" that Hawthorne so often posited. But guilt was not all: just because she recognized and acknowledged it, she could be saved, could "ascend" at last.

The final portion of the tale begins when Giovanni, hearing from Baglioni the story of the terrible result of Rappaccini's "insane zeal for science" and being warned that he too may become a victim of it, decides to take a powerful antidote that Baglioni has distilled, get Beatrice to drink it, and thus see if he cannot work a radical cure. Buying Beatrice a bouquet to take to her with the medicine, he finds to his horror that the flowers wither at his touch. Angry and frightened, with all his love, which has never been of the same quality as Beatrice's love for him, changed to fear and hatred, he rushes into the garden to stand before "the bright and loving eyes of Beatrice." Again the sight of her beauty and the memory of her apparent sweetness and purity move him. But he is as blind in his fright as he had been in his infatuation. He bursts out with questions and accusations. She tells him all she knows of her "awful doom," of the plant that her father created, and of its obscure connection with her own being. Giovanni responds to her frank statements with contempt and loathing. He speaks of his "unutterable hatred" of her and mocks her broken prayer with "fiendish scorn."

Beatrice asserts once more her innocence of intention: "Not for a world of bliss would I have done it!" To Giovanni's suggestion that they both drink the antidote, she says that she alone will drink it and he must await the result. As she does so, her father approaches and tells her that she is no longer alone, that she now has a companion in her isolation. Addressing her as "daughter of my pride and triumph," he denies that he has inflicted great misery on her: has he not given her greater power over others than any woman has ever had before, power even to kill at a touch?

She replies that she would be loved, not feared. "But now it matters not," for she is going where the evil which her father has striven to mingle with her being will pass away. The pain of Giovanni's "words of hatred" will fall away too in a moment. She wonders whether there was not always more evil in Giovanni's nature than in her own. Then she dies, "a poor victim of man's ingenuity and of thwarted nature, and of the fatality that attends all such efforts of perverted wisdom." Her "earthly part," Hawthorne tells us, could not throw off the poison her father had implanted, so that "the powerful antidote was death." Baglioni, appearing with rather improbable timeliness, observes the scene in the garden and taunts Rappaccini with the unforeseen "upshot" of his experiment.

Several comments are necessary on this ending, which may seem to ring several false notes. First, the emphasis in the end is where it has been all along: on Rappaccini's daughter, her poisonousness and innocence, her awful doom, her awareness, her acceptance of death as the antidote, her escape from the poison. If the note about her "ascending" seems a flaw to the modern mind, it is at least consistent with the medieval setting, the elements of magic and myth, and the frame of ideas within which the entire story is told, though it must be noted that she, not Hawthorne, uses this physical imagery.

Second, as the tale has progressed Hawthorne has made us increasingly aware of Giovanni's unadmirable character.

He is not actively bad, he is only the natural man, unchanged by Grace, unaided by Revelation. With his Grecian head and his shallow heart, he is, in one dimension, an embodiment of the pagan vision. As Hawthorne said several times outside his fiction and in it, such a vision seemed to him to lack depth. Unillumined by Christian truth, lacking Beatrice's "quick spiritual sense," he was incapable not only of her "high faith" but even of correctly interpreting what lay before his eyes. Giovanni extends the implications of the ruined classical fountain.

But there is also another way in which we may take him. He is one of Hawthorne's "empiricists." Commenting on the young man's attempts to rationalize his experience and explain away what did not fit into his simple naturalistic view of man and nature, Hawthorne says he was forced for a time to deny the testimony of his own senses: a curious position for an empiricist to be in. But Hawthorne explains his paradox immediately: "There is something truer and more real than what we can see with the eyes and touch with the finger." This is "better evidence" than such tangible facts as those Giovanni normally based his judgments on. In both his classical and his empiricist roles, then, Giovanni is unfitted to understand what he finds in this garden.

The emphasis Hawthorne has placed on the father in his concluding sentence—" 'Rappaccini! Rappaccini! and is *this* the upshot of your experiment!' "—may seem to run counter to what has been said about the centrality of Beatrice in the tale. Is Hawthorne faltering here, or should we take the story after all as simply another variation on the theme of the pride of intellect? Is this another false note, or is Beatrice still the most important character?

If we were to understand Hawthorne's intention in his final sentence as that of making Rappaccini central, then we should have to assume, not that he faltered here by throwing out a misleading clue but that he wrote weakly throughout the earlier part of the tale by revealing Rappaccini's character fully in the opening pages and adding nothing new to the portrait from that point on. In a sense, to be sure, Rappaccini frames the tale as the first person seen by Giovanni and the last person named by Baglioni; but in between, he exists only in the background, and after we have learned of his cold intellectuality, his scientific pursuits, his sickly aspect, and his love of his daughter, there is nothing more to learn about him. The portraits of Beatrice and Giovanni, in contrast, develop in action and are more than one-dimensional. But not only are they revealed to us gradually, the characters themselves come to significant recognitions. To make Rappaccini the protagonist is necessarily to conclude that the story is weak. We know him too well, too abstractly, too soon, and he, so far as we know, learns nothing from his experience.

It is the death of his daughter that is the "upshot" of his experiment that his rival taunts him with. This is what it comes to, that only death would prove an antidote powerful enough to release her from the poison her father's "fatal love of science" had created. So in an earlier Garden the desire to be godlike in knowledge had brought sin and death into the world. Beatrice is Hawthorne's symbol of man and his situation in a fallen world. *This* is the upshot. The final sentence, rather than removing Beatrice from the central position in the story, reinforces her centrality once for all.

4

"The Man of Adamant" has considerably more literary value than we should expect of an apologue, and "Rappaccini's Daughter" has the kind of value we do not find in pure allegory. In both, the texture supplies a complexity that qualifies and deepens the meanings implied in the structure. In both, the degree of aesthetic distance is great and the illusion of reality slight by contemporary standards; the appeal is to the contemplative side of the aesthetic experience. Yet even "The Man of Adamant" provides material for contemplation that a philosophic statement on the nature and effects of bigotry could hardly provide.

As for "Rappaccini's Daughter," it is like "Roger Malvin's

Burial" in moving from the literal to the symbolic and finally to the mythic. If it seems less a product of the passive sensibility than "Roger Malvin's Burial" and "My Kinsman, Major Molineux," its texture is more intricately wrought. In this it is more nearly like *The House of the Seven Gables* than like *The Scarlet Letter*; it may be used to define one of the modes of Hawthorne's fiction. That he preferred this mode to that which sprang more directly from the type of sensibility he described in "The Haunted Mind" is not surprising in view of what we have seen of the visions that so often haunted him between sleep and waking.

All the best of Hawthorne's tales exist in the area bounded by allegory and history, archetype and myth. They convey the kind of knowledge poetry conveys, in symbolic terms not essentially different from those poetry uses. The less successful tales fall short of greatness as "The Great Carbuncle" falls short, by not establishing firmly enough the concrete, the actual, the historical; or they fail as some of the "Legends of the Province House" do, by not infusing history with sufficient meaning. "The Great Carbuncle" and "Howe's Masquerade" are both memorable stories in their different ways, but they are not in the same category of greatness with "Roger Malvin's Burial" and "Young Goodman Brown" and "Rappaccini's Daughter." The difference between the lesser and the greater seems to lie in this: that the greater, whether they spring from the depths or the top of the mind, have both the universality of "The Man of Adamant" and the historicity of "Howe's Masquerade." Hawthorne's best tales have as much illusion of reality as they need to set up significances we cannot easily exhaust.

CHAPTER FIVE

THE SCARLET LETTER

Hawthorne's masterpiece has aroused many different reactions in its readers and inspired many interpretations. An early reviewer was shocked by the gentle way it treats an adulteress and, by implication, the light view it takes of adultery. A critic of our day has found it worth only an A minus because of the reservations Hawthorne seems to have about identifying himself entirely with Hester's antinomian views of a new order of society. Readers have not even agreed on the central subject. Is it the individual in relation to society, or the effects of hidden as contrasted with open guilt, or neither of these? Should the novel be called allegory or symbolism?

This continued variety of response testifies of course to its richness as a work of art. If some of the responses seem inappropriate, many of them seem just; with all their special emphases, they still are responses to what is there, the work itself. Insofar as they are mutually corrective and complementary rather than incompatible, they seem to me to exhaust the possibilities, for our time at least, of "interpretation." At least I have no "new interpretation" to offer.

What seems to me to need doing at this point in the development of Hawthorne criticism is to show *why* the work is more enigmatic than Hawthorne's other finished romances, even though there is a sense in which one would think it ought to be clearer. It ought to be clearer because it has less action and more exposition devoted to analysis of meaning. Expository writing is a way of "telling," narration a way of "showing." If symbolism is always more ambiguous than allegory and art contains a functional ambiguity that would be a defect in logical statement, why is this novel, which leans so heavily on statement, so ambiguous? Why has there been less agreement about its meaning than there has about the meaning of *The House of the Seven Gables*, in which there is more action, less expository analysis?

2

One may begin to shape an answer to this question simply by looking at the opening chapter. Hawthorne may be doing more telling than showing here, if we allow "telling" to include description as well as exposition and think of "showing" as meaning narration, but he is "telling" in a very special way. He is in fact letting his images do most of the work for him, even while he reserves the right to comment abstractly on them and, in later chapters, on the rare but significant actions. In the three short paragraphs that make up his opening chapter Hawthorne introduces the three chief symbols that will serve to give structure to the story on the thematic level, hints at the fourth, and starts two of the chief lines of imagery. The opening sentence suggests the darkness ("sad-colored," "gray"), the rigidity ("oak," "iron"), and the aspiration ("steeple-crowned") of the people "amongst whom religion and law were almost identical." Later sentences add "weatherstains," "a yet darker aspect," and "gloomy" to the suggestions already begun through color imagery. The closing words of the chapter make the metaphorical use of color explicit: Hawthorne hopes that a wild rose beside the prison door may serve "to symbolize some sweet moral blossom, that may be found along the track, or relieve the darkening close of a tale of human frailty and sorrow."

A large part of the opening chapter is allotted to this rose-bush and to some weeds that also grow beside the prison. Having learned to respect the economy with which Hawthorne worked in his tales, we should guess, even if we had not read beyond this first chapter, that these will turn out not to be merely "realistic" or "atmospheric" details. We should expect to meet them again, with expanded connotations. Actually, the flower and weed imagery is second in importance only to the color imagery in the novel. The more than thirty occasions on which it is subsequently found are not, like the even more frequent heart images, casual, or partly to be accounted for as stylistic mannerisms, the reflexes as it were of Hawthorne's style, but chief keys to the symbolic structure and intention of this work.

Finally, in addition to the Puritans themselves, the jail before which they stand, and the weeds and the rose, one other object, and only one, is mentioned in this first chapter. In the only generalized comment in a chapter otherwise devoted to objective description, Hawthorne tells us that "The founders of a new colony, whatever Utopia of human virtue and happiness they might originally project, have invariably recognized it among their earliest practical necessities to allot a portion of the virgin soil as a cemetery, and another portion as the site of a prison." The three climactic scenes of the novel take place before the scaffold in front of the prison. The cemetery, by contrast, remains in the background. We are not allowed to forget it, we learn that Chillingworth has a special interest in it, but we are not encouraged to make it the center of our attention until the end, when it moves into the foreground as the site of the tombstone with the strange inscription.

The cemetery, the prison, and the rose, with their associated values and the extensions of suggestion given them by the image patterns that intersect them, as the ugliest weeds are later discovered growing out of graves, suggest a symbolic pattern within which nearly everything that is most important in the novel may be placed. The cemetery and the prison are negative values, in some sense evils. The rose is a positive value, beautiful, in some sense a good. But the cemetery and the prison are not negative in the same sense: death, "the last great enemy," is a natural evil, resulting as some theologies would have it from moral evil but distinguished by coming to saint and sinner alike; the prison is a reminder of the present actuality of moral evil. Natural and moral evil, then, death and sin, are here suggested. The rose is "good" in the same sense in which the cemetery is an "evil": its beauty is neither moral nor immoral but is certainly a positive value. Like the beauty of a healthy child or an animal, it is the product not of choice but of necessity, of the laws of its being, so that it can be admired but not judged. Pearl, later in the story, is similarly immune from judgment. There is no strong suggestion of moral goodness in this first chapter, nor will there be in what is to follow. The cemetery and the weeds contrast with the rose, but only the suggestions of worship in the shape of the hats of the Puritans contrast with the prison, and those steeple-crowned hats are gray, a color which later takes on strongly negative associations.

Among the ideas implicit in the opening chapter, then, are, first, that the novel is to be concerned with the relationships of good and evil; second, that it will distinguish between two types of good and evil; and, third, that moral good will be less strongly felt than moral and natural evil. A symmetrical pattern is theoretically suggested here, and as we shall see, in the rest of the novel. But what is actually felt is an asymmetrical pattern, an imbalance, in which the shapes of moral and natural evil loom so large as to make it difficult to discern, or to "believe in" once we have discerned, the reality of moral goodness or redemption. The rose, in short, is finally not sufficient to relieve "the darkening close of a tale of human frailty and sorrow." The celestial radiance later seen gleaming from the white hair of Mr. Wilson is not sufficient either, nor the snowy innocence said to exist in the bosoms of certain maidens. In writing *The Scarlet Letter* Hawthorne let his genius take its course, and death and sin turned out to be more convincing than life and goodness.

3

The extremes of Mr. Wilson's "light" and Chillingworth's "blackness" meet not only in the gray of Hester's dress and the Puritan hats, and in the indeterminate drabness of the Puritan clothing, but also in the ambiguous suggestions of red. Images of color, and of light and shade, are more numerous than any other images in the novel. Readers have always been aware that Hawthorne has used these images "artistically," and sometimes that he has used them "expressively"; yet precisely what they express and how they express it have never, even in the extended treatments of the subject, been adequately analyzed. Some of them Hawthorne makes explicitly symbolic, others seem obscurely to be so, while still others resist every effort at translation into abstract terms. Faced with this profusion and complexity of evidence, most commentators have wavered between the opinion that the color images are used "allegorically" and the even less discerning opinion that they are only in the vaguest sense, as realistic background, functional. Here, as on a number of other aspects of Hawthorne's work, criticism is forced to make something like a fresh start. I think it will prove useful as a preliminary to later analysis to distinguish among three ways in which images of color and light and shade appear in the novel.

There is, first, the pure sensory image used literally, not figuratively, though the literalness of its use will not destroy whatever intrinsic symbolic value it may have. Second, there is the color or shade of light or darkness that must be taken literally but that also has explicit symbolic value. Finally, there is the image that has only, or chiefly, symbolic value, so that it cannot be taken literally. I shall call these pure, mixed, and drained images. It will be clear that this sort of classification cuts across other types of analysis, such as that which distinguishes between emphatic and casual imagery and that which seeks to isolate implicit paradox or distinguish types of ambiguity. The strategy here is intended to bring out the degree of "literalness" with which Hawthorne writes, and this matter in turn has an important bearing on the question of whether *The Scarlet Letter* is symbolism or allegory.

But first it must be clear that there is a real basis in the novel for making such distinctions—or that the data will lend themselves to such manipulation without forcing. A look at the first several chapters will be enough I think to give us an answer. Thus on the first page the grayness of the hats and the "weatherstains" of the jail are pure images, sense impressions to be taken quite literally. Only after we have become conscious of the part played by color in the tale are we apt to be aware of the appropriateness of these colors, though to be sure they may have had their effect on us before we became conscious of that effect. So likewise the "bright" morning sun and the "ruddy" cheeks of the spectators in the next chapter are first of all, and always fundamentally, to be understood in a perfectly literal sense. Again, the first time the scarlet letter is mentioned, the color image is pure: "On the breast of her gown, in fine red cloth, surrounded with an elaborate embroidery and fantastic flourishes of gold-thread, appeared the letter A."

Mixed images, on the other hand, have more than that suggestion of figurative extension that any image, however pure, will have: they may be said to *denote* both literal and figurative colors, so that in them the natural symbolism of color becomes explicit. The jail is "gloomy," that is, both physically and emotionally dark. The second time the letter is mentioned, its color has acquired a moral connotation from its context: Hester stood before the crowd with "desperate recklessness" while everyone looked at the sign of her ignominy, "that SCARLET LETTER." More clearly an example of this mixed type of image is the beadle's statement that here in this righteous colony "iniquity is dragged out into the sunshine": for Hester has just been brought from the literal darkness of the jail into the literal sunshine of the square, and this action is an example of "iniquity" which has been hidden or unknown being made public, brought into the (figurative) light. The speaker has meant his remark as a figure of speech, while the reader sees that it is literally appropriate too; there is a two-way movement, from the literal to the figurative, and from the figurative back to the literal, going on here and elsewhere in the color images in the novel. One final example in this preliminary survey of the mixed type of image: "his face darkened with some powerful emotion." Now powerful emotion may literally darken the face by flushing it, but here the symbolic effect of darkness, as that which is feared and evil, is also clear. This is the first reference to the "darkness" of Chillingworth.

The third or drained type of image is much less frequent than the other two. (There are ten times as many pure images as drained, and about twice as many mixed, according to my count.) On the first page we hear of the "black flower" of civilized society, a prison, and we realize that "black" is here figurative, for though the jail has been described as dark and weatherstained, it is not black in any literal sense. Again, in the last sentence of the first chapter we hear of the "darkening close" of the tale, and we read "darkening" to mean gloomy (in the emotional sense), sad. Finally, when the Reverend Mr. Wilson speaks to Hester of the "blackness" of her sin, the primary significance of the word, both for Hester and for the reader, is intensive and qualitative in a moral sense; the residue of literal meaning merely adds to the emotional overtones. Here, as in the "smile of dark and self-relying intelligence" displayed by Chillingworth, there is hardly any literal meaning left.

The colors presented in these three types of images are associated with natural good (beauty, health), moral and spiritual good (holiness), natural evil (ugliness, death), and moral evil (sin). With the exception of the yellow starch on the linen of Mistress Hibbens, in which I can discern only historical verisimilitude, all the colors in the novel, including yellow as used elsewhere, are associated with one or more natural or moral values, positive or negative. The most frequent colors are red in its several shades and black, pure or mixed, as in "gray," "shadowy," and "darksome." Red is ambiguous throughout, suggesting both sunlight and roses, on the one hand, and the traditional associations called up by "the scarlet woman" on the other. Pearl, a "natural" child, is dressed in red, Hester's letter is red, the roses are red, the bloom on healthy cheeks is red, and the glow in Chillingworth's eyes is thought to be red with the light of infernal fires. Black, dark gray, brown, all the darker shades, ordinarily suggest both natural and moral evil. Green and yellow are associated with natural good, with life and beauty.

Light is of various kinds. Sunlight suggests both truth and health. It is analogous to the spiritual Light of Revelation, which in Hawthorne's scheme of values should "illumine" nature, and to the light of grace. But there are also the "false light" of meteors and the "red light" of evil. Mr. Wilson, the most saintly of the Puritan ministers and the most sympathetic of the lesser characters, has "white" hair and light-colored ("gray") eyes, in marked contrast to the only colors assigned to Governor Bellingham, who has a "dark" feather and a "black" tunic. Thus too Dimmesdale, a mixed figure of lofty aspirations and base conduct, is seen as having a "white," lofty, and impending brow and "brown," melancholy eyes. Dressed in "black," he walks by choice in the "shadowy" bypaths. Hester is seen as red (her letter and her vivid complexion), gray (her dress), and black (her hair and eyes), the first two ambiguous in their associations, the last saved from being wholly negative by the glints of sunlight often seen in her hair. Pearl, though she has her mother's black hair and eyes, is usually seen as a flash of red and light: the "deep and vivid tints" of her "bright" complexion and "gorgeous robes" often throw an absolute circle of "radiance" around her. Chillingworth is compounded of shades of "darkness," except for the red, or reddish blue, glow thought to be seen in his eyes.

The relationships between the three types of images, the several colors, and their associated moral and natural values are highly complex, but I shall risk a few generalizations, the first of which is the most obvious. The use of colors in the novel is rhythmic, but it is more than that, for the rhythm is functional and expressive. In "The Interior of a Heart," for instance, there are twenty-two color images, all but two of which are black or white. The heart is Dimmesdale's, and Dimmesdale wavers between good and evil, we might almost say between the supernatural and the unnatural. It is conceptually right that he should be associated with both the radiance of Wilson and the darkness of Chillingworth. He is never associated with the greens and yellows and reds of sunlit nature.

Again, the chapter called "Hester at Her Needle" has eighteen color images, eleven of them red, seven black, dark, and white. Hester stands in an ambiguous position between Chillingworth and the white maidens, as Dimmesdale does between Chillingworth and Wilson, but she differs from him in her relation to nature. For a final example, on one page of "The Minister's Vigil," when the approach of Mr. Wilson and the threat of disclosure coincide, there are nine color images, eight of which are of light or whiteness. Recalling the beadle's earlier remark about the Puritan effort to drag iniquity out into the sunshine, in which light was associated with an uncharitable violation of the human heart, we become aware of what is sometimes obscured in discussions of Hawthorne: that color imagery is functional *in context*, not static or determined by some abstract scheme.

The most significant use of color in the novel is in the three key scenes, Hester on the scaffold with the infant Pearl, Dimmesdale with Hester and Pearl on the scaffold at midnight, and the three on the scaffold again at the end. In the first, Hester is dragged into the light and stands there "with the hot, mid-day sun burning down upon her face, and lighting up its shame; with the scarlet token of infamy on her breast. . ." In the second there is at first only the darkness of the "obscure night," which renders Dimmesdale's gesture ineffectual. Then two kinds of light appear. First there is the gleam of the lantern of the saintly Mr. Wilson, who appeared in his illuminated circle to be radiant with the "distant shine of the celestial city"; but Mr. Wilson's light does not reach Dimmesdale, who is thus "saved" by a narrow margin from disclosure. After Mr. Wilson's light recedes in the darkness, a meteor flames in the sky, making all visible, but in a "false" light, so that what Chillingworth sees by its aid is not true. Neither light in this scene accomplishes the necessary revelation. That is left for the final climactic scaffold scene, in which the three come together voluntarily in the light of the sun.

The second generalization I should like to suggest about the light and color images is this: their significance is enriched by the relations between the three types of images. In the first place, the pure images are so much the most numerous that they tend to establish, by sheer weight of repetition, the reading of the others. Where there is so much blackness, "gloomy" is bound to carry its physical as well as its emotional denotation. This becomes clearer when we compare the use of darkness in, say, *Dr. Grimshawe's Secret* with its use here. When in the later novel Redclyffe is said to exist in a darkened dream, we do not know quite what to make of it, for darkness has not been established as a motif in the novel. But when Governor Bellingham says that Pearl is "in the dark" concerning her soul, the expression means far more to the reader than that she is not, in the opinion of the governor, properly instructed: it calls up the whole range of colors, and the moral and other values attached to them, which the reader has absorbed by this time. We have another of those sudden expansions from image to symbol that is so conspicuous a feature of the novel.

In short, the marked predominance of pure images keeps the mixed and drained ones from losing force by becoming abstractly figurative, and this in turn is one of the reasons why the novel never becomes allegory. Though we must say that there is a struggle going on in the novel between the forces of darkness and of light, the preponderance of pure images keeps this struggle from becoming neatly dichotomous. When we read that Chillingworth had conceived "a new purpose, dark, it is true, if not guilty," we do not read this as a pleonasm, for darkness has acquired many associations beyond the guilt it may hide. Again, the "light" of the church is saved from being a mere figure for "the teaching of the church" by the fact that light has become associated with a cluster of positive values, both natural and moral, that cannot be translated adequately as "doctrine."

Finally, two drained images will illustrate the point. "The holy whiteness of the clergyman's good fame," in reference to Dimmesdale, draws a part of its meaning from the light constantly associated with Mr. Wilson and Christian Revelation, but another part from the false light of the meteor, which has only recently ceased to cast its distorting glare over the scene. And the smile that "flickered" over Chillingworth's face "so derisively" that the spectator could see his "blackness" "all the better for it" is also a false light which nevertheless may reveal some things truly, as the light of the meteor had revealed "the black, freshly turned earth" of the garden plots near the scaffold.

But the movement flows in another direction too, for the presence of the mixed and drained images underlines the symbolic value of the pure images. When Pearl, inspired by her mother's example, makes a letter out of eelgrass for her own breast, and Hester says that "the green letter, and on thy childish bosom, has no purport," we realize that the statement is true in several different senses: from Hester's point of view, the green letter has none of the "purport" that her own letter has, and she, of course, is preoccupied with just that kind of meaning; but from the reader's point of view, the greenness of the letter is an appropriate reminder of Pearl's association with nature. And when we see the Indians in the square on Election Day, the predominant reds and yellows of their barbaric finery and the black of their "snakelike" eyes carry associations with nature and with evil, but none at all with "celestial illumination." Like the weathered wood of the jail, the Indian costumes gather meaning from their context.

The point of my third generalization about the three types of images has perhaps already become sufficiently clear from what has been said, but it is so important that I should not like to let it rest on implication. The movement of the different colors back and forth between pure and drained images helps to keep what Hawthorne calls his "mesh of good and evil" a true mesh, with the strands intricately interwoven. Hawthorne usually presents a pure image first, establishing the sensed color, then expands it into a mixed image, exploring its connotations, then at last uses the color in a drained image that out of the total context of the novel would be bare and lifeless, or merely whimsical, but that in context is rich in the associations it has acquired along the way. But sometimes he reverses this process, and sometimes he jumbles the order, so that the colors are never completely fixed in the degree of their literalness or the extension of their symbolic values. When we read, for instance, of the "radiant halo" surrounding the head of Mr. Wilson as he walked through a "gloomy night of sin," the image that we should expect to be merely figurative, the "halo" of sanctity, turns out to be literal as well, for the light is shed by Mr. Wilson's lantern; and the one that we should at first expect to be literal—for we already know that it is a dark night, and as we start reading "this gloomy night . . ." we think we are getting a mere restatement of the darkness—turns out to be also figurative, forcing us to revise the reaction we had prepared.

The relations between the light and color images and their symbolic values are, then, neither static and schematized nor wholly free and arbitrary, but contextual within a general framework supplied by traditional patterns of color symbolism. The traditional associations of light and dark, for example, are apparently archetypal. Literature is filled with the darkness of death and sin and the light of life and goodness; and the common speech allows us to "throw light" upon a problem as often as we "explain" or "clarify" it. Perhaps the most nearly fixed in its symbolic values of all the colors in the novel is black. Yet even it is sometimes used ambiguously. Hester's black hair, that glistened so often in the sunlight before she covered it with a cap, and Pearl's "dark, glistening curls," so well set off by her scarlet costume, are examples. On the other hand, the red that runs through the book as a motif is almost always used ambiguously. Only a few examples, like the "red glare" in Chillingworth's eyes, are wholly clear, with one set of suggestions canceled out and another emphasized. The wild roses and the scarlet letter, Pearl's costume and her mother's complexion do not exhaust the possibilities. Chillingworth's light is thought to be a reflection of the infernal fires, but Pearl is also said to be a flame. When the forest, seeming to recognize a kindred spirit in Pearl, offers her partridgeberries "red as drops of blood" the gift carries with it memories not only of the rose bush but of the scarlet letter.

In short, red, black, gray, sunlight, firelight, and the less frequent green, yellow, blue, and purple are not simply descriptive of the setting and characters. In a very real sense they are themselves actors in the story that moves through and behind the story. Even in their absence they help to tell the tale. When we find that the most strongly and frequently presented colors are those most commonly associated with negative or ambiguous moral values, or with positive natural values, and that the light of positive moral and spiritual values is both less vivid and less frequent, we are not surprised. The first chapter prepared us for this. Perhaps the largest generalization we may draw from a study of the approximately 425 light and color images is that Hawthorne conceived, but when writing the novel did not strongly feel, the possibility of escape from evil and the past.

4

The "burdock, pigweed, apple-peru, and such unsightly vegetation" growing beside the prison, that "black flower of civilized society," where grass should have been, begin the flower and weed imagery, which, in some thirty images and extended analogies, reinforces and extends the implications of the imagery of color and light. Since these implications have already been drawn out, I shall simply call attention briefly to four relationships Hawthorne has set up.

First, and most clearly, the unnatural flowers and unsightly vegetation are aligned with moral evil, and with

Chillingworth in particular. He too with his deformity is "unsightly." Low, dark, and ugly, he suggests to some people the notion that his step must wither the grass wherever he walks. The sun seems not to fall on him but to create "a circle of ominous shadow moving along with his deformity." It is natural enough then to find him explicitly associated with "deadly nightshade" and other types of "vegetable wickedness," to see him displaying a "dark, flabby leaf" found growing out of a grave, and to hear that prominent among the herbs he has gathered are some "black weeds" that have "sprung up out of a buried heart." When his evil work was done "he positively withered up, shriveled away . . . like an uprooted weed that lies wilting in the sun." Flower and weed imagery unites with light and color imagery to define Chillingworth's position as that of the chief sinner.

But Chillingworth is not the only one so aligned. Less emphatically, the Puritans themselves are associated with weeds and black flowers. The implications of color imagery first set up the association: as their "Puritanic gloom" increases in the second generation to "the blackest shade of Puritanism," we begin to see them as cousins to the "nightshade" and so are prepared for Pearl's pretense that the weeds she attacks in her solitary games are Puritan children. Accustomed to her apparently infallible instinct for the truth, we see in her game something more than childish imagination.

The second relationship deserving of note also starts in the first chapter. We recall Hawthorne's saying of the wild rose-bush in bloom beside the prison that he hoped it might "relieve the darkening close" of his tale. No "sweet moral blossom" plays any significant part in the main story, but the happy fortune of Pearl, related in the concluding chapter, does offer a contrast with the "frailty and sorrow" of the tale proper. Thus Pearl's final role is foreshadowed in the first chapter. But Hawthorne does not wait until the end to make this apparent. He constantly associates her not only with the scarlet letter on her mother's dress but with the red rose. The rose bears "delicate gems" and Pearl is the red-clad "gem" of her mother's bosom. Her flowerlike beauty is frequently underscored. And naturally so, for we are told that she had sprung, "a lovely and immortal flower," out of the "rank luxuriance" of a guilty passion.

The position thus defined is repeatedly emphasized. Pearl cries for a red rose in the governor's garden. She answers the catechetical question who made her by declaring that she had not been made at all but "had been plucked by her mother off the bush of wild roses that grew by the prison door." She decorates her hair with flowers, which are said to become her perfectly. She is reflected in the pool in "all the brilliant picturesqueness of her beauty, in its adornment of flowers." Her "flower-girdled and sunny image" has all the glory of a "bright flower." Pearl is a difficult child, capricious, unintentionally cruel, unfeeling in her demand for truth, but she has both the "naturalness" and the beauty of the rose, and like the rose she is a symbol of love and promise.

These are the associations Hawthorne most carefully elaborates, but there are two others worth noting briefly. Weeds or "black flowers" are on several occasions associated with Hester. The most striking instance of this occurs when Pearl pauses in the graveyard to pick "burrs" and arrange them "along the lines of the scarlet letter that decorated the maternal bosom, to which the burrs, as their nature was, tenaciously adhered." The burrs are like Pearl in acting according to nature, and what they suggest in their clinging cannot be wholly false. Hester implicitly acknowledges the truth of what the burrs have revealed when she suggests to Dimmesdale that they let the "black flower" of their love "blossom as it may."

But a more frequent and impressive association is set up between Hester and normal flowers. Even the badge of her shame, the token of her "guilty" love, is thus associated with natural beauty. The scarlet letter is related to the red rose from the very beginning. As Hester stands before her judges in the opening scenes, the sun shines on just two spots of vivid color in all that massed black, brown, and gray: on the rose and the letter, both red. The embroidery with which

she decorates the letter further emphasizes the likeness, so
that when Pearl throws flowers at her mother's badge and
they hit the mark, we share her sense that this is appropriate.
Burrs and flowers seem to have an affinity for Hester's letter.
Hawthorne was too much of a Protestant to share the Catholic attitude toward "natural law": the imagery here suggests
that moral law and nature's ways do not perfectly coincide,
or run parallel on different levels; they cross, perhaps at
something less than a right angle. At the point of their cross-
ing the lovers' fate is determined. No reversal of the implied
moral judgment is suggested when nature seems to rejoice
at the reaffirmed love of the pair in the forest: "Such was the
sympathy of Nature—that wild, heathen Nature of the
forest, never subjugated by human law, nor illumined by
higher truth—with the bliss of these two spirits! Love,
whether newly born, or aroused from a death-like slumber,
must always create a sunshine."

Hester's emblem, then, points to a love both good and bad.
The ambiguity of her gray robes and dark glistening hair,
her black eyes and bright complexion, is thus emphasized
by the flower and weed imagery. As Chillingworth is associated with weeds, Pearl with flowers, and Dimmesdale with
no natural growing thing at all, so Hester walks her ambiguous way between burdock and rose, neither of which is alone
sufficient to define her nature and her position.

5

There are nearly twice as many heart images as there are
flower and weed images, but with one exception Hawthorne
insists upon them less. If they are in some respects even
more revealing, we may guess that that is because they
spring from Hawthorne's deepest concerns and most abiding
insights, not from the top of his head but from his own heart.
It is even more difficult to imagine Hawthorne's style
stripped of its heart images than to picture Dimmesdale
without his hand over his heart. The minister's gesture is
both consciously emblematic and a stylistic reflex.

But the heart imagery begins before we meet the minister. When Hester brings Pearl out of the dark "dungeon or . . . prison" we have veiled heart imagery, for the heart in Hawthorne is nearly as often a dungeon as it is a cavern or tomb. But this bringing out of the heart's secrets into the light is not voluntary, it is forced. It cannot then in Hawthorne's scheme of values be beneficial. One must "be true," but one cannot force others to be true. When the Puritans insist on "dragging" Hester into the public gaze—and get, clearly, a good deal of pleasure out of so doing—and then try to extort her secret from her, what they are doing constitutes an attempt at what Hawthorne calls elsewhere "a violation of the human heart"—the sin of Brand, Chillingworth, and other Hawthorne villains. To those who might be inclined to think that society has a right to do what the individual should not, Hawthorne has an answer, given in his comment on the stocks, that more common Puritan instrument for punishing by making the culprit publicly display his shame: "There can be no outrage, methinks, against our common nature,—whatever be the delinquencies of the individual,— no outrage more flagrant than to forbid the culprit to hide his face for shame."

The judges then stand in need of judgment. The Puritan people are here playing the role later played by Chillingworth. The heart imagery of the opening scenes establishes a tension that continues throughout the novel and is central to its meaning. That this interpretation does not constitute an overreading is suggested by the way light imagery reinforces heart imagery at this point: when we first see her, Hester's beauty shines out and makes a "halo," and Hawthorne says that to some she might have suggested an "image of the Divine Maternity." "The people's victim and life-long bond-slave," as Hawthorne calls her, is not sinless, but neither is she a sinner among the righteous. She is involved in a mesh of good and evil.

Many of the other uses of heart imagery are, as we should expect them to be, casual, almost incidental. They serve chiefly to keep us aware that we are here concerned finally with nothing less significant or permanent than the truths of the heart. Running reminders of the central heart images, they deepen and extend the reverberations of the action, sometimes into areas that defy analysis. The governor's mansion, for example, seems obscurely to be the heart of the Puritan rulers: behind a façade that glitters with fragments of broken glass, there is a suit of armor that reflects Hester's badge in magnified and distorted form. Despite the sunshine on the stucco walls, there would seem to be in this mansion an exaggerated consciousness of sin and almost no awareness of goodness, so that if we read this passage as a heart image we are reminded of "Young Goodman Brown."

Many of the others among the running heart images are clearer. The heart is a grave, in which corpses are buried. The heart is a chamber, in which the minister keeps his vigils in utter darkness; when Chillingworth enters the chamber, he is violating the heart. The heart is a hearth, in which one is wise to keep a fire. The heart is tomblike, or a niche in which images are set up and surrounded by curtains. The heart (or breast or bosom) is the place where the devil is most apt to set his mark. Of the fifty or so distinct heart images I have noted in the novel, most are of this order.

But those associated with Chillingworth are of special interest, for, along with the imagery of light and color and of weeds and flowers, they are the chief indications of his place in the scheme of values in the novel. What they do principally, of course, is once again to counter the judgment implied by the overt situation. Chillingworth, the "wronged" husband, does not cease to be the victim of injury when he strives "to go deep into his patient's bosom . . . like a treasure seeker in a dark cavern," but he makes it necessary to ask who is more greatly injured, he or the man who has "wronged" him. As the images continue the implication becomes clearer, so that, long before Dimmesdale has risen through his final act of honesty and courage, Chillingworth is seen as more sinning than sinned against, as more sinful even than the minister. "He now dug into the poor clergyman's heart, like a miner searching for gold; or, rather, like a sexton delving into a grave . . ." He stole into the chamber of the heart like a thief and there turned over, without valuing, "many precious materials, in the shape of high aspirations for the welfare of his race, warm love of souls, pure sentiments, natural piety, strengthened by thought and study, and illuminated by revelation." As he does so he imagines that his interest in what he finds is purely objective and disinterested, even scientific: "He had begun an investigation, as he imagined, with the severe and equal integrity of a judge, desirous only of truth, even as if the question involved no more than the air-drawn lines and figures of a geometrical problem, instead of human passions, and wrongs inflicted on himself." He is aided in his rationalization by the fact that his own heart is like a "cheerless habitation," cold in the absence of any household fire. But all the while it is becoming clearer that he is like Ethan Brand, who with "cold and remorseless purpose" conducted a psychological experiment on the heart of a young girl and "wasted, absorbed, and perhaps annihilated her soul, in the process."

Partly then as a result of the impact of the heart imagery, the reader feels his principal concern altered once again. First he was in suspense about the identity of Hester's partner in sin. Then, as that question begins to be answered, he wonders whether the minister will be publicly exposed and justice be done. But almost immediately, in "The Leech" and "The Leech and His Patient," he becomes concerned to have the minister escape somehow the persecutions of his tormentor. The central chapter on the relation between the two men, "The Leech and His Patient," begins and ends in heart imagery.

The most extended heart image is the forest scene. The forest in which Hester and Pearl take their walk has all the attributes common to normal human hearts in Hawthorne's work. It is black, mysterious, dismal, dim, gloomy, shadowy, obscure, and dreary. It is thought by the public to be where the Black Man meets his accomplices. It has in its depths a stream which as it mirrors the truth whispers "tales out of the heart of the old forest." But when Hester and Dimmesdale decide to follow the dictates of their hearts and, escaping man's law, live by nature, then "the wood's heart of mystery" becomes a "mystery of joy" and sunshine lights up the gloomy spot. In the four chapters concerned with this meeting, heart imagery plays a leading part, so that no analysis of the incident is likely to be adequate which does not take it into account.

6

Probably the implications contained in the names of the characters are more important than the remaining patterns of imagery. Pearl, of course, gets her name from the "pearl of great price" used in St. Matthew to suggest the incomparable value of the hope of heaven. Hester's initial mood of bitter rebellion against her situation is clear in the naming of her child. And the other chief characters too have significant names. "Hester" is a modern form of "Esther"; and the Old Testament Esther is gifted with beauty, strength, and dignity. Courageous and loyal, she defends a weak and oppressed people. The obvious parallel between the two women contributes one more implication that Hester is to be seen as finally "in the right." And it offers another bit of evidence to those who like to stress the feminist implications of the novel, for we may see the "weaker sex" defended by Hester as but a variant of the weak people defended by Esther.

The minister's first name, Arthur, tends to suggest that devotion to a high ideal associated with King Arthur. It is at once descriptive and ironic as the name of Hester's partner in adultery. His last name falls naturally into two parts, with the root of the first part, "dim," suggesting both weakness and darkness, and the second part, "dale," suggesting, in its meaning of valley, the heart, of which Hawthorne is so frequently reminded by any hollow, opening, or cavity.

Finally, "Chillingworth" is also made up of two parts, the first of which suggests coldness and the second merit or worthiness. It is a name more transparently descriptive of this man than Dimmesdale is of the minister. For Chillingworth has, as he acknowledges to Hester, a cold heart, and his sin is one of the cold sins. Yet he was once a worthy man: decent, self-controlled, law-abiding, scholarly, "good" as the world tends to measure goodness, with nothing lacking except the most important thing of all, the ability to love.

Names, then, are symbolic here, as they so frequently are in Hawthorne. There may be more name symbolism in the novel than I have indicated; there is certainly not less.

Of the other image patterns one of the most prominent is that of circles and chains. Considering the two as making up one pattern, since Hawthorne seems to think of them together, we find that each of the five times a circle or chain appears, it has the effect of increasing the guilt of the Puritan people and decreasing, or qualifying, Hester's. In the first few pages, for instance, we learn that the letter "had the effect of a spell, taking her out of the ordinary relations with humanity, and enclosing her in a sphere by herself." Hester then is in something like the position of Wakefield, who also was outside all "ordinary relations with humanity." But she has not chosen her fate, she has had it imposed upon her. The Puritan people who imposed it must be guilty of a very grave wrong indeed in Hawthorne's catalogue of sins. She is guilty of adultery, they of lack of charity. And since they had created "a sort of magic circle" around her, so that even in the crowd she was always alone, the reader can hardly blame her for casting away "the fragments of a broken chain" and thinking that "the world's law was no law for her mind." She had been literally forced into practicing Emerson's greatest virtue, self-reliance, in the isolation of her "magic circle of ignominy." No less excuse, in Hawthorne's world, would have exonerated her for breaking the connections in the "electric chain" of mutual sympathy and interdependence that should bind us together.

As circle and chain imagery is associated with Hester and helps to define her position, serpent imagery is associated with Chillingworth. At his first appearance we see a "writhing" horror "twisting" itself across his features. We are asked to visualize his figure as "low," a strange adjective surely if it means only "short," but appropriate to one who is said to "creep" along the ground. His ultimate transformation into a fiend should not take us by surprise if we have noted the snake imagery associated with him.

Another of Hawthorne's favorite image patterns, that of mirrors and pools that reflect, is used in the novel more prominently than the snake imagery, but with scattered rather than concentrated effect. The most telling instance is one we have already noted in passing in another connection: the reflection of Hester's letter in the polished suit of armor in the governor's house. As Yvor Winters was the first to point out, the convex surface so magnifies and distorts the letter that she is quite obliterated by it: she is changed from a person to an abstraction, a walking sin. Again the imagery connects the Puritan people and Chillingworth: compare his detached, "scientific" interest in Dimmesdale, not as a unique person but as an object to be investigated, with the Puritan view of Hester.

Unlike the curved mirror made by the armor, suited only to distort, natural mirrors, and especially those formed by water, whether of pools, streams, or fountains, normally tell the truth in Hawthorne, especially the hidden truth of the heart. We may presume that Dimmesdale saw something of the truth of his heart when for protracted periods he stared at himself in the mirror under the strongest possible light. And we may be sure that the brook in the forest mirrors truths otherwise hidden as well as the flowery beauty of Pearl. (Three chapters later it *becomes* a heart.) Thus, whether distorted or "true," the revelations of the mirrors in the novel are significant.

Finally, geometrical forms and patterns, the *shapes* of things, seem to me to be quite consistently functional throughout. Clearest are the images of the pointed arch, which draws the eye upward, or the less concrete images of height, suggesting aspiration, piety, or loftiness of purpose, and the low and twisted, suggesting evil. We note the "steeple-crowned" hats in the first sentence, and Hawthorne reminds us of them again. They suggest, not only in their obvious association with churches and so with worship but in the intrinsic character of their shape, the lofty aspirations and devotion to what was taken to be religious duty that conceived and created the New England theocracy. Again, Dimmesdale is so presented that the reader pictures him as tall and thin, in marked contrast with Chillingworth, who is seen as "low," "twisted," and "deformed."

With these hints that whenever shape is prominent it is significant, we may be justified in seeing in the scarlet letter itself something more than the first letter of *adultery*, something more than the first letter of the alternative reading *angel* preferred finally by some of the people: a design like that of steeples and the pointed arches of Gothic "cathedrals," a shape leading the eye upward toward heavenly things: all nature seemed to rejoice when the lovers reaffirmed in the forest a love that under different circumstances would have taken a place very high among positive moral values. That these implications do not "justify" adultery is clear. Hester's scarlet letter remains as ambiguous in its implications as her social position as outcast and sister of mercy, adulteress and light of the sickroom. Hester remains, as Hawthorne might have said, a "type" of those paradoxes of human nature that we have seen earlier in Rappaccini's daughter.

7

The Scarlet Letter is the most nearly static of all Hawthorne's novels. There is very little external action. We can see one of the evidences for this, and perhaps also one of the reasons for it, when we compare the amount of space Hawthorne devotes to exposition and description with the amount he devotes to narration. It is likewise true, in a sense not yet fully explored, that on the deepest level of meaning the novel has only an ambiguous movement. But in between the surface and the depths movement is constant and complex, and it is in this middle area that the principal value of the work lies.

The movement may be conceived as being up and down the lines of natural and moral value, lines which, if they were

to be represented in a diagram, should be conceived as cross-
ing to form an *X*. Thus, most obviously, Hester's rise takes
her from low on the line of moral value, a "scarlet woman"
guilty of a sin black in the eyes of the Puritans, to a position
not too remote from Mr. Wilson's, as she becomes a sister
of mercy and the light of the sickroom: this when we measure by the yardstick of community approval. When we apply
a standard of measurement less relativistic, we are also
likely to find that there has been a "rise." I suppose most of
us will agree, whatever our religion or philosophy may be,
that Hester has gained in stature and dignity by enduring
and transcending suffering, and that she has grown in awareness of social responsibility. Like all tragic protagonists, she
has demonstrated the dignity and potentialities of man, even
in her defeat.

Dimmesdale is a more complicated, though less admirable
and sympathetic, figure. He first descends from his original
position as the saintly guide and inspiration of the godly
to the position he occupies during the greater part of the
novel as very nearly the worst of the sinners in his hypocrisy
and cowardice, then reascends by his final act of courageous
honesty to a position somewhere in between his reputation
for light and his former reality of darkness.

There are allusions to the Crucifixion in the description
of his final moments, but they are very delicately suggested,
may or may not have been consciously intended by Hawthorne, and in any case do not really destroy the ambiguity
that has characterized Dimmesdale's situation all along. He
stretches out his arms in a Christ-like gesture, forgives his
persecutors, and accepts his death as one of "triumphant
ignominy," the only way open to him of ceasing to be "lost
forever." As he himself sees it, at any rate, he has emerged
at last not only into the light of day but into that which
shines from the celestial city. He sees Chillingworth's persecution as Providential: he has been saved despite himself,
by the very intensity of his suffering. But we note that the
words that characterize his death as triumphant and suggest a salvation in a life beyond death are his, not Haw-

thorne's. Hawthorne's last word on the subject comes in the description of the tombstone, in the novel's closing sentences, and there the ambiguity is complete. The description of the minister's death here reminds us of the ending of "Roger Malvin's Burial," though the presentation of the religious paradoxes implicit in Hawthorne's tragic vision seems if anything a little less hopeful here than in the short story.

As for Chillingworth, he of course descends, but not to reascend. As in his injured pride and inhuman curiosity he devotes himself to prying into the minister's heart, whatever goodness had been his—which had always been negative, the mere absence of overt evil—disappears and pride moves into what had been a merely cold heart, prompting to revenge and displacing intellectual curiosity, which continues only as a rationalization, a "good" reason serving to distract attention from the real one. He becomes a moral monster who feeds only on another's torment, divorced wholly from the sources of life and goodness. He is eloquent testimony to the belief that Hawthorne shared with Shakespeare and Melville, among others: that it is possible for man to make evil his good.

Thus the three principal characters move up and down the scale of moral values in a kind of counterpoint: Chillingworth clearly down, Hester ambiguously up, Dimmesdale in both directions, first down, then up, to end somewhere above the center. But this is not the end of the matter. Because there are obscure but real relationships, if only of analogy, between the moral and the natural (I am using "natural" in the sense of those aspects of existence studied by the natural sciences, which do not include the concept of freedom of choice among their working principles or their assumptions), because there are relations between the moral and the natural, the movements of the characters up and down the scale of moral values involve them in symbolic movements on the scale of natural values. The moral journeys are, in fact, as we have abundantly seen, largely suggested by physical imagery. Chillingworth becomes blacker and more twisted as he becomes more evil. Hester's beauty withers under the scorching brand, then momentarily reasserts itself in the forest scene, then disappears again. Dimmesdale becomes paler and walks more frequently in the shadow as his torment increases and his sin is multiplied.

But the moral changes are not simply made visible by the changes in the imagery: in their turn they require the visible changes and determine their direction. The outstanding example of this is of course Chillingworth's transformation. As we infer the potential evil in him from the snake imagery, the deformity, and the darkness associated with him when we first see him, so later his dedication to evil as his good suggests the "fancy" of the lurid flame in his eyes and the "notion" that it would be appropriate if he blasted the beauty of nature wherever he walked. So too the minister's moral journey suggests to the minds of the people both the red stigma which some think they see over his heart and the red A in the sky, with its ambiguous significance of angel or adultery.

Perhaps in this day of psychosomatic medicine, we should not too hastily conclude that Hawthorne's technique in this matter is as "fanciful" as, protectively, he says it is—a mere device for aesthetic ends, with no justification at all in experience. And it would be well to remember too that the implications of his "correspondences" between the spiritual and the physical are supported by the total structure of the novel, which implies that the relations between nature and man, fact and value, and the physical and the spiritual are neither those of identity nor those of total disparity. Here as elsewhere in Hawthorne's work, neither set of terms is reducible to the other, yet they are not wholly distinct. Hawthorne is not a naturalist, but he knows that man is a creature—a creature with a soul. His implications here are like those he attributed to the Christian world, as distinct .from the classical, in "Rappaccini's Daughter."

All three of the chief characters, in short, exist on both of our crossed lines, the moral and the natural. They are seen in two perspectives, not identical but obscurely related.

Pearl's situation, however, is somewhat different. She seems
not to exist on the moral plane at all. She is an object of natural beauty, a flower, a gem, instinctively trusted by the wild
creatures of the forest. She is as incapable of deceit or dis-
honesty as nature itself, and at times as unsympathetic. She
is not good or bad, because she is not responsible. Like the
letter on her mother's breast, she is an emblem of sin. Like
the red spot over the minister's heart, she is also a result of
sin. But she is not herself a moral agent. Even when she
torments her mother with her demands for the truth, or refuses to acknowledge the minister until he acknowledges
them, she is not bad, she is merely natural. She is capricious
with an animal's, or a small child's, lack of understanding of
the human situation and consequent lack of responsiveness
to emotions which it cannot understand.

Pearl is more than a picture of an intelligent and willful
child drawn in part from Hawthorne's observations of his
daughter Una. She is a symbol of what the human being
would be if his situation were simplified by his existing on
the natural plane only, as a creature. Hawthorne tells us that
Pearl is potentially an immortal soul, but actually, at least
before the "Conclusion," she seems more nearly a bird, a
flower, or a ray of sunlight. Because of this "naturalness,"
this simplification, she can reach the patches of sunlight in
the forest when Hester cannot: she is first cousin to the
sunlight in moral neutrality as well as in brightness. From
one point of view it seems curious that most readers find it
harder to "believe in" Pearl than in any other major character in the book except perhaps in Chillingworth in his last
stages, for Pearl is the only character drawn from Hawthorne's immediate experience with a living person. If the
naturalistic aesthetic of the late nineteenth century were a
correct description of the nature and processes of art, we
should expect to find Pearl Hawthorne's most "real" character. That she is not (though it is easy to exaggerate her "unreality") is I suspect partly the result of the drastic simplification of life Hawthorne has here indulged in, in giving
Pearl existence only on the natural plane. He has surely ex-

aggerated a child's incapacity for moral action, its lack of involvement in the demands of right and wrong, and so has produced in Pearl the only important character in the book who constantly comes close to being an abstraction. In creating Pearl, Hawthorne wrote partly out of the currents of primitivism of his age, suppressing or refusing to extend his normal insights, much as he made an exception to his convictions about the nature of the human heart when he created his blonde maidens, who are equally hard to "believe in," and for rather similar reasons. Oversimplified conceptions of experience cannot be made convincing.

Since "history" is created by the interaction of natural conditions and human choice, there is a significant sense in which Pearl has no history in the story. She moves in and out of the foreground, a bright spot of color in a gloomy scene, serving to remind Hester of her sin and the reader of the human condition by the absence of one of its two poles in her being, but never becoming herself fully human. In the final scaffold scene Hawthorne shows us Pearl weeping for the first time and tells us that her tears "were the pledge that she would grow up amid human joy and sorrow, nor forever do battle with the world, but be a woman in it." In the "Conclusion," when Hawthorne gives us a glimpse of the years following the real end of his tale in the minister's confession, he suggests that Pearl grew to happy womanhood abroad. If so, she must have taken her place with Hester and Dimmesdale and Chillingworth in the realm of moral values, making her history and being made by it.

But the others, including the Puritan populace, have histories and are involved in the larger movements of history created by all of them together existing in nature as creatures and moral beings. Hester might not have committed adultery had Chillingworth had a warmer heart, or perhaps even had he been younger or less deformed. He might not have fallen from a decent moral neutrality to positive vice had she not first fallen. Hester is forced to become stronger because the minister is so weak, and he gains strength by contact with her strength when they meet again in the forest. Chillingworth is stimulated by his victim's helplessness to greater excesses of torment and sin, and the Puritan women around the scaffold are stirred by Hester's youth and beauty to greater cruelty than was implicit in their inquisition anyway. St. Paul's "We are members one of another" could be taken as a text to be illustrated by the histories of human hearts recounted in the novel.

Yet with all this complex movement on two planes, with all this richness, this density, of history, when we ask ourselves the final questions of meaning and value we find the movement indecisive or arrested in one direction, continuing clearly only in the other. The Puritan people and Chillingworth are condemned, but are Hester and Dimmesdale redeemed? It is significant in this connection that Pearl's growth into womanhood takes place after the end of the story proper. It is also significant that though Hester bore her suffering nobly, it is not clear that she ever repented; and that, though he indulged in several kinds of penance, it is possible to doubt that the minister ever did. The redemptive love and knowledge that worked the cure of Roderick Elliston in "Egotism" do not enter the picture here—though, to be sure, Elliston's was a less complicated case than Hester's and Dimmesdale's.

The "darkening close" of this "tale of human frailty and sorrow" is only slightly relieved by the conclusion, which affords us a glimpse of happiness for Pearl in another time and place. The novel's darkness is related to "history" in another sense than the one in which I have been using the word—to history as the specifically Puritan past, as Hawthorne interpreted it. Because Puritan society was as it was, and because Hester and Arthur were both, in different degrees, of it as well as in it, there could be no really happy ending for them. Personal factors in Hawthorne's life may have entered into the mood of the work, to be sure. He wrote it while grief over the death of his mother was still intense and he was depressed by his dismissal from the Custom House position. It was a dark time for him. But more relevantly from the standpoint of judging the inner integrity of the novel he produced, the darkness is demanded by the nature of the materials. When he tells us that the Puritans were a people among whom religion and law were almost identical, the implication is clear: such a combination spoiled both the religion and the law, especially when the religious legalism rested on Biblical literalism. No wonder a jail, a gallows, and a cemetery dominate the scene in the first chapter, with only a single rose bush, blooming in an unpropitious site, suggesting the reality of anything else than sin and death.

We can now see that the opening chapter contains not only the thematic material that Hawthorne will develop but, implicitly, his final judgment of the Puritans. Hawthorne is expressing a view very typical of him when he says that "the deep heart of Nature," expressing itself through the rose, the traditional symbol of love, could "pity and be kind" to the prisoner, but the Puritans could only condemn and punish. We know what Hawthorne thought of those who could not pity and be kind. No wonder that at the very center of this society burdock and other ugly weeds flourished mightily. As Hawthorne explicitly tells us, they "evidently found something congenial in the soil." The rose of love and beauty, by contrast, was an anomaly here, and Hawthorne presents it as such.

Hawthorne is judging the Puritans by their own Christian standard and judging that they failed. When the woman taken in adultery was brought before Jesus, the one among her would-be judges who knew himself to be without sin was invited to be the first to stone her. No stones were cast, and Jesus himself refused to judge her. The point of the story is its condemnation not of adultery but of moralism. As he had made clear in "The Man of Adamant," Hawthorne thought the Puritans had misread their Bible. His own religion was no more moralistic than it was legalistic or literalistic. He took seriously the Biblical injunction, "Judge not, lest ye be judged." Once again, for him, the General Revelation of Nature and the Special Revelation of Scripture agreed: both suggested a very different treatment for Hester

from the one the Puritans accorded her. Nature and true
religion would have us pity and be kind.

But if Nature and Scripture agree on this, they differ on
the significance of sexual love. The Puritans, Hawthorne
knew, were attempting to follow Biblical precedents when
they punished adultery harshly; in the Old Testament death
was the prescribed punishment. If Nature passes no judgments on the subject, Scripture does. The tension resulting
from this conflict Hawthorne could not resolve and did not
attempt to; but as long as the natural and the moral are in
conflict, there can be no unalloyed happiness or complete
fulfillment without guilt. To a degree, Hawthorne agreed
with the Puritans on sexual love. This fact, too, made it
impossible for him to lighten his dark work more than he
did.

But he did not wholly agree with them. He thought that
adultery was a serious matter, but there are many passages
in his work that suggest that he thought the Puritan attitude
toward sex false and wrong. When he read of the fate of the
Mary Lathams and the Hester Crafords, his sympathies
were with them, not with their judges, just as it was with
all the other victims of Puritan theocratic rigor, whether
they were Quakers or antinomians. This is the implication
of his description of the women who crowd around Hester
on the gallows: the oldest and ugliest condemn her the most
harshly because they are not young enough or beautiful
enough to be loved as she has been. Sexual repression or
deprivation motivates their aggressive moralism. Hawthorne
had no more sympathy with the Puritans in this respect than
he had with the celibate Shakers, of whom he said that the
sooner they were extinct the better.

One of the clearest expressions of this attitude of Hawthorne's is found in "The Maypole of Merrymount." Among
the tale's many meanings is the one that grows from the
elaborately wrought contrast between the "natural" sexuality
of the Merrymounters and the stern repression of the Puritans. Between bestiality and ascetic repression, the ending of
the tale implies, there is a middle ground where the phallic

is not denied but hallowed. The young couple get married and go off to love and make love, with Hawthorne's blessing. Like the young couple in "The Canterbury Pilgrims," they have chosen the middle way between the heights of the unnatural and the depths of the merely natural, the unredeemed and unhallowed.

That the implications of these other stories are relevant here becomes very clear at one point in the novel. Toward the end of "The Governor's Hall," describing the governor's garden, Hawthorne says the garden contained a few rose bushes and apple trees, both probably planted "by the Reverend Mr. Blackstone . . . that half mythological personage, who rides through our early annals, seated on the back of a bull." Mr. Blackstone may be only half mythological, but the roses and apples he planted and the bull he rides on are wholly so. Once again, as in "Rappaccini's Daughter," Hawthorne has juxtaposed a classical and a Christian garden. The bull of unrestrained sexuality, the rose of a love ambiguously both human and divine—the red rose of passion and the rose window of the church—and the apple that was forbidden in the Garden of Eden—all are here held up for our contemplation.

The Eden allusion becomes even clearer when Pearl "began to cry for a red rose, and would not be pacified," for her mother quiets her by saying that she hears "voices in the garden." In Genesis we hear "the voice of the Lord God walking in the garden." Whether the voices Hester hears in this garden are capable of truly speaking for the Lord is one of the questions Hawthorne raises.

Unless Pearl is acting in a way quite untypical of her in the novel, Hawthorne wants to suggest that they are not. Pearl has demanded truth, always, and what she tries to accomplish is right, and finally is accomplished—bringing her father and mother together in the light of day. Pearl speaks for Hawthorne, as he in effect tells us when in the end he states the one moral among many he might have stated, "Be true!" When she cries for a rose in this scene, her choice is not only her own but Hawthorne's as well.

Not the apple, with its possible implication that sex is wicked
and therefore asceticism is justified, and not the bull, suggesting bestiality, but the rose, nature redeemed. Hawthorne's attitude toward sex was a long way from that of
D. H. Lawrence, but neither was it Puritanical, as he understood the Puritans.

The implication of Pearl's crying for a rose at this point
is strengthened if we return once again to the first chapter.
There the single rose beside the jail was presented as wholly
untypical of the place and time. The Puritans could not be
conceived to have planted it and did not value it. Instead,
it was rumored to have sprung up by a miracle under the
footsteps of an enemy of the Puritan society, an antinomian
first jailed and then exiled by the grim interpreters of the
Voice, an antinomian Hawthorne calls the "sainted Ann
Hutchinson." What unites Ann Hutchinson with the Anglican clergyman who planted the roses in the governor's
garden is opposition to the Puritans. When they bring roses
into this society, they bring something quite out of place
here. So much the worse, of course, for the Puritans! In the
context of such contrasts, we can almost imagine Hawthorne's liking Mr. Blackstone's bull!

But the negative judgment of the Puritans does not destroy the ambiguity of the novel on its more universal level
of meaning. The Puritans were wrong in their treatment of
Hester; more significantly, wrong in their whole attitude
toward nature and sex. But what if Hester had been able to
live in the better society of her dreams? Would there be
then no problem, no conflict between nature and man, the
natural and the moral? Would the crossed lines of our
diagram become parallel, or even cease to be two and become one?

Hawthorne did not think so. This would have seemed
to him a pagan vision, to be repudiated for both philosophic
and moral reasons. He had already repudiated the pagan
garden in "Rappaccini's Daughter." He was not likely to
approve it here, despite the nod of approval he seems to
give to Mr. Blackstone and his bull. The Puritans needed

what the Anglicans had to offer, but for Hawthorne the Voice in the garden was a real one, and the apple had been the agent of the Fall. As Giovanni in "Rappaccini's Daughter" had at first failed to see the snakey vines for what they were, so the Puritans could see nothing else. Both views, Hawthorne thought, were unbalanced. Neither pagan nor Puritan himself, he could be described as a Christian humanist. But since it was not his *views* that were in control when he wrote *The Scarlet Letter* but the material he had to work with and his deeper sensibility, there could be no final breaking of the ambiguous balance maintained throughout between the claims of nature and the claims of the moral law. The bull and the voice of God in the garden continue to conflict in a fallen world.

In the ending the imagery once more, for the last time, tells the story, a tragic story containing not much hope for those involved, and perhaps not much for the rest of us. The ambiguity at any rate is not dispelled by the dark light that falls on the tombstone or by the colors named in the heraldic motto. This light that is "gloomier than the shadow" hardly seems to come from above, and the scarlet letter loses none of its ambiguity when seen against a background of utter darkness. No wonder Hawthorne preferred *The House of the Seven Gables*.

CHAPTER SIX

THE HOUSE OF THE SEVEN GABLES

The House of the Seven Gables was written far more deliberately than *The Scarlet Letter*. If Hawthorne's first novel was, as he said, "wrung from the heart," his second was the product in much greater degree of conscious artistry. He was right, as he so often was in his judgment of his work: it was indeed more representative of the whole man. It was more comprehensive, more like the man his family knew. In it he achieved more perfectly than in the earlier novel that balance of the light and the dark that was characteristic of his response to life.

But if Hawthorne was not wrong in thinking that this work represented him better, neither is the modern reader wrong in his preference for the earlier novel. For Hawthorne recognized aspects of himself that he did not like, traits and tendencies that were hard to live with, insights and feelings that left him ill at ease. The traits he liked, on the other hand, were those his age also admired. It is little wonder, then, that whereas *The Scarlet Letter* shocked his contemporaries, and to some degree Hawthorne himself, *The House of the Seven Gables* pleased everybody. But to say that for the modern reader it is not wholly convincing is almost certainly to understate the case.

Yet for all its archaisms, there are reasons for calling it inferior in interest only to *The Scarlet Letter* and *Moby Dick* among American novels before the work of James. The variety of the ways in which it has been interpreted by perceptive critics is one clue to its richness. It can be read as a parable on the nature and effects of Original Sin. It can be read as a more complete working out of the theme of "Lady Eleanor's Mantle," that pride and death are inseparable companions: they sit together in the darkening room that is at once the heart of the old house and the tomb of the judge's ambitions. It can be read as the most impressive artistic statement of Hawthorne's democratic beliefs: the aristocratic Pyncheons discover that death and suffering are no respecters of persons and that they must give up their pretensions to superiority and mingle with "the common life" and the plebeian Maules. It can be read as a statement of the archetypal theme of withdrawal and return, which Hawthorne interpreted as isolation and redemptive reunion. It can be read as Hawthorne's maturest statement on man's relation to the past, considered as determinative of the future, and on whether, or how, he can escape from the bondage the past imposes. It can even be read as Henry James seems to have read it, as a piece of charmingly poetic realism, a sort of forerunner of the "local color" tales of old New England that were so popular after the Civil War, a delicate evocation of a way of life that James remembered having known as a boy.

It can be read in all these ways, and others too, but they are all partial readings. Hawthorne himself provided hints for a no less partial reading. In his preface he tells us that the subject of his romance is wrong and retribution, sin and suffering, carried on through generations. He seems only partially serious as he tells us that the "moral" he has provided for his romance is that "the wrong-doing of one generation lives into the successive ones, and, divesting itself of every temporary advantage, becomes a pure and uncontrollable mischief." In a somewhat more serious tone he adds that he wishes the work might convince mankind "of the folly of tumbling down an avalanche of ill-gotten gold, or real estate, on the heads of an unfortunate posterity, thereby to maim and crush them, until the accumulated mass shall be scattered abroad in its original atoms." The romance provides, then, in Hawthorne's view of the matter, texts for sermons on the sins of pride and avarice and on the fact of mutability, illustrating meanwhile the ways of Providence.

But Hawthorne knows, as he also says in his preface, that "when romances do really teach anything, or produce any effective operation, it is usually through a far more subtle process than the ostensible one." He knows that what he wants to say cannot after all be said in the preface, that the real meaning of his work cannot be expressed in a generalization. For all its moralizing then, this preface, in which Hawthorne comments more freely on his intentions in the work than was customary with him, tells us to read the romance attentively if we would know the meaning.

2

The opening sentences, familiar though they are, are worth quoting:

Half-way down a by-street of one of our New England towns stands a rusty wooden house, with seven acutely peaked gables, facing towards various points of the compass, and a huge, clustered chimney in the midst. The street is Pyncheon Street; the house is the old Pyncheon House; and an elm-tree, of wide circumference, rooted before the door, is familiar to every town-born child by the title of the Pyncheon Elm.

In view of what we have discovered of Hawthorne's habit of emphasizing in his descriptions only those details that are most significant, we shall do well to note certain images here. Hawthorne opens his story of the house that, as we later discover, was built by pride and possessed by death on the very day of the housewarming with a description that stresses the darkness and angularity of the structure and the "wide circumference" of the great tree that is said later to "overshadow" it. A careful reading of the story will disclose no significant feature of structure or texture, image or concept, that is not associated in some way with the suggestions contained in the house and the elm.

The outward appearance of the house, Hawthorne tells us in the sentences immediately following those I have quoted, had always reminded him of a human face. The interior, especially the great chimney in the center, he repeatedly presents in terms of heart imagery. The elm introduced in the second sentence is described more fully later in the first chapter and again in chapter nineteen, where we are once more reminded that it has the shape of a "sphere." It is the source, we learn, of whatever beauty the house possesses, and it makes the house "a part of nature." At the end the few leaves left it by an autumn gale "whisper unintelligible prophecies" as the last of the Pyncheons leave the house forever.

The associations clustered around the house and the elm, and particularly the straight lines and angles of the one and the curves, circles, and cycles of the other, are not equally present everywhere or scattered at random throughout. In the first ten chapters angular images predominate, from their introduction in the title and the first sentence through the portrayal of Hepzibah to their last new embodiment in the Pyncheon fowls in the tenth chapter. Meanwhile, however, images of curve and circle, though subordinate, are also present, especially in the several reminders of the shape of the elm, in the introduction of Phoebe, and in the treatment of Clifford's portrait. In the last eleven chapters the action is dominated by the presence of Phoebe and Clifford, both clearly associated with images of curve and circle. When in the last chapter Pyncheon and Maule are united and depart from the house, the theme which has been rendered visible by straight lines and angles is overcome by that embodied in curves, circles, and cycles.

This contrast between two strongly contrasted patterns of imagery, one of which diminishes in frequency and emphasis while the other increases in both, seems to me to lead us to the heart of the novel. The house is both setting and symbol: it is the antagonist in a drama of good and evil.

But the elm is taller even than the house, and overshadows it: appropriately enough, it has the last word. Hepzibah, in whose gaunt angularity and frown we see again the features of the house, is in the spotlight in the opening chapters, only to be supplanted by Clifford after his return from prison. As the climax approaches and the two victims of the past make an abortive attempt at flight, it is he who takes command. At the end he too retires into the background while Phoebe and Holgrave lead the way to the new life. The soft lines of Clifford's oval face, the rounded grace of Phoebe, the seasonal-cyclical prophecies of the elm—these replace the rigid angles of the house and of Hepzibah and of the Pyncheon fowls as the revolution of the hands on the face of his watch mock the dead judge's ambitious plans and delusions of permanence.

3

Because, as he says in his Preface, he is writing a Romance rather than a Novel, because he is not aiming at a "very minute fidelity, not merely to the possible, but to the probable and ordinary course of man's experience," because he feels that he has the right to present the heart's truth under circumstances of his own choosing and creation, Hawthorne is able so to design his work as to keep these images and their symbolic implications always before us. So much are they in control, indeed, that readings of the romance which ignore them are very likely to miss the point of what Hawthorne was trying to say. A closer look than we have yet taken at the structure of the work, and particularly at the plot and the characters, will show the extent to which Hawthorne subdued his materials to the demands of his pattern.

The recounting of family history in the first chapter is in essence a summary statement of the cycles of mutability. Prosperity, we learn, has given way to poverty before, so that Hepzibah has only to *reopen* the shop once before resorted to by an impoverished ancestor. The cycles of nature embodied in the yearly "death" and "rebirth" of the elm are apparent, to the long view, on the human level also: original injustice has been re-enacted as original retribution will be re-enacted. The same things have happened over and over again as generation has followed generation, so that in this glance at the past in which time is foreshortened until death seems almost immediately to follow birth we see what Hawthorne says he wants us to see, "how much of old material goes to make up the freshest novelty of human life." We see the past alive in the present. The wheel of fortune revolves before us and circles not apparent to the mind that lacks memory take shape. But the Pyncheons do not see them, for their vision is taken up with the more palpable reality of their great house and the social position of which it is a symbol.

The Pyncheon withdrawal from the mass; their willed isolation within the mansion "withdrawn," as Hawthorne says, "from the line of the street, but in pride, not in modesty"; their attempt to build a house and a fortune that would always endure—all this is negated by Hepzibah's forced opening of the cent shop. This act, so crucial and central in the rising action of the novel, and presented with emphatic circle imagery, may be seen as connected with the concept of the cycle in three ways. First, it is a simple repetition of an action that occurred in the past. Second, it means that for this branch of the family the wheel of fortune has turned full circle, from poverty to riches to poverty again, as it will later turn in another way for the branch represented by the judge. And third, though Hepzibah's pride is yet undiminished, her contacts with her first customer mark the beginning of that return after withdrawal which is one of the basic themes of the novel.

The coming of Phoebe, a Pyncheon reduced to plebeian status and so renewed in vitality and grace that now she seems to shed a circle of light around her, is another movement in the same direction, and one that is even more clearly a part of a cyclical process. Her presence, bringing new life and color and happiness to a house that had long known only isolation and darkness and death, subtly modifies Hepzibah's point of view as it partially destroys her isolation after her long solitude; and for Clifford, after his still more complete alienation, it becomes the very principle of life. Clifford's attachment to Phoebe, so cruel in its implications for Hepzibah, is the first willed, and so efficacious, step in the Pyncheon regeneration.

Chapter eleven, "The Arched Window," is perhaps the most explicit key to thematic structure. Hawthorne's chapter titles are seldom without significance, and sometimes, as here and in "May and November" and "The Flower of Eden," the modern reader will surely feel that they point too insistently to the deeper import of the chapters they introduce. For from beneath the only segment of a circle to be seen in the angular house, Clifford looks out at the "stream of humanity" in the street, and from this window he makes, in his attempt to jump out, what is in effect his first violent effort at reunion. Still later, seeing from it the throngs of churchgoers, he persuades Hepzibah to start with him for church, not from any sense of piety, but from a compulsion to participate in a common activity. Clifford's extreme suffering and ruin have prepared him for escape from the house of the Pyncheons.

But escape is not possible, in Clifford's way, by merely willing it. Even after the death of the judge, the flight precipitated by Clifford fails. The two old people return, unable to escape their past until after the engagement of Holgrave and Phoebe. This union of Pyncheon and Maule makes possible their reattachment to "the magnetic chain of humanity."

4

The texture of the novel is such as constantly to reinforce the themes thus embodied in the larger aspects of structure. After the opening sentences the continued description of the house centers on the contrast of its evidences of former grandeur with its present darkness and decay. But flowers grow from the rotten shingles of a roof kept moist by the overshadowing elm, visible emblems of that cycle whereby life requires death for its nourishment. Again, there is a suggestion that the overhanging second story, rendering the rooms below doubly gloomy by casting them in its shade, represents a predominance of head over heart, an imbalance later reversed in Clifford, whose sympathy, we are told, was unchecked by judgment. And the references to vegetable and seasonal cycles first introduced by the mention of the elm are continued in the descriptions of the garden, in the continuous light and shade imagery, particularly in the opening of chapter five, with its reminder of the diurnal revolution, in the description of the sun dial, and in the elaborate attention given to the judge's watch. "The shadow creeps and creeps, and is always looking over the shoulder of the sunshine."

Maule's well, introduced early and later made to supply the title of a chapter dealing with the relations of Phoebe and Holgrave, symbolically unites the two contrasting image patterns of house and elm. For though its waters are continuously renewed, still they carry the taint first noticed at the time of the building of the house. In the waters of this spring past and present are somehow one. As Hawthorne said of another spring in "Egotism," "How strange is the life of a fountain!—born at every moment, yet of an age coeval with the rocks, and far surpassing the venerable antiquity of a forest."

Frequent circle imagery, particularly after the arrival of Phoebe, continues, defines, and expands some of the implications. When, for instance, Hepzibah received payment from her first customer in the cent shop, the coin itself is a reminder of the cycle she is now taking her first step to complete:

The little *circlet* of the schoolboy's copper coin—dim and lustreless though it was, with the small services which it had been doing here and there about the world—had proved a talisman, fragrant with good, and deserving to be set in gold and worn next her heart. It was as potent, and perhaps endowed with the same kind of efficacy, as a galvanic *ring!*

Out of context, the words I have italicized in this passage

may seem so casual and "natural" as to be hardly worth noting, but when we recall the way Hawthorne worked in *The Scarlet Letter*, and then consider that the theme of this romance asks us to consider whether history should be conceived in cyclical, linear, or some other terms, we see that they serve as textural enrichments of a motive that is embodied everywhere, on all levels, from the most abstract to the most sensuous. They are a part of a running stream of circle images of all degrees of literalness and emphasis. Phoebe, for instance, is said to move in a "circle," where the drained image means literally a group of acquaintances. And we have pure images when we are told that she wears her hair in "ringlets" and that she appears to Clifford, whose intuitions seem unfailing though his reason is weak, to shed light around her "like the circle of reflected brilliancy around the glass vase of flowers that was standing in the sunshine."

The circle imagery is united with the imagery of lines and both are translated into abstract terms by Clifford when he talks to the strangers on the train. Having attempted to jump from an "arched" window in order to "plunge into the surging stream of human sympathies," and having attained his present illusory identification with mankind by passing through the "arched" entrance to a railway station, he now speculates, as he attempts to flee straight away from the old house, on the nature of time and history. Explicitly the passage presents a hopeful, "progressive" view of history, a view marked by full confidence in the beneficent effects of scientific and technological advances which increase man's freedom and power. The passage reminds us of a side of Hawthorne's own thought—what he tended to think of as the "hopeful" side—that found frequent expression later in the English Notebooks when he encountered what sometimes seemed to him the oppressive weight of tradition in English society and contrasted this with the more open and free society of America. But even while he lets Clifford express the "optimistic" view in its most extreme form, he undermines the hope it seems to present. Clifford is "possessed and swayed by a powerful excitement," intoxicated by his first taste of freedom; though his intuitions have proved trustworthy, his judgment is not to be relied on. He speaks "wildly" when he expresses his hope of leaving the past behind completely. The very words he uses to express his momentary faith have implications he does not note.

Clifford's chief emphasis is on history as straight line ascent. The past, he thinks, was coarse and sensual; in it, men were in bondage to ideas that restricted their freedom. It is his "firm hope that those terms of roof and hearth-stone, which have so long been held to embody something sacred, are soon to pass out of daily use, and be forgotten." Though the increasing mobility afforded by inventions like the railroad, which has given him and Hepzibah wings to soar straight up and away from the past, may "bring us around again to the nomadic state," the result will surely be desirable, for it will do away with "those stale ideas of home and fireside."

Yet even while he voices his hope that science and technology will bring a better world, he recognizes that there is much that is old in present novelty. The forward movement of progress includes the circles of repetition, so that "while we fancy ourselves going straight forward, and attaining, at every step, an entirely new position of affairs, we do actually return to something long ago tried and abandoned, but which we now find etherealized, refined, and perfected to its ideal. The past is but a coarse and sensual prophecy of the present and the future." If this is the case, the meaning of history may be visualized best by combining images of line and circle, with line dominant and circle subordinate: "all human progress is in a circle; or, to use a more accurate and beautiful figure, in an ascending spiral curve."

The measure of Clifford's error here is the extent to which he lets the line dominate the circle when he combines the two in his "accurate and beautiful figure." He is talking like Holgrave before Phoebe converted him to the truth. Hawthorne's irony in letting Clifford's hopefulness about the future rest on his welcoming the destruction of the "stale" ideas of "home and fireside" gives the reader an insight that Clifford himself attains only later, after he gets off the train and confronts the visible embodiments of what his hopeful words really entail. Then he and Hepzibah realize that flight from the old house in this way is impossible. I shall return to Clifford's speech for a closer analysis later, but for the moment it is enough to note that in this most explicit statement of what the work is, finally, all about, the themes find their expression in images that Hawthorne introduced in his opening sentences.

One aspect of the implications of the circle imagery is strongly reinforced by the imagery of light and darkness that Hawthorne scatters so profusely through his story. The "black" old house that "never lets in the sunshine" admits a very brilliant ray indeed when Phoebe enters. One of the stumbling blocks in the novel for the modern reader is in fact the way in which Hawthorne has made Phoebe, "the bright young girl . . . whose fresh and maidenly figure was both sunshine and flowers" and whose name in Greek meant *shining*—the way he has made her seem more like a ray of sunshine than like a person. As Hawthorne had drawn on his daughter Una in creating Pearl in *The Scarlet Letter*, so here he drew on his wife Sophia in creating Phoebe. In both cases the portrait done from life has seemed to many readers the least lifelike one in each book.

But if he fails with Phoebe in his color and light imagery, he is sometimes successful, particularly, and symptomatically, in handling the darker shades. When he feels the darkness of time and death in the "Governor Pyncheon" chapter, when he places before us again and again the cold and the darkness of the house, when he describes the "gloom of sky and earth" during the great storm in which Clifford and Hepzibah fled, when he visualizes death as a descent into the black depths of water in the opening of "The Departure"—here and elsewhere he succeeds in imparting the life of the imagination to a chain of color images that sometimes seems forced and merely ingenious. But on the whole I think we shall have to decide that the light and color imagery is handled too emphatically and that its chief effect—aligning with positive values those things and persons associated with circles, and with negative values their angular opposite numbers—would have been clear anyway.

More sparingly and subtly used to reinforce the circle and angle images are the running allusions to Eden. They begin in connection with the color and flower symbolism of chapter five, on the morning of Phoebe's first day in the house. Outside her window the girl discovers a bush covered with "a rare and very beautiful species of white rose." She discovers also that "a large portion of them . . . had blight or mildew at their hearts; but, viewed at a fair distance, the whole rose-bush looked as if it had been brought from Eden that very summer, together with the mould in which it grew." The references continue in chapter seven with a description of the sunshine which Phoebe has let into the house—"as fresh as that which peeped into Eve's bower while she and Adam sat at breakfast there." And these two apparently casual references are revived and reinforced in chapter ten when the Pyncheon garden becomes the Christian Garden and Clifford a new Adam: "It was the Eden of a thunder-smitten Adam, who had fled for refuge thither out of the same dreary and perilous wilderness into which the original Adam was expelled." Finally, this line of reference is explicitly united with the stream of flower imagery in the chapter called "The Fower of Eden." Then Phoebe and Holgrave "transfigured the earth, and made it Eden again."

These connections with the Eden myth take us of course to the heart of the story. For Adam's sin, like that of the Pyncheons, was pride; the penalty, alienation from God and man and the corruption of man and nature—the introduction, as it has been interpreted, of death; and the cure, love. And the Christian myth of the origin and cure of evil embodies the concept of a cycle as surely as the ancient figure of the wheel of fortune and the pagan vegetation myths do.

For the story told is one of union, alienation, and reunion, withdrawal and return. The Eden allusions then help to expand Pyncheon history into man's history.

Even the rhythm and syntax of the style contribute to the symbolic pattern Hawthorne is creating. Again and again at crucial points the sentences move to a rhythm more regularly undulatory than is common in prose: they rise and fall and return upon themselves with a controlled movement in contrast with the first and consistent with the second, the finally triumphant, motive. Frequently the longer sentences start with modifiers, move slowly to the main clause, and end with modifiers: "At the moment of execution—with the halter about his neck, and while Colonel Pyncheon sat on horseback, grimly gazing at the scene—Maule had addressed him from the scaffold, and uttered a prophecy, of which history, as well as fireside tradition, has preserved the very words." Or through balance, repetition, and antithesis they achieve a circular effect with main clauses: "Beauty would be his life; his aspirations would all tend toward it; and, allowing his frame and physical organs to be in consonance, his own developments would likewise be beautiful." Frequently, as in the foregoing sentence, the last word, after the accretions of insight and qualification achieved by the development, repeats or alludes to the first: "He had no right to be a martyr; and, beholding him so fit to be happy and so feeble for all other purposes, a generous, strong, and noble spirit would, methinks, have been ready to sacrifice what little enjoyment it might have planned for itself,—it would have flung down the hopes, so paltry in its regard,— if thereby the wintry blasts of our rude sphere might come tempered to such a man." Or the effect is achieved more subtly by rhythm alone: "But no sooner was she a little relieved than her conscience smote her for gazing curiously at him, now that he was so changed; and, turning hastily away, Hepzibah let down the curtain over the sunny window, and left Clifford to slumber there."

This is the antithesis of Emerson's staccato sententious style, his pulpit exhortation—which was, of course, as suited to his purpose of arousing the youth of the land to nobler lives as was Hawthorne's to his purpose. It is the style of a man whose insights are too qualified to be succinctly summarized. What Hawthorne wrote of Donatello's progress in *The Marble Faun* could be said of the style of the *Seven Gables*: it travels "in a circle, as all things heavenly and earthly do." The very sound and structure of the predominantly loose and heavily modified sentences express the returns and contradictions, the ambiguities and cycles of a reality which he saw as containing at its very core an "entanglement of something mean and trivial with whatever is noblest in joy or sorrow."

Now it is true of course that Hawthorne's style is basically the same in all his work, and that the rhythm in it might always be called in some sense "cyclical." Which is to say that the style of the *Seven Gables* is not wholly organic to the structure of the novel. But that it should be "wholly organic" is of course impossible, unless we were to assume that a novelist could create a completely distinct style for each of his works and that the works themselves were not each a partial expression of persistent attitudes and ideas and a persistent sensibility. Hawthorne's style is obviously Hawthorne's style, everywhere; and on the other hand, many of his works embody the theme of withdrawal and return. But such qualifications do not invalidate the conclusion that here the style is functional to a degree not usual in novels, even in Hawthorne's novels.

Finally, several other devices characteristic of Hawthorne's technique are here put to use to enrich the theme. The "ambiguity device," for instance, allowing multiple interpretations of a single incident, is an expression of Hawthorne's way of viewing things from all possible vantage points, circling round them to discover all the implications. Hawthorne tells us in his preface that his work is not a novel but a romance because it takes liberties with actuality in order to "connect a by-gone time with the very present that is flitting away from us," to show, that is, the cyclical reality which, as Clifford says, we do not normally perceive. To do this in an ordinary realistic novel Hawthorne thinks is impossible; so, as he tells us in his preface, he will base his work on legend and superstition, take the superstition seriously without believing in it, and examine it to see what human truth it may contain.

Tradition, legend, and superstition, then, are the heart of the tale, but the tale itself is not superstitious. It is ambiguous, with an ambiguity as deeply intertwined with its meaning as the ambiguity of *Moby Dick*. The "village gossips . . . hinted" that the house of the Pyncheons was built over an unquiet grave. "Some people thought" that the digging of the foundation disturbed the waters of the spring, as Rappaccini's pride had brought death into the garden. There was a "tradition, only worth alluding to," that a voice spoke out at Colonel Pyncheon's death saying, "God hath given him blood to drink." "There were many rumors" about the cause of the death, rumors no doubt unfounded in "fact" but very possibly grounded in the moral law.

Now it is commonly pointed out that this characteristic device of Hawthorne's represents a late and serious use of a Gothic tradition for moral and psychological purposes. "Modern psychology, it may be, will endeavor to reduce these alleged necromancies within a system, instead of rejecting them as altogether fabulous," Hawthorne tells us in his first chapter. Less commonly remarked is the fact that the method itself is basically mythopoetic, the end here being the creation of epiphanies of cyclical reality. So Joyce in our time linked myth with actuality, Ulysses and a Dublin Jew, to create epiphanies of a reality he conceived in terms of Vico's cyclical theory of history. Hawthorne's naturalization of the supernatural, his serious, but not superstitious, examination of those profoundly revealing expressions of the human mind and soul by which man in his ignorance of the true and final "facts" creates an interpretation of the raw data of experience, his candid, rational, and sympathetic analysis of the irrational—these connect him with the present century's discovery of the fundamental importance of myth. And the premise of the method was a sense, and the purpose a demonstration, of the cycles in which we are involved but which we do not see.

This is also one of the effects of another characteristic of Hawthorne's writing as we find it here: his habit of slowing down the action until we can study its minutest aspect, analyze it from all sides, and realize, among other things, its connections with the past and its foreshadowing of the future. Between the time when Hepzibah leaves Judge Pyncheon to summon Clifford and the time when she returns, only a few minutes elapse but it takes a full chapter to present them. In "The Pyncheon Garden" no overtly significant actions occur: the characters meet and talk a little, Phoebe reads to Clifford, the summer afternoons seem, as James remarked, drowsy and motionless, with time suspended and reality concentrated here and now; yet what finally emerges is a keener sense of the revolutions in which we are all involved.

In short, the images of angle and circle implied in the description of the house and the elm which opens the romance are, like the images in the opening chapter of *The Scarlet Letter*, the first suggestions of a pattern that may profitably be thought of as the figure that Hawthorne worked into the carpet. Though an alternative reading could be made which would give the central place to images of light and dark—for they are very numerous and prominent—yet it seems clear that Hawthorne himself has given us the clue we need to decide this question by beginning and ending his work with the house and the elm and by making his theme explicit in Clifford's speech. It requires no forcing to see that all the motives, on whatever level of abstraction or concreteness, are connected with this basic pattern of circle and angle. The secular movement of light and dark, the rhythm of flower and blight, the allusions to prelapsarian innocence and post-Adamic sin, the themes of isolation and reunion and permanence and change, even the contrasts of head and heart and pride and humility, all are linked in some way with the basic image pattern. Phoebe, for instance, is associated throughout with roundness, light, flowers, inno-

cence, the heart, humility, and a balance between permanence and change. Clifford finds in her the principle of life,
Holgrave the correction of his ingenious speculations. Her
arrival is the coming of grace after sin and suffering. In her
marriage with Holgrave we see both the end of the male
Pyncheon line and of the name, and the promise of renewal.
She carries the redemptive theme of the romance. Though
the burden is too heavy for her to bear, she is certainly supported by every device Hawthorne knew how to use.

5

It is paradoxically true of *The House of the Seven Gables*
that it is at once more realistic and more consistently allegorical than *The Scarlet Letter*. It has a richer evocation of
atmosphere, a more palpable recreation of a definite time
and place and way of life than Hawthorne's masterpiece.
But it is also more directly and completely controlled by a
conscious conceptual framework, a framework involving the
most abstract levels of thought. If the work is to be recovered
for mature readers in our time, it can only I think be through
an appreciation of its symbolic structure. This may not be
possible, but we shall not know whether it is possible or not
until we see how far Hawthorne succeeded in conveying
"more of various modes of truth" than he could grasp "by a
direct effort."

The first of the themes to demand comment is the one
that Hawthorne emphasizes in the preface and continues to
underscore throughout, the relation of past and present.
Superficially, the relation seems to be one of contrast. Past
evil makes present suffering, past wealth leads to present
poverty, the house once magnificent is now decayed. When
the inadequacy of this insight becomes clear, we find another, which turns out to be its very antithesis, emerging
from the pattern: there is nothing new under the sun, past
and present are essentially identical, as seen in the deaths of
colonel and judge. But this too turns out to be only a partial
insight, needing correction. The correction, we discover, has

been foreshadowed from the very beginning by the symbolism of the elm, which experiences yearly death and rebirth, and by the symbolism of Maule's well, which combines permanence and change.

But when we relate these conceptions to the image patterns we discover what seems to be an essential ambiguity. The angles of the house are associated only with death and the *illusion* of permanence and linear progress, but the circles of the elm are associated both with sterile repetition and redemptive renewal, with the death of the judge and with Phoebe's coming. We must somehow distinguish between the movement of the hands around the face of the dead judge's watch and the circles of light shed by Phoebe.

The "light" shed by the judge's sultry smile is deceptive. Despite his appearance he is really a creature of darkness. If he had his way he would continue and compound the original injustice. He is therefore unable to escape the compulsive cycles of nature. The circles in which he is involved are his only reality; his dreams of achievement, his plans for his day and for the continued building of his fortune, are as illusory as the dreams of permanent magnificence his ancestor embodied in the house. The circles associated with Phoebe, on the other hand, are not compulsive but liberating. Her light is as real as the sunshine and as healing as love. Hers are the circles of nature, but nature completed and illumined by grace. She is natural, but as the flowers are natural: like the lilies of the field, she is not worried about achieving security or ambitious to achieve distinction. She is emblematic, Hawthorne might have said of her, as he said often of his wife in his love letters, of the redemptive power of love, by which alone man may break out of the cycles of futile repetition and participate by choice in a cycle of a different kind.

But if Phoebe illumines and transforms nature by the power of love, we are still left with a difficulty. How can the circles of nature and grace be so different and yet look so much the same? If we conceive of the circles of history in terms of the ancient figure of the wheel of fate, then the death of the judge and much else in the history of the family would make it appear that the wheel is merely going around. But the union of Pyncheon and Maule suggests that the wheel is moving somewhere as it revolves.

Is progress real or merely apparent? A closer look at Clifford's speech on the train will yield a partial clue. Hawthorne's irony in this scene is constant and much more subtle than we have yet noted. Its final effect is to reinforce the meanings he had expressed earlier in "The Celestial Railroad." Thus in reading Clifford's words about how the past is only a "coarse and sensual prophecy" of the present and future, we may emphasize, as Clifford does, the inferiority of the past because it was coarse and sensual. But if the past provides a *prophecy*, it must be because the repetitions of history suggest that man's nature and condition are essentially unchanged. If so, hope for real progress now must rest where it has always rested.

Again, in Clifford's phrase about the present repeating the past, but the past "etherealized, refined, and perfected to its ideal," we may, with Clifford, take "ideal" to mean simply "better," more desirable. But there are implications here that Clifford does not see. "Perfected to its ideal" may also mean "made more truly itself." Evil as well as good may be purged, refined, rendered purer, in short "spiritualized," as Hawthorne very well knew. His really evil characters are guilty not of the gross and sensual sins, not of obvious expressions of self-centeredness like murder, but of intellectual and spiritual pride. "Spiritual" is not necessarily a plus-valued word, though it tended to be for Hawthorne's age. It may be quite neutral: there are spiritual enormities as well as physical ones. That Hawthorne thought so is implied everywhere in his work. But if it is possible to read Clifford's phrase as meaning that evil as well as good continues, both being gradually "refined" or rendered more "spiritual," then "progress" becomes a very equivocal term and the irony of history has not really been dissolved. History itself then would offer no adequate basis for hope.

One of Hawthorne's own comments as narrator in his last

chapter corroborates our impression that "perfected to its ideal" is a more ambiguous phrase than Clifford knew. Commenting on the fact that it was too late in his life for Clifford to benefit from any formal vindication of his good name, Hawthorne broadens the observation to include all wrongs done and suffered: "It is a truth (and it would be a very sad one but for the higher hopes which it suggests) that no great mistake, whether acted or endured, in our mortal sphere, is ever really set right." If this is true, whatever meaning the idea of progress has in the novel, it cannot be that of utopianism or secular liberalism.

Yet both internal and external evidence suggests that the ideas Clifford voiced on the train—ideas central in the liberalism of the time—had a strong appeal for Hawthorne. The structure of the novel as a whole, with the departure from the house and the marriage combining to make a happy ending, would seem to suggest that Hawthorne approves of Clifford's understanding of history as figured in an ascending spiral curve, even if he does not approve of the reasons Clifford gives for his hopeful view. But how can he do so if he also believes that no great wrong is ever set right? Does the leaving of the old house for a new one at the end mean real progress or does it not? Is the novel confused because Hawthorne simply cannot make up his mind?

There is certainly a conflict of attitudes involved here but there is also, I think, a sufficient resolution of the conflict to keep the paradox from becoming a complete antinomy. Hawthorne demonstrates a Keatsian sort of "negative capability" in entertaining sympathetically two opposed views, but there is finally as much clarity in the implications of his work as we have any right to demand. He provides a partial resolution of the conflict both on the level of belief and on the level of feeling and imagination. On the level of belief, the resolution is dependent on our taking more seriously than we have yet the parenthetical part of the statement I have quoted about the great wrong Clifford suffered. The truth the narrator asserts would be a very sad one—and one thoroughly in conflict with the hopeful cast of Clifford's view of history—if it did not inspire "higher hopes." In short, the irremediable injustices of this life are a reason for believing in the life eternal, in which there will be perfect justice. Hawthorne's belief in immortality comes to the support of his desire to believe in progress.

But Hawthorne was no philosopher, and his ideas about progress tend to fit his mood and the occasion rather than add up to a consistent theory. Truth for him was to be found in the image, as well as conveyed by the image. When we turn from the statements we have been considering, we find that most of what seemed like inconsistency disappears. Here as elsewhere, Hawthorne was able to convey through his art "more of various modes of truth" than he could grasp by direct effort—or state philosophically.

The common impression that the work simply wavers between belief in progress and despair of any escape from the past may be corrected by a closer look at the implications of the emphatic Eden imagery and at what Hawthorne has said, chiefly through imagery, in the chapter on the flight in which Clifford's words occur. By his references to Eden, Hawthorne locates the house of the seven gables in the spiritual geography of his imagination. When Phoebe returns after her visit to the country and goes into the garden, she finds it ruined and deserted. The idyllic summer afternoons she spent there reading to Clifford will never come again. Hawthorne devotes a paragraph to describing the garden's emptiness and disarray, making this the most emphatic reminder in the book of the mythic overtones of his tale.

The implications of this passage and of the explicit references to Eden elsewhere in the book are clear enough. Man is a fallen creature in a fallen world. Any redemption possible for him is offered only on condition that he recognize this fact. Clifford's brief dream of an easy escape made possible by the newest thing in locomotion is a delusion. There is and will be no celestial railroad so long as man's essential condition remains unchanged. Like R. P. Warren's characters who find that flight westward changes nothing, does not permit escape from the guilt of the past, Clifford and Hepzibah must return to the house.

What has already been implied by his Eden allusions Hawthorne amply reinforces by the way he manages the abortive flight. In the first place, the "two owls" have to leave the house in the middle of a great storm, and Hawthorne makes it clear that his image is a metaphor for a stormy world. As Hepzibah and Clifford face the east wind, its pitiless blast makes them "death-a-cold." Hepzibah, more sensitive than Clifford on this occasion, experiences "a moral sensation, mingling itself with the physical chill, and causing her to shake more in spirit than in body. The world's broad, bleak atmosphere was all so comfortless!" And Hawthorne makes sure that we do not dismiss Hepzibah's impression as one appropriate only to the Hepzibahs of the world. Exercizing his right as intrusive author, he comments in the next sentence, "Such, indeed, is the impression which it makes on every new adventurer, even if he plunge into it while the warmest tide of life is bubbling through his veins."

Fallen man in a stormy world: the combination makes what Hawthorne calls "a very sombre picture." In such a world it would be a delusion to suppose that progress would be easy. And Hawthorne suggests the extent of Clifford's delusion by having him support his argument for progress by espousing two opinions that were precisely the opposite of Hawthorne's and one which he found at least questionable. Clifford thinks that mesmerism represents a great advance, since it will do much "towards purging away the grossness out of human life." Hawthorne himself lumped mesmerism with spiritualism and considered them both to be, if not fraud, then both religiously irrelevant and morally dangerous. Clifford also thinks it an unmitigated advantage to "do away with those stale ideas of home and fireside, and substitute something better." The extent of his delusion may be tested by noting the symbolic implications of the hearth or family fireside image throughout Hawthorne's work, from beginning to end. The opening of this chapter parallels the situation in "Night Sketches," as the two old people who have been sheltered from life plunge into a stormy world and discover what it is really like, but Clifford's several references to the advantages of giving up the outmoded hearth reverse the meaning of the end of the sketch, in which the light of faith is known to be trustworthy just because its flame was kindled at the hearth.

But if Clifford's words are ironic, containing meanings the opposite of those he intends to express, they should not be taken as completely destroying the tension Hawthorne has set up between the conservative and the liberal views of history. Clifford may speak wildly and without recognizing all the implications of what he is saying, but that Hawthorne does not mean to undercut Clifford's hope entirely is implied in many ways in the book, perhaps most clearly in the implications, on the political and social level, of the marriage of Phoebe and Holgrave. This is a marriage of conservative and radical, of heart and head. Woman is the conserver and the conservative, man the speculator whose thought may undermine even that which is most sacred, even the hearth and the altar. The marriage of Phoebe and Holgrave, then, though we see more of its effect on Holgrave than we do on Phoebe, still at least theoretically preserves some sort of balance between the two attitudes. Hawthorne makes explicit what, in his view, Holgrave's "error" was. It was excessive confidence in man and lack of respect for the past. "As to the better centuries that are coming, the artist was surely right." Marriage to Phoebe should not lessen his "faith in man's brightening destiny" but increase his feeling for the values of the hearth, so that he might come to realize that "God is the sole worker of realities." Only on the religious level, in the higher hope motivated by the spectacle of history, did Hawthorne dissolve his ambiguity.

The best evidence of what the hearth meant to Hawthorne is to be found in "Fire Worship." There, in a tone that at least partly takes back what he is saying, he declares he will never be reconciled to the "enormity" of the iron stove that has replaced the open hearth.

Truly may it be said that the world looks darker for it. In one way or another, here and there and all around us, the inventions of mankind are fast blotting the picturesque, the poetic, and the beautiful out of human life. . . . While a man was true to the fireside, so long would he be true to country and law, to the God whom his fathers worshipped, to the wife of his youth, and to all things else which instinct or religion has taught us to consider sacred.

Fire, in short, at least fire in the open fireplace, is "the great conservative of Nature." But if the tone of the sketch did not make it sufficiently clear that Hawthorne's views are not confined within the limits of such conservatism, evidence elsewhere would do so. Only in a playful tone could Hawthorne write of "these evil days" in which "physical science has nearly succeeded in extinguishing" the "sacred trust" of the household fire. He is exaggerating as much as Clifford when he asks, "What reform is left for our children to achieve, unless they overthrow the altar too?" The conflicting claims of liberal and conservative are being balanced here as they are in the comment on reformers in "The Hall of Fantasy," where Hawthorne writes, "Be the individual theory as wild as fancy could make it, still the wiser spirit would recognize the struggle of the race after a better and purer life than had yet been realized on earth. My faith revived even while I rejected all their schemes."

Still, the irony in Clifford's words about the hearth prepares us to find his discussion of the significance of the new theories of electricity similarly mistaken. Yet once again, the ideas he voices are not *entirely* mistaken. Electricity, he thinks, supports idealism in its view that the world is essentially mind, not matter. Its implication is that "the world of matter has become a great nerve." Indeed, it is even more thoroughly spiritual, more nonmaterial, than would be suggested by "nerve": it is "instinct with intelligence," not material at all, really, but "a thought, nothing but thought, and no longer the substance which we deemed it." Metaphysical idealism seems to Clifford so thoroughly to support his hope of escape that he is not disturbed by the old gentleman's warning that the practical application of electrical theory in the newly invented telegraph may merely make the work of bank robbers and murderers easier.

The reader, if not Clifford, is prepared then for what faced "the two wanderers" when they got off the train:

They gazed drearily about them. At a little distance stood a wooden church, black with age, and in a dismal state of ruin and decay, with broken windows, a great rift through the main body of the edifice, and a rafter dangling from the top of the square tower. Farther off was a farm-house, in the old style, as venerably black as the church . . . uninhabited.

No wonder "Clifford shivered from head to foot" now, as Hepzibah had at the beginning of their flight. The realities of a stormy world have supplied an answer to the question of whether his momentary idealism was justified or not. The deserted church and the deserted house measure the extent of his and Holgrave's delusions and prepare us for the way Hawthorne ends the chapter. Hepzibah kneels and prays, lifting her hands to the sky.

The dull, gray weight of clouds made it invisible; but it was no hour for disbelief,—no juncture this to question that there was a sky above, and an Almighty Father looking from it! "O God!"—ejaculated poor, gaunt Hepzibah,—then paused a moment, to consider what her prayer should be,—"O God,— our Father,—are we not thy children? Have mercy on us!"

If Clifford in his disdain of the hearth has reversed the meaning and imagery of "Night Sketches," Hepzibah in her final prayer has repeated both. She has not, like the narrator in the early sketch, been granted a glimpse of a true light. The storm still hides the sky toward which she directs her prayer. But she takes the lead now in guiding Clifford back to the hearth. The hearth even of such a house as the one she thinks she must return to for good is better than what she has discovered in her first real experience of the world. In as stormy a world as this, one learns the true value of the hearth.

6

Hawthorne ends his novel by refusing to declare himself on the reality of secular Progress, falling back instead on the "higher hopes" he had said were inspired by the vision of time as unredeemable. "The Pyncheon Elm . . . with what foliage the September gale had spared to it, whispered unintelligible prophecies." "Wise Uncle Venner," meanwhile, imagines Alice Pyncheon, the most pathetic victim of the evil of the past, floating "heavenward from the HOUSE OF THE SEVEN GABLES!" She at least has escaped what Hepzibah and Clifford could not escape by physical flight. As for the living characters, Hawthorne seems to want to encourage us to hope.

But why should not the fine new house in the suburbs generate the same evils the old house did? There is, after all, even a new fortune to go with it—or rather, an old, tainted one, newly acquired. Must we then read the ending as ironic? Or should we simply say that it is unconvincing?

If the book itself were thought not to make it sufficiently clear that the ending is meant to be taken seriously, without irony, all that we can find out about Hawthorne and his beliefs and attitudes from the total record he left us would show that he intended no irony here. Before he wrote it, he decided he wanted his next book to be more hopeful than *The Scarlet Letter*, and when he had finished it he thought he had succeeded. A more careful reading than it has generally been given will show that in it he made no unqualified declarations that he *needed* to undercut with an ironic ending. Thematically, the ending follows from what precedes it and in no way changes the meaning. Hawthorne has both shown us and told us that it is a stormy world that Holgrave and Phoebe will have to live in. Whether they will be destroyed by it or not is left as undecided here as was the fate of the young lovers in "The Canterbury Pilgrims." In both cases we are invited simply to hope that their love will last and prove redemptive. Hawthorne has implied that the new house will be an improvement over the old, but he has even more strongly implied that, as man's condition remains essentially unchanged, those who inhabit it will have to face problems as old as Eden itself.

He has said, in effect, that both change and permanence are real, and that we are not to think of them as being one good and the other bad. Instead, we must think about them in terms of the necessary distinctions between superficial and profound, external and internal, physical and moral. He has said that what his century chiefly meant by progress, that is, technology, solves some problems but not others; and that the ones it does not solve are more important than the ones it does. The way he handles Clifford's reference to the telegraph epitomizes all he has to say on technology: "it is an excellent thing,—that is, of course, if the speculators in cotton and politics don't get possession of it."

As for what he has said about redemption through love, it would never have occurred to him to be ironical about that. If the prophecies of the elm at the end are "unintelligible," that is because in a dark world where much must remain obscure, the only meanings worthy of the heart's trust are those that emerge when Scripture corroborates and completes Nature: the "higher hopes," again, and the flowers growing from the rotting roof, life coming out of death. Here nature and Scripture agree. The voice of Nature alone is either undecipherable or insufficient. It is September, and the great storm has torn off most of the elm's leaves. Nature is undergoing its seasonal death even as Uncle Venner fancies Alice Pyncheon ascending in corroboration of our higher hopes. Hawthorne meant his ending to be taken seriously.

But the modern reader inevitably finds it difficult to do so, for two reasons. First, he is likely to bring to his reading a stubborn skepticism directed toward both Hawthorne's idea of the redemptive power of married love and his faith in immortality, his higher hopes. That of course is not Hawthorne's fault, but suspension of disbelief may be even more difficult than suspension of belief.

And Hawthorne makes it unnecessarily difficult by the

way he handles Phoebe, Holgrave, and their courtship and marriage. Hawthorne felt he had been "saved" by his own marriage, and he idealized Sophia much as Mark Twain idealized Libby. Writing the novel, he felt little need to convince the reader that Phoebe ought to be taken as a visible sign of Grace, that marriage to her would transform Holgrave's views, or that marriage itself was a blessed state. Did he not know it to be true, from his own experience? So he lavished his care on Hepzibah, principally, though also on Clifford and the Judge, as more difficult problems for the artist, and gave the less challenging portraits less attention.

But with a Phoebe who is both too good to be believed and too quickly symbolic in her goodness, a Holgrave who is much more interesting on a thematic level than he is convincing as a created character, and a marriage that comes too suddenly and may seem a mere contrivance, so that we have as much trouble believing in the love as we do in the lovers, it is not very surprising that many readers have failed to be convinced of the validity of the hope Hawthorne proffers in his ending. It is hard to believe that love will save us if we cannot believe in *the* love that is supposed to have saved the Pyncheons and the Maules.

But it is too easy to emphasize the failure. It is, anyway, I suspect, as much ours as Hawthorne's. And insofar as it is Hawthorne's, the reasons that have been given for it have not always been good ones. Hawthorne said in his Preface that he was writing a romance, but we tend to demand of him the very "minute fidelity . . . to the probable and ordinary course of man's experience" he said it was not his aim to produce. Whether it is possible to grant him his aim without feeling that it is inferior even while we grant it, is an open question. But at any rate it should be clear that it is only on this "novelistic" level that the work fails, if it does. As a mythopoetic fiction, it is one of the greatest works in American literature.

CHAPTER SEVEN

THE BLITHEDALE ROMANCE

We do not often read *The Blithedale Romance* nowadays. If we do read it, or, more likely, plan to read it, it may be because we are interested in its portrayal of life at Brook Farm, that abortive experiment in communal living in which Hawthorne rather inexplicably joined for a while. Read this way, it is very disappointing. Where we had hoped for a gallery of portraits and a re-creation of historic details, we find instead the most Gothic of Hawthorne's romances, with only one historical character we are likely to recognize and even that one greatly disguised. For Zenobia is not Margaret Fuller, as Hawthorne was careful to point out in his preface; she is a literary creation in some respects suggestive of Margaret Fuller. And if the work proves disappointing as history, it is equally, or at least so we are likely to feel at first reading, disappointing as a romance, for its Gothicism is too evident and its machinery too contrived.

But there is another way to read *The Blithedale Romance*, a way which, while it will not make it seem a great historical novel, will make it seem an acute analysis of the meaning of history; and while it will not completely salvage it as a romance, will make it appear a very interesting work of art. I mean reading it with the closest attention to texture, as though it were not a novel but a poem. To read it this way is to read it the way Hawthorne wrote it. It is also to read it in the only way likely to give us a fresh insight into its meaning and value for us.

2

We may fairly begin with the title. *Blithe dale* may be read as Happy Valley, and the body of the novel suggests that we not only may but should read it this way. The title contains, then, an echo of one of Hawthorne's favorite authors, for Johnson's *Rasselas* tells how the Prince of Abyssinia, reared in a secluded happy valley where there was no sin or suffering of any kind, journeyed through the outer world in search of a man both happy (for he had not been contented in the happy valley) and wise, only to have to return at last, disillusioned, to his refuge from the world. Hawthorne's book uses a similar journey plot, but inverted. Coverdale the narrator goes from the real world of Boston to the happy valley of Blithedale and then, disillusioned, returns to Boston. Johnson set up a mythical Happy Valley in order to test the nature of the real world against it; Hawthorne started from the real world of Boston in order to test the reality of Blithedale. Johnson ended on the theme developed in his poem "The Vanity of Human Wishes"; Hawthorne ended on a theme that may be partially suggested by such phrases as "the failure of reform" and the folly of expecting utopias if the heart of man remains unchanged, the same theme, essentially, as that developed in "Earth's Holocaust."

That sketch had ended, we remember, after the reformers had attempted to do away with all the world's "trumpery" and injustice and superstition, with the warning that unless we could find some way to purify the heart of man, all reforms would prove in the end to have been in vain, for it is from the heart that evil springs. There is no happy valley to be found or created merely by altering man's outward habits of living or getting a living. The title *Blithedale* then is ironic: the happy valley turns out to be a fool's paradise.

So much emerges from a literal reading of the two parts

of the word. But the second part is also a covert heart image.
We have seen Hawthorne use a valley (or dale) to suggest
a heart before.* This reading points not to the conclusion
Coverdale came finally to share with the Prince of Abyssinia
but to a fallacy he came to see as lying behind the failure at
Blithedale. The reform rested finally on the assumption of
the natural goodness of man's heart: if man is good "at
heart," then by changing those social arangements that
corrupt him we can create utopia. All hope for man rests
in political and economic, or, more broadly, social manipulation. The Rousseauists are right: man's heart is "blithe" in
the sense of happy, fortunate, just as we should desire it to
be. Whether read in this way, then, as an ironic reference to
the error at the root of the matter, or as an allusion to
Rasselas, the title is revealing. Ignoring the tendency to evil
in man's "foul cavern," from which the old evils or their
duplicates would issue all over again even if we should
succeed in eliminating their superficial manifestations, the
experiment was doomed to failure from the start.

Coverdale, whose voice and personality are central in the
work, has a name as suggestive as that of the community.
The first part suggests what is perhaps his most striking
characteristic, his tendency to cover up, to be secretive, to
hide and withdraw. He is constantly keeping out of sight;
he peers and peeks and eavesdrops. What he is finally covering, we come to suspect, is the secrets of the heart, as he
conceals his love for Priscilla until the end of the story and
as the last part of his name suggests. The concealment motive suggested by his name is connected, as we shall see, with
a good many other disguise images that run through the
novel.

Hollingsworth's name suggests both "holy" and "worthy."
But here too, as in the title, there is irony. For despite his
devotion to what is, abstractly considered, a good cause, the
reform of criminals, he is an egotist who is blind to all that

---

* For a thorough treatment of the subject of heart imagery, see John
Shroeder, "'That Inward Sphere': Hawthorne's Heart Imagery and Symbolism," *PMLA*, March 1950.

is most holy and worthy of our devotion. He loves mankind in the abstract but not actual men. His flaw comes finally to reveal itself to Coverdale as spiritual pride, which blinds him to the real complexity and mixed nature of man and the world. His name, though it points to a real nobility in his character, is finally ironic.

Zenobia bears the name of a queen both splendid and tragic, and she herself is regal in appearance and manner and comes to a tragic end. She is described in terms of her natural vitality and her luxuriant womanhood, and her name carries the significance of "one having life from Zeus." But here too there is a touch of irony, for the flower that she always wears in her hair, and that Coverdale finds emblematic of her nature, is at first a hothouse bloom, an exotic, and later a piece of jewelry wrought in imitation of a flower. She too, though less obviously than the others, is somehow false.

These are the clearly symbolic names in the work, though there may be vaguer, or more debatable, suggestions in some of the others, especially in Westervelt. But they are enough to make it clear that there is more here than just a straightforward recounting of Hawthorne's memories of Brook Farm.

3

The texture of *The Blithedale Romance* is remarkably rich and interesting, even for Hawthorne. Two main streams of imagery clarify, reinforce, and expand the themes suggested by the name symbolism. In the early chapters fire imagery is dominant. Hawthorne insists on it so much, in fact, that at the beginning of chapter four he apologizes for "harping on it." But the imagery of masks, veils, and disguises, though subordinate to the fire imagery in most of the opening chapters, is introduced earlier. It is doubly present in the first sentence of the first chapter, explicitly in the reference to the Veiled Lady and implicitly in the reference to Moodie; and thereafter it dominates the chapter. It is apparent, as we have seen, in the name of the narrator. And it finally overshadows the fire imagery. Both it and the fire imagery are enriched by being associated with other image patterns, but the two of them are so much more frequent and emphatic than the others that they establish the pattern within which all the images have their place.

Readers often find Hawthorne's first chapter puzzling and unsatisfactory. He devotes it to introducing, first, the Veiled Lady, who except for Coverdale is the first character to appear, and second, old Moodie, whose name supplies the chapter with its title. Toward the end of the chapter we hear of Zenobia. One of the peculiarities of the chapter for the modern reader is that it is devoted to introducing three people of whom only one, Zenobia, is apparently a character of any consequence in the novel. I say "apparently" because we eventually discover that the Veiled Lady is really Priscilla and old Moodie is the father of both Priscilla and Zenobia. But by the time we discover this we are likely to have ceased to care, for the "mysterious" aspects of Hawthorne's plot are certainly not likely to hold our attention long today. Is this chapter then, we wonder, simply a rather extreme example of the trouble Hawthorne often had with the mechanics of his stories?

I think we may assume that Hawthorne felt he was gaining a valuable addition to suspense by this device of introducing characters whose identity remains hidden. But the chapter served Hawthorne in another way, and for us this is surely the more important. It introduces and places in the foreground of our attention veil and fire images. And it is typical of Hawthorne that the images which will be the chief carriers of the theme grow out of the plot, which thus functions symbolically even though it remains clumsily contrived and Gothic on the literal level.

The introduction of a mysterious Veiled Lady in the first chapter of a work that is to be full of disguises is obviously appropriate, but the thematic function of the chapter does not end there. Old Moodie, too, wears his own kind of veil. "He was a very shy personage, this Mr. Moodie." He wears a patch over one eye, and he never, as Coverdale immediately notices, reveals more of himself than is absolutely necessary. When he visits Blithedale and eats lunch in the field with Hollingsworth and Coverdale, he eats "with" them but not in sight of them, for he manages to sit so that a screen of leaves hides everything about him but his shoes. When he follows the two to the farmhouse he walks behind Hollingsworth so that Hollingsworth "could not very conveniently look him in the face." Coverdale notes that he gave the impression of "hiding himself behind the patch on his left eye." At the funeral of Zenobia he keeps his face "mostly concealed in a white handkerchief." He is as much a veiled character as the Veiled Lady and more obviously so than Coverdale.

The only other character introduced in the first chapter is Zenobia, and from what we learn of her later we first get the impression that she is unlike Coverdale, Moodie, and the Veiled Lady in being quite lacking in a veil. (Coverdale pictures her once lacking not only a veil but any other sort of drapery or covering.) She does not share Moodie's tendency to hide behind bushes or Coverdale's to peer out of thickets or into windows; she seems in fact to Coverdale to be rather immodestly open in her manner, disturbing him with her frank acknowledgment of her womanliness. Yet there is one secret she will not reveal, the secret of her very identity. So it is that Coverdale remarks to Moodie in the first chapter that "Zenobia . . . is merely her public name; a sort of mask in which she comes before the world . . . a contrivance, in short, like the white drapery of the Veiled Lady, only a little more transparent." Every character in the first chapter, then, wears his mask. When finally we discover that Priscilla is the Veiled Lady and half-sister of Zenobia, we realize that these two who are so unlike in almost every respect are connected in a significant way: one wears a veil by choice, the other by necessity. It is not difficult, knowing Hawthorne, to guess which will serve as heroine.

But we are not quite through with this first chapter yet. When Coverdale replenishes his fire we have the unobtrusive beginning of a chain of fire imagery that does not cease until the end of the romance. Thus the opening chapter does in fact accomplish a good deal: it introduces all but Hollingsworth among the principal characters and it first states the leading images. The distance between this and the opening chapters of *The Scarlet Letter* and *The House of the Seven Gables* is after all not so great as it at first seems.

After this Hawthorne never lets us forget for long the theme signalized by the veil imagery. We are reminded of it on some thirty-five of the subsequent pages. But to say that we are "reminded" is not to convey adequately what is really going on. For the veil is not a static or allegorical symbol, and the first chapter merely introduces it, it does not define it. Twenty-two of the twenty-nine chapters develop the theme explicitly, and all of them, of course, do so implicitly.

Coverdale, for instance, journeys to Blithedale in a snowstorm that veils the "conventionalism" of the world against which Blithedale is a protest. Zenobia wears her unnatural flowers, which Coverdale decides are a "subtile expression" of her character. Westervelt hides his true character behind a false laugh and false teeth: his laughter, "brief, metallic," reveals that his "remarkably brilliant" teeth are "a sham." Coverdale feels "as if the whole man were a moral and physical humbug; his wonderful beauty of face, for aught I knew, might be removable like a mask." Even the pair of spectacles Westervelt later puts on are masking devices: they "so altered the character of his face" that Coverdale "hardly knew him again." The reformers spend an evening at charades and Zenobia remarks that the identity of the actors is too apparent through their improvised disguises. Later the whole company, with the exception of Coverdale, put on masks and play at being Arcadians. Coverdale does not need a mask. He remains hidden as usual even without one, peering at the others through the leaves and later retreating, when he is discovered, to his "bower," from which he observes Priscilla, Zenobia, and Hollingsworth without disclosing his own presence. Everyone at Blithedale except

Silas Foster, the hired farmer, has a mask, veil, or disguise on at some time in the story.

4

The fire imagery is only slightly less prominent than that of veils, masks, and disguises. Chapter one closes with Coverdale building up his fire. Chapter two opens with his admission that he is not likely ever again to know so cheery a blaze as that which he remembers from his first day at Blithedale. The remainder of the chapter develops the implications of this initial imagery. The fire that first day warmed the heart as well as the body. The cheer it provided in contrast to the cold outside strengthened Coverdale and his companions in their hope that here they might begin "the life of Paradise anew." After several reminders of the presence of the fires in chapter three, chapter four turns again to extended treatment of the subject. The great old kitchen fireplace, with its "cavernous" opening, is now described. The fire that burns in it is very cheery, but it is not such as any real farmer would build: it is too large to be perfectly natural even in such a fireplace, and, as Silas Foster sardonically points out, it is built of brushwood, which burns very brightly but will not last.

Silas Foster's doubt about the permanence of the fires at Blithedale is paralleled by Priscilla's inability to be warmed by them. She finds "the sense of vast, undefined space, pressing from the outside against the black panes of our uncurtained windows . . . fearful . . . The house probably seemed to her adrift on the great ocean of the night." And so it was later to seem to Coverdale. Very soon after arriving, indeed, he was forced to go shivering to his "fireless chamber" with a cold in the head.

While Coverdale is still confined to his sickbed, Hollingsworth builds a fire to warm the room, and it is very welcome to the sufferer from cold. Yet "there never was any blaze of a fireside that warmed and cheered me, in the down-sink-

ings and shiverings of my spirit, so effectually as did the
light out of those eyes, which lay so deep and dark under
his shaggy brows." When it becomes clear to Coverdale later
that his friend has given way to "the terrible egotism which
he mistook for an angel of God," the light that warms disappears. Coverdale is left thereafter with more cause than
ever to deplore the coldness of his own heart. His "cold
tendency," which has gone far as he thinks toward "un-
humanizing" him, leads him to want fires everywhere, even
when he does not need them: "Summer as it still was, I
ordered a coal-fire in the rusty grate, and was glad to find
myself growing a little too warm with an artificial tempera-
ture." The cold from which Coverdale suffered was more internal than external. Like that of Gervayse Hastings in "The
Christmas Banquet," it was the cold that proceeds from a
frozen heart.

Several other image patterns are related, some obviously and some obscurely, to the veil and fire clusters. It
has already become clear how coldness comes in as the counterpart of the fires and warmth, and how these two lead
naturally, as always in Hawthorne, to heart imagery. These
four, veil and fire, coldness and the heart, take on added
meaning in their relationships with the iron imagery associated with Hollingsworth, the flower imagery and the frequent allusions to the theater and acting associated with
Zenobia, the images of laughter that make an interesting
connection between Westervelt and Coverdale, and the
images of dreaming that are associated with Coverdale
alone. And all these running metaphors are tied in with the
frequent allusions to Eden, Arcadia, and Paradise. Some,
like the iron imagery that helps to characterize Hollingsworth, grow naturally out of the main image patterns, ex-
tending and reinforcing them; others, like the flower imagery associated with Zenobia, serve to qualify or counter the
suggestions of the dominant images. Though each of these
might profitably be given separate treatment, I shall comment on only two of them, the heart and cold clusters, which
may be treated together.

The cold is at first external. We see it in a set of pure images which at first reading have no obvious metaphorical force: Coverdale and his friends begin their enterprise in a snowstorm, and as they gather around their fires the cold seems to press in from without. Then, following a brief spring and summer which some of the less perceptive of the utopians seem to expect to last forever, Coverdale returns to the farm in the fall. Once again the weather is cold, but by now the metaphorical implications are clearer, so that the images are like those I called "mixed" in *The Scarlet Letter*: Coverdale finds the "ice-temper" of the air invigorating because he is experiencing a momentary resurgence of faith. When his heart is warm, he can defy, or even enjoy, the outer cold. And what is implicit here, the uniting of the streams of heart, fire, and cold imagery, is also made explicit. Zenobia is talking to Priscilla about the latter's probable future as Hollingsworth's wife:

"Poor child! Methinks you have but a melancholy lot before you, sitting all alone in that wide, cheerless heart, where, for aught you know,—and as I, alas! believe,—the fire which you have kindled may soon go out. Ah, the thought makes me shiver for you! What will you do, Priscilla, when you find no spark among the ashes?"

We were prepared for "that wide, cheerless heart" by the descriptions of the kitchen hearth, with its "old-fashioned breadth, depth, and spaciousness," much earlier. We see now that the hearth has been a symbolic heart all along. And the brushwood fires prepared us for the ardor which Priscilla has awakened in Hollingsworth and which Zenobia believes is bound to be short-lived. We can now see that the groundwork for all this was laid as early as the first chapter and elaborated in the meditation of Coverdale which opens chapter two:

There can hardly remain for me (who am really getting to be a frosty bachelor, with another white hair, every week or so, in my mustache), there can hardly flicker up again so cheery a blaze upon the hearth, as that which I remember . . . at Blithedale. It was a wood-fire, in the parlor of an old farm-house, on an April afternoon, but with the fitful gusts of a wintry snow-storm roaring in the chimney. Vividly does that fireside re-create itself, as I rake away the ashes from the embers in my memory, and blow them up with a sigh, for lack of more inspiring breath. Vividly, for an instant, but, anon, with the dimmest gleam, and with just as little fervency for my heart as for my finger-ends! The staunch oaken logs were long ago burnt out. Their genial glow must be represented, if at all, by the merest phosphoric glimmer, like that which exudes, rather than shines, from damp fragments of decayed trees, deluding the benighted wanderer through a forest. Around such chill mockery of a fire some few of us might sit on the withered leaves, spreading out each a palm towards the imaginary warmth, and talk over our exploded scheme for beginning the life of Paradise anew.

5

When the novel opens Coverdale is returning to his apartment after having spent an evening watching "the wonderful exhibition of the Veiled Lady." Though he suspects that mesmerism and its attendant clairvoyance and telepathy are rather "the revival of an old humbug" than "the birth of a new science," yet he has asked the Veiled Lady to predict the success or failure of the Blithedale enterprise. In view of his skepticism about the new "science," he is not surprised when the answer he receives is "of the true Sibylline stamp, —nonsensical in its first aspect, yet, on closer study, unfolding a variety of interpretations, one of which has certainly accorded with the event." The answer, in short, is a kind of riddle, with its "truth" hidden behind a veil of ambiguities. Like the identity of the Veiled Lady herself, the meaning of her reply will become clear only as time uncovers it. The most obvious thing a veil does is to cover, hide, or disguise.

Yet this raises an interesting question. Why, if this is so, is veil imagery introduced at the beginning, then pushed into the background to make way for the fire imagery that predominates in the next four chapters, then later brought back into the foreground again? Why, in other words, as the meaning of the answer to Coverdale's question becomes clearer, as the veil of obscurity is lifted from the prophetic words, does the veil imagery increase? There would seem to be movements in opposite directions going on here: the identity of the characters is being gradually unveiled, as is the answer to the initial question about the success of the enterprise; but Coverdale, after the first flush of his enthusiasm has worn off, covers his tracks more completely than ever, Zenobia takes to wearing artificial flowers in place of her hothouse bloom, Westervelt comes into the picture with his profusion of masks, and at last all the utopians together put on disguises.

One thing such a statement of the problem seems to me to make clear is that the veil imagery does not function in terms of an allegorical sort of symbolism. Like the laughter in "My Kinsman" and the colors in *The Scarlet Letter*, it functions symbolically in terms of context. The veil which is at first merely a piece of gauze hiding the features of the mesmeric subject quickly expands to metaphor as it gets associated with the obscurity of her answer to Coverdale's question, then becomes a metaphor for the mystery surrounding the identity of Moodie and Zenobia—all this in the first chapter. As the tale progresses it takes on the character of a snowstorm, a hothouse flower, a set of false teeth, a pair of spectacles, a window curtain, a "leafy retreat," the black water of a river at night hiding a body, and even Coverdale's habits and personality. It becomes finally, perhaps, whatever hides from us the frustration, the futility, which lie hidden, suspected but not clearly seen, in the future.

As the years darkened around Coverdale he saw, one supposes, the meaning of the veil changing from that which hides a truth one wants to know to that which hides a reality one fears to know. Thus it was, perhaps, that though he knew, when he wrote, the folly of the kind of utopianism he had taken part in at Blithedale, yet he could not wholly regret having been involved in it; for it had been a generous folly, resting upon a belief in the possibility of progress.

And his words and his tone suggest that it came to seem to him, in some of his moods at least, that without the veil that mercifully conceals reality we could undertake no generous or noble action whatever. If the reality of Blithedale had been clear to him at the beginning, he never would have been warmed, even momentarily, by the blazing fires in those early weeks of the adventure.

If this is the final meaning of the veil, then the content of the fire symbol must be modified accordingly. The brush-wood fire, even the fire of great logs, long since reduced to ashes, suggests in such a context not so much true comradeship and "holy sympathy" and faith as a mere illusion of these things. The outer cold, the blackness Priscilla saw pressing in upon the little group, must have been more real, then, than the flames all along. The comradeship, the sympathy, and the faith were indeed made possible only by the presence of the veil. If this is what Coverdale comes finally to suspect, as his tone seems often to imply, then here certainly is the ultimate failure of hope—for "the world's improvability," surely, and for another life (our "higher hopes") in which the world's wrongs will be rectified as they cannot be at Blithedale, probably.

Hawthorne's belief in immortality seems to play no part in this novel, certainly not in the way it did in *The House of the Seven Gables*. It is simply not relevant to his subject here, which is the possibility of achieving planned social reform. I would not mention it at all, except for two facts. First, its presence in the ending of *The House* contributed something to the hopeful tone of that work—to the intended one, at least, if not to the achieved one for the modern reader—and its absence here may help to account for the generally hopeless tone of this work. *This* is how Hawthorne felt when he looked at history simply by itself, apart from what Revelation had to say about it. As he wrote later in "Chiefly About War Matters," "No human effort . . . has ever yet resulted according to the purpose of its projectors"; or, as he put it in his biography of Pierce, "There is no instance, in all history, of the human will and intellect having perfected any great moral reform by methods which it adapted to that end."

The second fact that makes Hawthorne's belief in immortality worth mentioning at this point even though it in no way enters the novel directly is that the imagery that I have been commenting on, the darkness and the cold, strikingly parallels the imagery of "Night Sketches," which *does* directly concern the chief tenet of Hawthorne's faith. It is as though what we had here were the discoveries of the narrator of the sketch before he found any trustworthy light in the cold and dark world outside his chamber. Once again, the implication is clear: except for the light that faith provides, the world is completely cold and dark. To Hawthorne it seemed that even the man of faith was bound to find his light guiding him precariously through a dark world, lighting up just enough of it to make his next steps possible. To reason alone, the ways of Providence seemed to Hawthorne unintelligible. Blithedale was concerned with reason alone, or rather with the reforms dictated by "will and intellect" together. No wonder this is the most negative of all Hawthorne's novels.

But if Coverdale suspects at times that the experiment would never have been tried if reality had not been veiled, he does not *believe* it—quite; nor, we may suppose, does Hawthorne. For the veil is also, always, that which isolates man from man and the desired truth from our perception of it. It destroys the connections in "the magnetic chain of humanity." As Mr. Hooper, in an earlier story, had been cut off from his congregation by his black veil, so the partners in the Blithedale attempt at practical brotherhood are isolated from one another by their veils. And if the veils cannot be removed, if it is not possible to bring out into the light that which is hidden, to "be true" as Dimmesdale finally was true, then no experiment in brotherhood can ever succeed. Again, in so far as the veil hides the ultimate truth from us, it put us all in the unhappy position of Aylmer in "The Birthmark," whose scientific idealism led to such awful results; for we recall that he "failed to look beyond the shad-

owy scope of time, and, living once for all in eternity, to find
the perfect future in the present." Aylmer failed to look,
Coverdale suspects we may be unable to look beyond the
veil: whatever the cause, the result may be the same.

When we pursue this interpretation of the veil imagery
we approach Hawthorne's consciously intended meaning.
Priscilla is his redemptive character, whose love will save
Hollingsworth if anything can. She is, despite the veil
thrust upon her in her role as the Veiled Lady, the only
major character who does not either wear a veil by choice
or manifest spiritual and intellectual pride. She is the only
character motivated consistently by love. (Zenobia is "in
love" with Hollingsworth, but her love is a manifestation of
eros rather than *agape*; and Hollingsworth protests that he
loves humanity, but he doesn't care very much for actual
men.) Priscilla is a paler Phoebe, a more helpless Hilda of
The Marble Faun. Her love is redemptive so far as the others
will let it be.

But they will not let it be if they can prevent it. They
admit her to their circle at first somewhat reluctantly and,
as Coverdale notes, do very little to make her feel at home
with them. One remarkable thing about this community
founded on the theory of the brotherhood of man is the
almost complete absence in it of any actual brotherhood.
The leading characters, Zenobia, Hollingsworth, and Coverdale, are scarcely concerned at all about the fate of the
community; each uses it for his own purposes. And they
care less and less for each other as time goes on. So that in
addition to being set, as Coverdale says, in a "relation of
hostility" to the world outside in their effort to compete with
it commercially, they come finally to be hostile to each other.
Removal of their veils, being true, would have been no doubt
the first prerequisite to lasting success of the experiment; a
change of heart would have been the second. Certainly the
chief intended meaning of the work is that we cannot create
"Paradise anew" while maintaining our separateness, our disguises, and the fundamental self-centeredness or pride of
which they are a manifestation. Hawthorne is saying again

what he had said in "Earth's Holocaust," that all reform is superficial so long as the heart remains unchanged.

That something like this is the intended meaning of the work may be shown by an examination of the fire and veil imagery in such a way as to make clear the comparative weight Hawthorne has given to each of them in the various parts of the novel. The pattern that emerges looks like this:

Chapters	*Images*
I	VEIL—fire
II–V	FIRE—veil
VI–IX	fire—veil
X–XXIX	fire—VEIL

I have set chapter one apart from the others because it simply introduces what is to follow. And it is clear now that in addition to its other, already noted, introductory functions, it foreshadows the dominance of the veil imagery in the last chapters. It supplies in fact a veiled answer to the question Coverdale asks of the Veiled Lady.

Now this is an admirably balanced and functional structure. It suggests the cyclical pattern of *The House of the Seven Gables*, which starts with the HOUSE and the elm and ends with the ELM and the house. If this sort of thing ever happens by accident—which one may reasonably doubt—it does not happen by accident in Hawthorne's work: he knew what he was about, as we have ample evidence by this time to believe. What he was about in this instance was creating a work of art that would say again more fully and clearly what he had often said before. The largest pattern that emerges from the imagery here says that the reformers could not succeed in reorganizing society because they could not, or would not, put off their veils and emerge from their separateness. It says that the fires of faith, hope, and love burned brightly at first at Blithedale but were soon extinguished by the selfishness of men and women who could not afford to be "true."

The implication of this is of course that a redeemed society can only come when there are enough redeemed individuals. And the ending *means* to suggest the possibility of this: Priscilla may be able to "humanize" Hollingsworth. But this possibility is surely too slight to encourage us to pin our hopes on it. And there is another reason why the record of Blithedale's failure is so very much more impressive than the suggestion that another kind of effort might succeed. As we have noted, there seems to be some question in Coverdale's mind about what the veil finally is and does. Aylmer would have been wiser to look beyond, but that was because what he would have learned by doing so would have been the message of the Gospel. It would have chastened his hopes of man's achieving perfection by his own efforts, but it would not have overwhelmed him with any revelation of the final futility of all effort. But what if there is nothing but darkness and cold "beyond"? Then clearly the veil is a saving ignorance, making possible a precious illusion, permitting us for a little while to be warmed by the ephemeral fire. Whether the veil is this as well as that behind which individuals hide themselves from others, Coverdale does not seem able to make up his mind.

His ambivalence, and the resultant suggestion of uncertainty about the meaning of the veil as symbol on the most abstract levels, almost make it possible to read the novel in two different ways. Either the experiment failed because men could not sufficiently put away their veils and be true and loving; or it would never have been started had there not been a veil draped over the facts of life and death, making faith and hope momentarily possible. Of these two readings there can be no question about which one Hawthorne meant us to make. Even if there were no evidence at all available from his other works and his life, or if we decided to rule all that other evidence out, the structure and texture of this work should be decisive—unless we wish to assume that Hawthorne did not know what he was about and that the design he wrought is not meaningful. For if we were to decide that the primary meaning of the veil is that of a saving ignorance making possible a valuable illusion, then the largest pattern made by the images in the work would be at odds with the work's meaning. For in this reading we should expect that as the veiling effect increases, the fires, being dependent on the veil for their being, would burn brighter. But this is precisely the opposite of what happens: the veils become more prominent, and the fires go out. Form and content do not come apart in this way in Hawthorne. The veil cannot be intended, as the structure of the work itself shows, primarily to be that which makes hope possible.

Yet the doubt creeps back and will not be argued away. The ambiguity remains and will not be dissolved in paraphrase. It is not that there is any conflict here between intended and achieved meanings in the usual senses of those terms, for what we have decided is the primary intended meaning is "achieved"; it is thoroughly and consistently and even elaborately embodied in structure. It is not that form and theme are at odds but that image patterns and theme together are to some extent at odds with feeling, with tone. Coverdale, for instance, says he has been in love with Priscilla all along; and, considering Priscilla's role and his, we find this appropriate on the thematic level. But we have trouble believing him. Again, he does not say he has no hope left of any kind for man, but his tone speaks more eloquently than his words, and the disillusion he means to apply only to the kind of effort that was made at Blithedale we find difficult to restrict to that effort.

This is not the ambiguity of the "double mood." It is Hawthorne's own special brand of ambiguity, the ambiguity of head and heart. What Coverdale believes he cannot trust himself always to feel; and what he feels he does not believe. Hawthorne the conscious artist makes the fires die as the veils come to the fore. At the same time Hawthorne as Leonard Doane and Gervayse Hastings and Goodman Brown, Hawthorne of the haunted mind, was aware, or felt without being aware that he felt it, that the fires might have been impossible without the veils.

6

Even those who may find the work less ambivalent than these speculations suggest can hardly deny that it is very cold. Hawthorne wrote only one novel and very few stories with happy endings that are even partially convincing, but surely this is more negative and hopeless than most of the works. As Coverdale writes he seems to be chiefly aware of the death that is involved in time, with the "years that are darkening around" him. He says he does not want to regret his part in the Blithedale enterprise, but his tone suggests a great weariness. "Whatever else I may repent of, therefore, let it be reckoned neither among my sins nor follies that I once had faith and force enough to form generous hopes of the world's destiny."

We are invited to assume that Coverdale means only that the generous hopes were misdirected at Blithedale, that this kind of effort at redemption is a mistake. But this is not always what he seems to mean, despite his recognition that Priscilla points the way to a more fruitful effort:

Therefore, if we built splendid castles . . . and pictured beautiful scenes, among the fervid coals of the hearth around which we were clustering, and if all went to rack with the crumbling embers and have never since arisen out of the ashes, let us take to ourselves no shame. In my own behalf, I rejoice that I could once think better of the world's improvability than it deserved.

Does Coverdale's doubt about the "world's improvability" go beyond Fourierist reform to include any co-operative effort, or even any individual effort? There are times when he makes it seem so. There is a sense in which it may be said that what finally emerges from the novel most vividly is death. It is not surprising that the most powerful scene is the midnight search in the river for the body of Zenobia, in which Hawthorne drew upon an experience he had had while living in the Old Manse. There were a good many kinds of experience that Hawthorne could not use successfully in his writing, but this he could use. The stream that hid the body, that veiled it from the searchers, Coverdale called, fittingly in his character as minor poet, the "Black River of Death." When the water's veil was finally lifted it revealed something so grotesque and fearful that Coverdale was moved, for once, to a profound emotion. "Ah, that rigidity! It is impossible to bear the terror of it."

Such meanings as these were almost certainly not the ones Hawthorne *intended* to express. Once again, the sketches may be drawn on to discover intention. If we add to "Earth's Holocaust" the section on reformers in "The Hall of Fantasy," we shall be able to reconstruct the views Hawthorne held on such matters, reconstruct them with considerable confidence. In the latter sketch the usual Hawthornesque balance is perfectly maintained. Though reformers are the victims of fantasy, to be understood as "representatives of an unquiet period, when mankind is seeking to cast off the whole tissue of ancient custom like a tattered garment," still, Hawthorne hopes that none "who believe and rejoice in the progress of mankind" will be angry with him for thus satirizing those who seek "a better and purer life." After all, he is not rejecting all reform but simply testing the practicability of reformers' schemes by bringing them out into "the white sunshine of actual life." Only when reformers lose touch with reality do they deserve our ridicule.

"Perhaps your faith in the ideal is deeper than you are aware," said my friend. "You are at least a democrat; and methinks no scanty share of such faith is essential to the adoption of that creed."

Perhaps if Blithedalers had been a little more realistic, particularly about the nature of the human heart, the enterprise might have succeeded. I think we may suppose that Hawthorne intended Coverdale to express only some such meaning as this. But if so, Coverdale was not the man to express it.

In creating Coverdale, Hawthorne isolated and projected a part of himself that he disliked. Coverdale is of course not Hawthorne. He is a minor transcendentalist poet, a slightly comic figure even in his own eyes. His tastes in reading are very nearly the opposite of Hawthorne's, and there is irony in the whole portrait. Yet the irony is partially self-directed, for he is that part of Hawthorne that Hawthorne had earlier projected in his cold, proud, faithless men. Since he is both narrator and analyst—"Greek chorus," he calls it—of the story, his character gives the work the tone of icy coldness it has. Whatever he may say of his own reactions, the reader is never warmed for a moment by the roaring fires at Blithedale.

And this is no doubt one of the reasons for the lack of popularity of the book, in Hawthorne's day and in our own. Others perhaps are the too sharp break between the chapters dealing with Blithedale itself and those relating Coverdale's stay in town; the too evident influence of the Gothic romance, with its machinery of mysterious persons, "marvels" like mesmerism, and very villainous villains; and the surprising revelation at the end that Coverdale is in love with Priscilla—for we had thought that he could not love anyone but himself.

But surely the chief difficulty in the way of a greater enjoyment of the novel is created by Coverdale. He is, as we are tempted to say today, a very Jamesian character, highly conscious, and self-conscious, a reflector rather than an actor, given to irony, which he as frequently directs at himself as at others. He is a preliminary sketch for some of James's later characters. But whereas James manages to make us feel sympathy for his characters, Hawthorne makes us feel little or none for Coverdale. Perhaps the basic reason is that Hawthorne disliked the Coverdale in himself too much, so that he was not in sympathy with his own central creation.

But today there is no good reason for emphasizing the failure. The flaws are perfectly evident: given contemporary taste in fiction, we are not likely to miss them. What we have tended to miss is the remarkable textural richness and beauty of the work. Missing this, we have missed too a great deal of the meaning. The book deserves to be read more carefully than we have generally read it.

CHAPTER EIGHT

THE MARBLE FAUN

Hawthorne's whole career had prepared him to write *The Marble Faun*, his "story of the fall of man." Loss of innocence, initiation into the complexities of experience in a world of ambiguously mingled good and evil, experiences of guilt so obscurely related to specific acts as to seem more "original" and necessary than avoidable, these had been his subjects in story after story. Eden had never been far in the background, whether he was writing of life in a decayed mansion in Salem or of the attempts of reformers to undo the fall in a utopian community. The analogy with the Garden of Biblical myth had supplied the basic metaphor in "Rappaccini's Daughter." When, just after his marriage, he had experienced a happiness greater than he had ever known before, he inevitably thought of Sophia and himself in the Old Manse as a new Adam and Eve in an unfallen world.

Several of his stories that we generally think of as stories of initiation are equally stories of the fall. Robin's encounter with sin becomes a fortunate fall in "My Kinsman, Major Molineux." The innocence of this self-reliant and naïve country boy proves inadequate to guide him to his destination through the mazes of the city's streets, but thanks to a kindly Providence, he finds he may rise, after his fall, without the help he sought. Young Goodman Brown's experience in the forest was a less fortunate fall. Whether the evil he found universal there was only a dream, or a mirage contrived by the Devil to destroy him, or a false conclusion based on his inability to see the significance of his being there himself, at any rate he was destroyed by it when he lost faith in the reality of the good. From being an Innocent, he became a Cynic and so was lost because he could not accept the world as it really is. He prepares us for Giovanni in "Rappaccini's Daughter," who cannot accept the ambiguous mixture of good and evil he finds in the garden. Brown's Faith wore pink ribbons until he lost it entirely; it never became mature. So Giovanni first thought Beatrice an angel, then decided she was a fiend, but never could accept her as a human being. The Adamic falls re-enacted by Brown and Giovanni led to no subsequent rise. "My Kinsman" is perhaps the only story Hawthorne ever wrote in which there is a fall that is clearly fortunate. "Roger Malvin's Burial" ends in a reunion with God and man after isolation, to be sure, but whatever "rise" there is here is a very sad one. The vision of life it implies remains tragic.

The last story reminds us of another way in which Hawthorne's career had prepared him to write *The Marble Faun*. Hawthorne had so obscured Reuben's guilt as to make it seem like a general human condition rather than the result of a specific act which he might well have avoided. All men, Hawthorne had implied, rationalize their self interest as Reuben does, and none of us tells all the truth all the time —though in the end our evasions catch up with us, as Reuben's did with him, until at last we are guilty in fact, by a kind of negative choice, as well as by virtue of our sharing the human condition. Our sin, in short, is both "original" and ever-renewed. We are like the later Pyncheons, in part victims of the house, in part perpetrators of fresh sins —until love releases us from our inheritance. Hawthorne was more interested in guilt as a necessary human condition than he was in any specific sinful act. So he treated the central action in *The Marble Faun* in such a way that it is just as impossible to decide that Donatello is really responsible for the murder he committed as it is to decide that Reuben clearly did wrong when he left Roger Malvin to die. Miriam, herself a victim of a dreadful evil, is at least as responsible as Donatello, and the murdered man both invited and deserved his fate. All Rome, all history, made the crime inevitable, and its spreading effects leave no one untouched, not even the spotless Hilda. This murder is no ordinary crime but a re-enactment of the archetypal fall.

2

If Hawthorne had told this story many times before, he had never told it quite so directly or with so conscious an effort to determine its ultimate significance. It had generally been in the background, perhaps not consciously intended at all, as in "Young Goodman Brown," or suggested in the form of enriching allusions, as in *The House of the Seven Gables*. Now it was made the explicit subject—the too explicit subject, the modern reader is likely to decide. When innocent, faun-like Donatello, who has grown up in a rural Arcadia where he has been "close to nature," encounters evil in the corrupt city and ends by committing a murder, but is apparently deepened and matured by the experience, Miriam sees the analogy with Eden and asks the question it prompts:

"The story of the fall of man! Is it not repeated in our romance of Monte Beni? And may we follow the analogy yet further? Was that very sin,—into which Adam precipitated himself and all his race,—was it the destined means by which, over a long pathway of toil and sorrow, we are to attain a higher, brighter, and more profound happiness, than our lost birthright gave?"

Should we think of Adam's sin as a Fortunate Fall, and therefore perhaps of each man's re-enactment of the Fall as equally fortunate? Was Donatello's murder, in fact, a blessing in disguise? "Was it a means of education, bringing a simple and imperfect nature to a point of feeling and intelligence which it could have reached under no other discipline?" If sin is not educational, how else account for the fact that God permits it?

Kenyon, to whom Miriam addresses these questions, replies that he finds this line of speculation "too dangerous." He will not follow her into such "unfathomable abysses." Yet a little later, contemplating the significance of the fact that Donatello since his crime has perceptibly changed for the better, he *does* follow her:

"Here comes my perplexity," continued Kenyon. "Sin has educated Donatello, and elevated him. Is sin, then,—which we deem such a dreadful blackness in the universe,—is it, like sorrow, merely an element of human education, through which we struggle to a higher and purer state than we could otherwise have attained? Did Adam fall, that we might ultimately rise to a far loftier paradise than his?"

When Hilda demonstrates "the white shining purity" of her nature and the orthodoxy of her religious faith by responding to the sculptor's questions with horror, declaring herself shocked beyond words, he quickly retracts, asks her forgiveness, and declares he never did really believe it. He is in love with Hilda and has no answer ready to give to the question she asks him. "Do not you perceive what a mockery your creed makes, not only of all religious sentiments, but of moral law? and how it annuls and obliterates whatever precepts of Heaven are written deepest within us?"

For once, in this reply to Kenyon, Hilda may seem to the modern reader to demonstrate that moral sensitivity and insight that Hawthorne so emphatically, and to us for the most part so unaccountably, attributes to her. For she seems to have realized that one of the implications of the version of the old idea of the Fortunate Fall that both Miriam and Kenyon have put forth is that, since sin is educational, we *ought* to violate our consciences in order to attain the improvement in us that will result. In effect, whether she knows it or not, she sees that her friends are confusing history and myth. The myth describes the constant human condition: sin is "original" in man's nature, shared by all alike, present even in those not clearly guilty of any specific sin. It has nothing to say about what man ought to do about this fact. Only when it is taken as history does the question arise, Ought we then to imitate Adam and sin deliberately, so that Christ, the Second Adam, may come to redeem us? The idea of the Fortunate Fall arose when devout men contemplated the story of the old and new covenants as interpreted by Christians and felt a need to express their gratitude to God for the way He had brought good out of evil. Man had fallen but God had raised him again. Calamity had turned out, then, because "God so loved the world," to have unforeseeable, fortunate consequences: God sent His only son to die on the cross for our sins. Fortunately, the Atonement does for us what we cannot do for ourselves. The idea of the Fortunate Fall has immense theological implications, but no moral ones at all, or else the wrong ones, just as Hilda says.

The question as posed by Miriam and Kenyon is never resolved in the novel. It could not be without violating both Hawthorne's sense of the truth of life as he understood it and his sense of the limitations of words and rational thought in such areas, his sense of the mystery in which man finds himself. True, Miriam, who implies that she believes the fall *is* fortunate, is a sympathetic character and often speaks for the darker side of Hawthorne's mind, but she cannot be taken as always Hawthorne's spokesman. Hawthorne presents her as warped by her tragic experience even while he gives her his full sympathy. If her view of life is closer to Hawthorne's own than is Hilda's, Hawthorne admired Hilda more and wished he might more fully share her unquestioning faith. Miriam raised a question which Hawthorne too had pondered, and decided, apparently, he could not answer, at least not with a *yes* or a *no*.

Kenyon is much more a spokesman for Hawthorne than is Miriam, and Kenyon too rejects the implication of his own and Miriam's question. A good deal of the time in the novel there is very little distance between Kenyon and Hawthorne. Essentially, Kenyon and Hilda are Nathaniel

and Sophia. When Hilda rebukes him for his speculation
and he explains that he never really believed it, Kenyon
goes on to explain his vagary:

"But the mind wanders wild and wide; and, so lonely as I live
and work, I have neither polestar above nor light of cottage
windows here below, to bring me home. Were you my guide,
my counsellor, my inmost friend, with that white wisdom which
clothes you as a celestial garment, all would go well. O Hilda,
guide me home!"

The parallel between this and many of Hawthorne's love
letters to Sophia is very close. One of the things Hawthorne
must have meant when he declared himself "saved" by his
marriage was that he had found Sophia's buoyant faith a
needed counterbalance to his own dark questionings. So
Kenyon might be wiser in the ways of the world but Hilda,
as we are often reminded, was wiser in religious truth.
Kenyon might well ask her to guide him home, in Hawthorne's view of the matter. His refusal to carry on his line
of speculation had Hawthorne's approval.

Depending on which aspect of it we look at, the plot
either supports or does not support the rejection by Hilda
and Kenyon of the idea of the Fortunate Fall. Though Donatello has been matured and humanized by his suffering, he
must go to prison. Though Miriam has been ennobled by
love, she ends in sad penitence, without hope of happiness
with Donatello. Kenyon and Hilda decide to leave Rome,
thus in effect putting the problem behind them. The plot
gives no clear answer to the largest question explicitly posed
by the novel.

3

But perhaps the question itself is illegitimate, impossible
to answer. Hawthorne has Kenyon say, after he has looked
from Donatello's tower at the landscape mottled with patches
of sunlight and shadow and seen it as a symbol of life, "It
is a great mistake to try to put our best thoughts into human
language. When we ascend into the higher regions of emo-

tion and spiritual enjoyment, they are only expressible by such grand hieroglyphics as these around us." By symbols, in short, and myths. Speaking in his own person as narrator, Hawthorne has already noted the loss now that man has grown beyond the archaic expressiveness of gestures, and "words have been feebly substituted in the place of signs and symbols." What words cannot do, the visual arts sometimes can. Speaking again in his own person, in one of the passages lifted from the Notebooks, Hawthorne says of Sodoma's Christ bound to a pillar that it shows what "pictorial art, devoutly exercised, might effect in behalf of religious truth; involving, as it does, deeper mysteries of revelation, and bringing them closer to man's heart, and making him tenderer to be impressed by them, than the most eloquent words of preacher or prophet." In his first chapter, describing the Faun, who was "neither man nor animal, and yet no monster," Hawthorne has despaired of putting his basic idea into abstract language: "The idea grows coarse as we handle it, and hardens in our grasp." The idea of the Faun, he decides, "may have been no dream, but rather a poet's reminiscence of a period when man's affinity with nature was more strict, and his fellowship with every living thing more intimate and dear." To discover what the novel finally, at its deepest level, means, then, we should turn from a consideration of the questions framed by Miriam and Kenyon to the myths which Hawthorne uses to shape his story.

Almost exactly in the center of his book Hawthorne has placed a chapter he calls simply "Myths." In it he gives us what Miriam, on another occasion, demands of Donatello, "the latest news from Arcady," which is, in effect, that nature has no cure for what ails us. However beautiful the old Arcadian myths are, however sad it is that we have lost our innocence, they are not true any longer in a fallen world. (In Hawthorne's terminology, the old pagan legends are "myths," the Biblical story in Genesis a symbolic truth, perhaps not literally true historically but true as a type of the human condition. He never refers to the Genesis story as

a "myth.") Donatello, now that he has known sin, cannot
re-enter Arcadia.

The chief substance of the chapter is the legend of Donatello's spring, which one of his ancestors found to be ani-
mated by a beautiful maiden, the spirit of the water, with
whom he fell in love. On summer days she would cool his
brow with her touch or make rainbows around him. Kenyon
interrupts the story at this point with a skeptical comment:

> "It is a delightful story for the hot noon of your Tuscan sum-
> mer . . . But the deportment of the watery lady must have had a
> most chilling influence in midwinter."

If this criticism seems the product only of the skeptical mind,
another is implicit in the story itself. Eventually the dryad
refused to appear to her lover, and Donatello explains that
her refusal was caused by the effort of his ancestor to wash
off a bloodstain in the water. While summer and innocence
last, in short, being "close to nature" is perhaps enough;
at least, Hawthorne says elsewhere, it is a very beautiful
idea. But winter and guilt come, death and sin are in the
world, and Arcadianism does not know how to deal with
them. Attempting to communicate with the wild creatures
as he once had, Donatello calls to them in the "voice and
utterance of the natural man," but he is frustrated when a
brown lizard "of the tarantula species" makes its appearance.
"To all present appearance, this venomous reptile was the
only creature that had responded to the young Count's efforts to renew his intercourse with the lower orders of nature." Donatello falls to the ground and Kenyon, alarmed,
asks what has happened to him. " 'Death, death!' sobbed
Donatello."

Kenyon himself supplies sufficient comment on the legend
of the spring: "He understood it as an apologue, typifying
the soothing and genial effects of an habitual intercourse
with nature, in all ordinary cares and griefs; while, on the
other hand, her mild influences fall short in their effect
upon the ruder passions, and are altogether powerless in
the dread fever-fit or deadly chill of guilt." After a little more

talk, the two friends part, Donatello to climb up in his tower once more, Kenyon to go inside to read "an antique edition of Dante." We have met the venomous reptile and heard Donatello's answer to Kenyon before, in Rappaccini's garden, where Hawthorne also alluded to Dante to help us to get our metaphorical bearings. Sin and death have entered the world, to spoil the Arcadian dream. Whether the fall is "fortunate" or not may be impossible to answer, but at least the world we know is no unfallen earthly paradise. Evil is in it, and nature itself offers no satisfactory cure.

The cure, insofar as there is any, lies partly in repentance and love in this world, and partly in the hope of another life. These meanings emerge from the plot considered as symbolic action or myth and from the implications of the leading images with which Hawthorne supports his myth. The plot gives us three of the characters at least, and perhaps by intention four, growing in moral and spiritual stature as they experience sin and suffering. Miriam ceases to suffer in isolation and think only of herself, falls in love with Donatello, and dedicates her life to penitence and to the service of the one she has wronged. Donatello gains in wisdom and understanding, becomes in fact human. Hilda comes down from the tower of her perfect rectitude, repents having turned away Miriam in her need, and becomes human enough to marry Kenyon. All, in fact, come down from the isolation of their towers; all fall in love. That there is no cure for suffering is clear from the careers of Miriam and Donatello, but that suffering and acknowledgment of mutual complicity in guilt are necessary preludes to any redemption possible to man is clear from the careers of all of them.

The "higher hopes" of another life that will rectify the wrongs of this one are implied in Kenyon's deference to Hilda, in his plea that she lead him home, and in Hawthorne's own too often expressed admiration of her. Hilda is "the religious girl" as well as the girl of a shining purity of character, Kenyon the "thinker," potentially the skeptic. Not just Kenyon but the whole novel stands in awe of Hilda, whose precise function is to keep the lamp of religious faith,

with its higher hopes, burning. (She can let the flame of the
old Catholic lamp go out at the end because she herself in
her own person emanates a better and purer light.)

Hilda is supported in her task of guarding religious faith
and hope by much of the imagery, sometimes with images
that Hawthorne makes very emphatic, sometimes with what
seem mere reflexes of his habitual style. I shall give just
two examples. At the end of the chapter called "The Owl
Tower," in which Kenyon and Donatello have climbed to
the top of Donatello's tower and Kenyon has had his vision
of the symbolic landscape, Kenyon finds, growing out of the
masonry of the tower, seemingly out of the very stone itself,
"a little shrub, with green and glossy leaves." Donatello
thinks, "If the wide valley has a great meaning, the plant
ought to have at least a little one." Kenyon asks Donatello
if he sees any meaning here and Donatello says he sees
none, but, looking at the plant, he adds, "But here was a
worm that would have killed it; an ugly creature, which I
will fling over the battlements."

Kenyon does not voice the meaning he sees, and Hawthorne makes no comment. But the context makes reasonably clear what Donatello missed. We are reminded of Melville's "Bartleby the Scrivener," in which, in the Tombs,
green grass could be seen by Bartleby if he would only turn
his face from the wall. Kenyon's view of the valley has increased his "reliance on His providence" (whereas Donatello has seen only "sunshine on one spot, and cloud in
another, and no reason for it in either case"), and he has
just explained to Donatello that he "cannot preach": words
will not express his "best" thoughts, that is, his religious
thoughts. He has seen, as he looked at the earth spread below them, something of the way of "His dealings with mankind." Now, in the rarefied "upper atmosphere" of the tower,
he finds a green shrub, the meaning of which he does not
even attempt to state for his companion. Green is the traditional color of hope, and the plant is growing in a very unlikely place: "Heaven knows how its seeds had ever been

planted . . ." But not only Heaven knew: Hawthorne knew
how the seeds of such hope as he cherished had been
planted. The chapter ends with Donatello's destruction of
the "worm" that would destroy the plant.

My second example comes at the end of chapter three,
"Subterranean Reminiscences," in which the four friends
have been exploring one of the catacombs, where they
"wandered by torchlight through a sort of dream." Hilda
and Donatello, both Innocents, find the darkness especially
repellent: their experience of life has in no way prepared
them for it. Miriam thinks that "the most awful idea connected with the catacombs is their interminable extent, and
the possibility of going astray in this labyrinth of darkness . . ." When Kenyon wonders whether in fact anyone
has ever been lost in the place, he is told of "a pagan of
old Rome, who hid himself in order to spy out the blessed
saints, who then dwelt and worshipped in these dismal
places." The pagan has been "groping in the darkness" ever
since, unable to find his way out.

At this point the party reaches a chapel carved out of the
walls and stops to look at it; "and while their collected
torches illuminated this one small, consecrated spot, the
great darkness spread all round it, like that immenser mystery which envelops our little life, and into which friends
vanish from us, one by one." Miriam, it turns out, has
"vanished into the great darkness, even while they were
shuddering at the remote possibility of such a misfortune."
Miriam shares Hilda's strict orthodoxy even less than Kenyon,
who at least longs for and admires what is not as much his
as he would like it to be. She has something in common
with the pagan of old Rome; she is not held by the brightly
illuminated consecrated spot. (As it turns out, though, she is
more a victim of persecution than an unbeliever.)

We are reminded of the brightly lighted chamber in
"Night Sketches," with the cold darkness all around, or of
the darkness that seemed to press in on the little company
at Blithedale. In the latter case, though, the hope suggested

by the warmth and light was a secular one. Here everything about the context unites to suggest a purely "religious" hope —in the sense of a hope for immortality. The darkness into which our friends vanish is the darkness of death. Later, Kenyon will protest the presence of a skull in Donatello's bedroom: "It is absurdly monstrous, my dear friend, thus to fling the dead-weight of our mortality upon our immortal hopes. While we live on earth, 'tis true, we must needs carry our sketetons about with us; but, for Heaven's sake, do not let us burden our spirits with them, in our feeble efforts to soar upward." (Kenyon's higher hopes may have seemed to him feeble, but Hawthorne characterizes him elsewhere as he would have characterized himself, "a devout man in his way.") Those who know the extent of "the blackness that lies beneath us everywhere," who know that we are "dreaming on the edge of a precipice," who know that sinking into nature is equivalent to sinking into the grave and have explored the "dark caverns" of experience, will not need to keep a skull in the bedroom to remind them of man's mortality.

They will be likely to agree with the point of Hawthorne's moral and theological criticism of Sodoma's Siena fresco of Christ bound to a pillar. Hawthorne felt sure the picture sprang from sincere religious feeling: a shallow or worldly man could not have painted it. The picture is "inexpressibly touching" in its portrayal of the weariness and loneliness of the Savior:

You behold Christ deserted both in heaven and earth; that despair is in him which wrung forth the saddest utterance man ever made, "Why hast Thou forsaken me?" Even in this extremity, however, he is still divine . . . He is as much, and as visibly, our Redeemer, there bound, there fainting, and bleeding from the scourge, with the cross in view, as if he sat on his throne of glory in the heavens! Sodoma, in this matchless picture, has done more towards reconciling the incongruity of Divine Omnipotence and outraged, suffering Humanity, combined in one person, than the theologians ever did.

4

The Marble Faun ought to have been Hawthorne's finest novel. His career had pointed toward it from the beginning. In it the heart imagery that is implicit in "The Hollow of the Three Hills" has become the underground world of Rome, the catacombs, the tomb or dungeon of the heart and of dreams. In it Robin's initiation has become consciously archetypal, to be seen in the dimensions of its largest significance. In it the implications of "Earth's Holocaust" and "The Celestial Railroad" have been combined within the framework of man's basic myth. The most persistent preoccupations and the recurrent images of a lifetime of writing have been brought together in what ought to have been a definitive recapitulation.

Instead, the novel is clearly inferior to *The Scarlet Letter* and even, it seems to me, to *The House of the Seven Gables*. Richer in many respects than *Blithedale*, it is less consistently interesting: there are frequent stretches of it one wants to skip. There is a very large gap in it between intended and achieved meaning. Hawthorne failed with Rome, and he failed with Hilda, and both were essential to the achievement of his intention.

Hilda is at once a nineteenth century stereotype and Hawthorne's tribute to Sophia. The only way of interpreting her that will "save" Hawthorne and his novel is to take the portrait ironically, but this will not do if we consider all the evidence. True, Miriam points out that Hilda's innocence is like "a sharp steel sword"; so white a purity makes for judgments that are "terribly severe." And Miriam often speaks for Hawthorne. Here we should probably assume that he thought so too. But this is only a minor qualification of what, for Hawthorne, is Hilda's awe-inspiring virtue and compelling attractiveness. Once again, as in the case of Miriam's implied assent to the idea of the Fortunate Fall, we may not assume that Hawthorne is completely committed to Miriam as his spokesman. In his own person, as narrator, he pays Hilda lavish, and tiresomely repetitious, tribute, and as Kenyon he marries her and asks her to guide him home.

Yet to the modern reader Hilda is either ridiculous or, if we can take her seriously, self-righteous and uncharitable. She is not only a far less impressive character, as a literary character, than Miriam, she is far less attractive, and even less "good," as a person. Throughout most of the course of the novel her chief concern is to protect the spotlessness of the innocence assumed by her and asserted by Hawthorne. She finds everyone else's faith and everyone else's conduct corrupt. When called upon for help, she turns her friend away lest she be stained by the contact. Though the idea would have shocked Hawthorne immeasurably, it is impossible not to see her as a feminine version of the man of adamant—at least until the very end, when the rigor of her moralism is softened somewhat.

There is no consistent or effective irony in the portrait. Though this "daughter of the Puritans," as Hawthorne repeatedly calls her, comes down from her tower to marry Kenyon, the change is not so much one from spiritual pride to humility as from priestess to goddess: "Another hand must henceforth trim the lamp before the Virgin's shrine; for Hilda was coming down from her old tower, to be herself enshrined and worshipped as a household saint, in the light of her husband's fireside." It is true that Hilda thought right and wrong completely distinct, never in any degree mingled or ambiguous—the error of judgment that Hawthorne's innocent young men have to grow out of, the idea they have to unlearn by painful experience. But Hawthorne thought such an error—if indeed error it was, as he would have said —charming and admirable in innocent young girls. Hilda is like young Robin before his "evening of ambiguity and weariness"; the difference between them is that Hawthorne does not require that young girls should grow in knowledge of the world.

His century placed women on a pedestal just *because*, in their role of guardian of values that were being threatened, they knew nothing of the world. If their innocence rendered them helpless to deal with reality, it was nevertheless to be both protected and admired, for reality was very nasty. If they did not truly partake of the human condition, it was a good thing they didn't. A comment Hawthorne makes in the novel on a work of art, without suggesting any connection with his portrait of Hilda, suggests the chief reason for his failure with his heroine: "It was one of the few works of antique sculpture in which we recognize womanhood, and that, moreover, without prejudice to its divinity." Womanhood's "divinity"? Since Hilda was more than normally pretty and good, no wonder her destiny was to be "enshrined and worshipped" at the fireside.

As he depended greatly on Hilda to give his novel an affirmative meaning, so Hawthorne depended chiefly on Rome and its art treasures to give it thematic density. Here too he failed, though for quite different reasons. Again, recent efforts to "save" the novel do not really work. To be sure, Hawthorne anticipates James in developing the Europe versus America theme: Rome is the past, experience, culture, and corruption, in contrast with America's present, ideals, morality, and innocence: Miriam versus Hilda. This is fine, theoretically. But Hawthorne too often simply lifts long passages of description from the Notebooks, and the passages remain inert in the novel. There is too *much* of Rome, and too much about art. They are a burden the story is simply incapable of carrying.

Examples could easily be given of passages in which Hawthorne succeeds in making his comments on art and descriptions of Rome work for his story. Perhaps the best one is Miriam's comment on Guido's "dapper" Archangel, whose feathers are unruffled in his struggle with Satan: "Is it thus that virtue looks the moment after its death-struggle with evil? . . . A full third of the Archangel's feathers should have been torn from his wings . . ." But for page after page there is nothing like this, nothing in fact that is not very tedious. And Hawthorne seems to know it. At least he keeps apologizing for his descriptions while the story halts, sometimes for a chapter at a time, to accommodate them. This is simply awkward novel writing and no amount of demonstration that, where there are symbolic implications in the Notebook material they are consistent with the general theme, will really save the romance as a work of art. Thematic considerations alone cannot save any novel.

The effect on the reader of all this inert material is to suggest that Hawthorne was not sufficiently interested in his *story*—an effect reinforced by his embarrassed and coy protestations at the end, in the added conclusion, when he refused to make more than a slight gesture toward clearing up the mysteries of his plot. What he is really saying in his "Conclusion" is that he doesn't *care* whether Donatello had furry ears or not or who detained Hilda, and we the readers shouldn't either. But he had cared about Hester, and Hepzibah, and Zenobia, cared about them as people and not merely as allegoric or mythic symbols. Despite the elaborate density of its background, it might well be argued that *The Marble Faun* is more allegorical than any of the three preceding romances.

5

Still, if it is true that the work has been generally underestimated, as I think it has, the reason is not hard to find. Its weaknesses are very obvious, impossible I should think to overlook, while its strength is subtle and delicate. It is easy to read this work in which "Adam falls anew, and Paradise . . . is lost again" without responding to a good deal of its multiple suggestiveness. There is nothing in its period quite like the way it plays theological, philosophical, and psychological perspectives against each other in the image of the catacombs. Here the characters wandered in "a sort of dream," a dark labyrinth of guilt, an "ugly dream" indeed: "For, in dreams, the conscience sleeps, and we often stain ourselves with guilt of which we should be incapable in our waking moments." The "dark caverns" of experience in Hawthorne's novel are so richly meaningful that we should have to read the work for this if there were nothing else to draw us.

There is of course much else. The scene at the precipice (we are all, in some sense, "dreaming on the edge of a precipice"), the whole series of chapters laid in Donatello's country, where the serpent is discovered in nature's garden, the descriptions of the several studios (Miriam's is said to be "the outward type of a poet's haunted imagination," and the description justifies the comment)—all these parts of the work, and more, make it more worth reading than most American novels of the nineteenth century, even if we are not already committed to Hawthorne before we start it.

If we are, we shall find it an even more rewarding failure. For on the thematic level it is, for the most part, such *good* Hawthorne. It is not just Donatello but all of us who "travel in a circle, as all things heavenly and earthly do." The loss of innocence is very sad, but it is at least naïve and may be disastrous to suppose that we haven't lost it. Guilt is original, a necessary aspect of the human condition, not something that sets conspicuous sinners apart from the rest of us. And it is mutual, so that in our inevitable complicity we may not relieve ourselves of its burden by pointing the finger, casting the stone. Still, we need not despair if only we will acknowledge our complicity and enter the human circle.

"Outraged, suffering humanity" must learn to live with "the blackness that lies beneath us, everywhere," but Kenyon, taking the long view from the height of Donatello's tower, saw, above the stormy valley, "within the domain of chaos, as it were,—hill-tops . . . brightening in the sunshine; they looked like fragments of the world, broken adrift and based on nothingness, or like portions of a sphere destined to exist, but not yet finally compacted." Kenyon's images give us Hawthorne's answer to the question whether the fall was fortunate or not, an answer that springs from his "best thought" and that was otherwise inexpressible.

CHAPTER NINE

THE LATE ROMANCES

In the last five years of his life Hawthorne tried to
write one more romance to bring his career to a fitting close.
He had lived long with a premonition of early death, and
now, with an increasing sense of urgency, he wanted both
to make money to provide for his family after he was gone,
and to say some things that he felt he had never yet succeeded in getting said.

He failed in both these aims. He failed miserably, desperately, shockingly. Against a growing certainty of failure he
forced himself to write on and on, to discard what he had
done and start afresh, writing in torment and desperation
of spirit, concealing from his family how much he was writing that they might not realize how completely he was failing. In five years he accumulated some twenty-two "studies"
for four romances which he left unfinished at his death:
twenty-two studies, four fragmentary romances—and, except
for the three chapters of *The Dolliver Romance* and a few
scenes in *Septimius Felton*, nothing with the power and
authority of the earlier work, almost nothing indeed that
was not positively bad, and that he did not, with his still
acute self-criticism, recognize as bad. His own comments in
the margins of his manuscripts tell the story: "Here I come
to a standstill! . . . I have not the least notion how to get
on. I never was in such a predicament before . . . There

must be a germ in this—I don't know . . . How? Why? What
sense?"

A large part of the evidence of the failure is now open for
inspection.* Only the causes of it still are hidden. We can
see the chaos, follow the fumbling and the false starts, watch
the old tricks being used without effect, without meaning.
We can watch Hawthorne parodying himself, recognizing
the parody, stopping, discarding what he had done, starting
again, only to fall into the same traps. We can watch him
returning to the apprenticeship of *Fanshawe* all over again,
as though he had never written the great tales and *The
Scarlet Letter*. We can watch him struggling against ill
health and inner desolation, forcing himself by sheer acts of
will to go on when he had no hope. The drama that we may
watch in Hawthorne's last period is as strangely and mov-
ingly tragic as anything in the life of any writer; tragic, not
merely pathetic, for Hawthorne as actor in his own drama
had been a great writer and now he could write nothing,
or almost nothing, of any worth.

What had happened to his talent?

2

In all the complicated, seemingly chaotic confusion of
Hawthorne's last five years of writing, only one element of
clarity is apparent. The twenty-two studies and four fragmentary romances treat just two themes. Hawthorne's English experiences had suggested to him the subject of the
American claimant to an English estate. He first tried to
treat the subject in *The Ancestral Footstep*, which he was
planning as early as 1855 and which he actually began in
1858; then he tried all over again in *Dr. Grimshawe's Secret*,
which he worked on in 1860 and 1861. When this subject
failed him, his own situation, which brought again into the
foreground a lifelong interest, suggested to him the subject
of the elixir of life, the subject both of *Septimius Felton*,

* See E. H. Davidson, *Hawthorne's Last Phase* (New Haven: Yale University Press, 1949).

which he worked on from 1861 to 1863, and of *The Dolliver Romance,* with which he was occupied in the last months before his death in March 1864. Though he tried, especially in *The Ancestral Footstep* and *Dr. Grimshawe's Secret,* to work in material from his English Notebooks on the differences between English and American cultures, as he had used his Italian Notebooks in *The Marble Faun,* and though he had some hope of capitalizing on the timely subject of civil war in *Septimius Felton*—for the Revolution he felt was also a civil war—yet the claimant and the elixir are the organizing centers of all his last efforts at fiction. And they were at once inevitable and impossible: inevitable because all his career had pointed to them, impossible because now that he tried to treat them directly in major works he no longer had any means of dealing with them.

Superficially, the subject of the first two of Hawthorne's unfinished romances was new to him and seems to suggest that he was trying once again to treat "present actuality," to use directly the English experiences just behind him. But a second look is enough to suggest that this lost English inheritance situation is more than a result of the English years and more than a stock device of the popular romance: it is the old Eden-Arcadia theme in a new, timely guise. For both the American claimant and man exiled from Eden or Arcadia share the memory of a lost birthright, the memory, conscious or buried, of a nobler condition. In both themes, man is sadly fallen from his former situation, whether to his final good or ill not being quite clear.* Hawthorne had been haunted all his life by a memory of a lost innocence. That memory lies behind and beneath the Gothic claptrap of *The Ancestral Footstep* and *Dr. Grimshawe's Secret.*

In his youth Hawthorne had thought a good deal about the fallen and shrunken estate of his family, exaggerating in his fancies no doubt their former affluence and social position as he contemplated his own poverty and obscurity and

---

* See, in *Hawthorne's Last Phase,* the various endings Hawthorne contemplated for the American heir in *The Ancestral Footstep* and *Dr. Grimshawe's Secret.*

the necessity of accepting help from his uncles. At the beginning of his writing career he had given compulsive expression to some of the deeper layers of these fantasies of a lost estate in "Alice Doane's Appeal." In the great tales written between 1830 and 1850 he had returned to the theme often, peripherally and indirectly, as in "My Kinsman, Major Molineux" and "Roger Malvin's Burial," through symbolic reference and allusion in "Rappaccini's Daughter," or directly, as in "The New Adam and Eve." Of the four novels, only *The Scarlet Letter* does not have the theme in a prominent position. Eden imagery is a major factor in the *Seven Gables* and *Blithedale,* and the fall of man is the explicit theme of *The Marble Faun.* The return of an American heir to claim his ancestral estate is, in short, only a variation on a theme that had often appeared in Hawthorne's works because it expressed an interest that lay close to the center of his deeper mind.

And now, as he approached the end of his life, with what seems to have been full consciousness of the fact, the idea came to the surface and refused to be dismissed, even when it was clear that he was not succeeding in doing anything with it. He had gone to England with a recurrent sense of "returning home": "My ancestor left England in 1630. I return in 1853." He had tried to look up the records of the family but he had found out little that he had not already known. Long ago he had identified himself in his imagination with an English relative when he had written stories of Jervase Helwyse and Gervayse Hastings, for there had been a Gervase Elwes, a baronet, in the family; the thread connecting the Jervase Helwyse of "Lady Eleanor's Mantle" and the Gervayse Hastings of "The Christmas Banquet" with Hawthorne's genealogical interests in England is unbroken.* Now he entitled his book about his English experiences *Our Old Home,* and he was quite sure in the end that the Wayside in Concord was not and never would be the home he sought. Once, after visting the English village of Eastham,

---

* See the *English Notebooks* for 1854.

he had written in his journal, "Eastham is the finest old English village I have seen, with many antique houses, and with altogether a rural and picturesque aspect, unlike anything in America, and yet possessing a familiar look, as if it were something I had dreamed about." Now he tried to write romances about Americans returning to claim estates they had never seen but knew instinctively.

The other theme too, the elixir of life, or earthly immortality, was also inevitable, and not only because Hawthorne knew he was dying. Septimius Felton's search for power and happiness in an unending future is but the reverse of the search for the lost birthright. Eden and Immortality are two sides of the same preoccupation. There is a sense in which we may say that Hawthorne's failure with *The Ancestral Footstep* and *Dr. Grimshawe's Secret* required that he reverse the coin and search the future for what could not be found in the past.

Hawthorne had always written of life with one eye on death. Fanshawe, his earliest clearly recognizable projection of himself in fiction, had been doomed to die young. "Alice Doane's Appeal" and "The Hollow of the Three Hills," probably his earliest surviving tales, have death at their center. And from these youthful pieces down to *The Marble Faun*, death, in one of its several disguises if not directly, occupies the center of the scene. Just as Hawthorne's negative or guilty characters are usually more vividly created than his good ones—Judge Pyncheon more so than Phoebe, Zenobia than Priscilla, Miriam than Hilda—so it might also be said that in nearly all of his works death tends to be *felt*, life only surmised, hoped for, or postulated. Judge Pyncheon's death is vivid and powerful; Phoebe's life and love pale, relatively unconvincing. The death of Zenobia in *Blithedale* is the strongest scene in the book.

And now that his own death appeared to Hawthorne very close, the theme of the elixir of life which he had long ago treated in "Dr. Heidegger's Experiment" appealed to him with a new urgency. Over and over he wrote on pieces of paper the number 64, which he had long since connected with "some destiny." "God himself," he had written in his English Notebooks in 1855, "cannot compensate us for being born for any period short of eternity." Now he made Septimius Felton reply to his friend's question as to whether their countrymen were "worthy" to live: " 'It is hardly worth answering or considering,' said Septimius, looking at him thoughtfully. 'We live so little while, that (always setting aside the effect on a future existence) it is little matter whether we live or no.' "

Mark Van Doren has commented very justly on Hawthorne's self-portraiture in the figure of Dr. Dolliver. But it should be added that an aspect—and, on the whole, a very important aspect—of Hawthorne is portrayed likewise in Septimius Felton, that morbid scholar-recluse who is first cousin to Fanshawe but who is not willing, like Fanshawe, to accept his doom. When Hawthorne deplored his well-loved Dr. Johnson's "morbid" dread of death, he was speaking from the top of his mind and protesting too much. His own frequent protestations of faith in immortality cannot be taken wholly at face value: he was more like Dr. Johnson than he cared to admit even to himself. As, in an increasing "intensity of desolation," he made himself write on and on, the subject of the elixir of life forced itself on him as naturally as the subject of the American heir had, until he had found beyond all possibility of doubt that he could do nothing with it. It seemed that he could do nothing with this, either.

3

Many reasons have been suggested for Hawthorne's final failure, some of them based on bad logic, others obviously superficial, all of them more or less inadequate. Among those that are worthy of comment, the one that seems, at first thought, most cogent is failing health. But there are several reasons why this is not sufficient to account for what happened. In the first place, Hawthorne's physical health did not begin to fail until about 1861 or even later, while his artistic failure is obvious in all the work he did on *The Ancestral*

Footstep, begun in 1858, and in *Dr. Grimshawe's Secret*, 1860–61. This consideration alone would be conclusive, but we may add to it a second: the kind of failure we find in the late romances is not such as simple physical illness could easily account for. It is, rather, a failure at the center, a failure at the very point where Hawthorne's creative greatness had lain, a failure of meaning and values. Something deeper than physical pain or lack of energy would be needed, one suspects, to produce this kind of failure.

The same line of reasoning is sufficient to show that it was not the Civil War that made Hawthorne unable to write as he once had. The war may have been for him, as Mark Van Doren has said, "pure disaster," though I suspect that this is overstating its effect. But the war did not break out until after he had stopped working on the two most completely bad of the last romances, *The Ancestral Footstep* and *Dr. Grimshawe's Secret*. And while it was in progress, at the very end of his life, he wrote the only thing in this whole period that has any sustained value, the fragments of *The Dolliver Romance*. The war, then, will surely not do as a sufficient reason for his failure.

Slightly more plausible perhaps on the face of it is financial worry. It is true that Hawthorne had not succeeded, for various reasons, including both bad luck and bad judgment, in building up enough savings from his consular income to make his family secure. But he had known, earlier in his life, that security is not possible in the world; and during a period of real financial distress he had written some of the greatest tales and sketches and *The Scarlet Letter*.

An explanation of about the same degree of plausibility is offered by the "twilight of romance" theory: that by the end of Hawthorne's career the rise of the realistic mode in fiction had rendered his type of writing obsolete, and that his realization of this confused and frustrated him. It is true that Hawthorne began his career rather late in the Romantic movement and that by the final years of his life the new realistic fashion was already under way in Europe and faintly stirring in America. It is likewise true that Hawthorne admired the work of the English Victorian novelists and sometimes regretted that he could not write like Trollope. But it is also, and more significantly, true that this was not a new development at the very end of his career. If his genius had been nourished on Scott, it had been nourished just as obviously on Bunyan, who can hardly be called a "romantic." Hawthorne's favorite writers at all periods in his life were what he called the "old time" authors, not, with the exception of Scott, men of his own century—Dante, Cervantes, Spenser, Shakespeare, Bunyan, Milton, Johnson. If he was "old fashioned" at the end of his career, he was not very much less so in the middle of it, when he was doing his best work. The "twilight of romance" had in fact already set in before even *The Scarlet Letter* was written, so it can scarcely be used to explain the total failure of almost everything written after the *Marble Faun*. It is, no doubt, one of the reasons for Hawthorne's increasing uncertainty in his last ten years, but it must not be used to explain too much.

There are, I think, two approaches to this problem which offer more reward. I mean the psychological and the theological or philosophic. The two are interrelated, but for convenience I shall treat them separately. In making the psychological approach I must beg to be excused from attempting any definite analysis. Psychology is a highly specialized study, and I am not a psychologist. But a few facts are clear, and one or two inferences from them seem inevitable.

Some psychological factor as yet unidentified by any of Hawthorne's biographers, presumably the Oedipus situation that Freud considered universal at some stage in male development, was apparently at work during all of Hawthorne's adult life to produce his lifelong restlessness, unease, and sense of guilt and estrangement. Toward the end of his life there seems to have been a resurgence of guilt feeling.* This is not to say that there were no objective bases for these feelings: simple moral realism and self-knowledge

---

* See Dr. John H. Lamont, "Hawthorne's Unfinished Works," *Harvard Medical Alumni Bulletin,* 36:13-20 (Summer, 1962).

should be sufficient to produce a sense of sin, and only the
insensitive are likely to be wholly contented. But no reader
of Hawthorne's letters and journals can escape, it seems to
me, the feeling that the cause of the discontent and dissatisfaction that amounted to spiritual malaise lay far deeper
than the causes constantly suggested by Hawthorne himself
and by his family—causes like the size and shape of the
houses in which they lived, the neighbors, the climate, the
need to work at uncongenial tasks.

Much of the time after 1850 Hawthorne found all tasks
uncongenial, even writing. He frequently protested that he
could not write in the winter because of the cold. In England his consular duties were extremely light, almost nomi-
nal, yet he got no creative work done. In the Salem Custom
House position he "worked" at earning a living only a few
hours each day, yet could do nothing on his writing during
the rest.

There was, to be sure, a period when Hawthorne seems to
have been relatively at peace: the first two or three years
after his marriage. But though his was an ideally "happy
marriage," the fact that Hawthorne was not very happy during twenty or so of the twenty-two years it lasted seems to
me undeniable. His restlessness, his dis-ease shines out
through the very attempts of his wife and son to deny it. In
the last ten years of his life the dissatisfaction in his letters
amounts at times to petulance and at times to hopelessness.
A very deep-seated ambivalence of feeling becomes apparent. Everything is Janus-faced, nothing is clear, nothing
gives any real satisfaction. As he had hated Salem, yet been
unable to turn from it and all that it stood for in his mind,
so later in England he both longed for and dreaded his return to America, longing and dreading not mildly, superficially, with the surface of his mind as moods and circumstances changed, as might be natural, but deeply, agonizingly.
He longed also for a real home, and one of the most moving
passages in the English Notebooks recounts his longing:

The house is respectably, though not very elegantly, furnished.
It was a dismal, rainy day yesterday, and we had a coal-fire in

the sitting-room, beside which I sat last evening as twilight came on, and thought, rather sadly, how many times we have changed our home since we were married. In the first place, our three years at the Old Manse; then a brief residence at Salem, then at Boston, then two or three years at Salem again; then at Lenox, then at West Newton, and then again at Concord, where we imagined that we were fixed for life, but spent only a year. Then this farther flight to England . . . during all which time we shall have no real home. For, as I sat in this English house, with the chill, rainy English twilight brooding over the lawn, and a coal-fire to keep me comfortable on the first evening of September, and the picture of a stranger—the dead husband of Mrs. Campbell—gazing down at me from above the mantel-piece,—I felt that I never should be quite at home here. Nevertheless, the fire was very comfortable to look at, and the shape of the fireplace—an arch, with a deep cavity—was an improvement on the square, shallow opening of an American coal-grate.

Yet the reasons he was never able to establish a permanent home were as much inward as outward. When circumstances, including the result of a former decision, forced him to live longer in the Wayside than he had ever lived in any house since his marriage, he protested vehemently that the place was a "prison" from which he would never escape. A good deal of the time he hated everything about it, as he had hated Salem and Rome and even, at the end of his stay there, the Old Manse.

The evidences of this dis-ease of his became more pronounced in the last decade, especially in the last five years— and several years before there were any visible symptoms either of his sudden "aging"—if that is really what it was— or of his final unidentified physical illness. The temper and tone of his English and Italian letters and journals provide the hint of the failure in the writings to come that is not provided by conditions of physical health, or money matters, or politics, including war. The secret that cannot be communicated, that estranges one even from those one loves and that takes the *life* out of everything, had provided the substance of many great tales and the principal theme of his greatest romance. When it ceased to be projected into

stories it did not cease to exist. There seems to me to have
been a very marked increase of ambivalence and hopelessness in Hawthorne's life in the final decade, and particularly
in the last American years. The mystery of the late cramped
handwriting, so suddenly changed, the greatly increased
manifest isolation, even in the midst of a loving family, the
altered tone of the letters, all suggest that the memory of
lost innocence and the sense of death have become almost
obsessive.

If this is so, it means among other things that Hawthorne
and Melville were more alike in their experiences than they
knew or we have realized. It is interesting, and perhaps instructive, to set up a parallel between Melville's *Typee* and
Hawthorne's "Alice Doane's Appeal"; and between *Pierre*,
with its evidences of breakdown of control, and *Blithedale*,
with its much less evident signs of trouble to come; and between *Billy Budd* and *The Dolliver Romance*, each of which
suggests a new control and peace coming just before the
end. Such a parallel is useful only in so far as it suggests
similarities in the psychological histories of the two great
writers. It could be highly misleading if misapplied. What
it suggests is the possibility that Hawthorne's personality
was not so much unlike Melville's as his greater self-control
and the different circumstances of his life would seem to
indicate. And if that is so, then a psychological explanation
of the failure of the last romances is as appropriate as is
Professor Henry A. Murray's psychological analysis of the
failure of Melville's *Pierre*.

When we turn from an attempt to survey all the evidence
to get at the inwardness of Hawthorne's experience during
his last years—that is, from a psychological approach—and
simply look closely at the fragments themselves, what we
find is no merely technical failure, and no turning to new
subjects that he did not know how to handle, but a failure
at the very center, a failure of meaning. The most striking
difference between Hawthorne's work before the late romances and the first three of the late romances themselves
is that the best of the early work is either directly or in-

directly moral and theological while the late romances for the most part are not. Even when the early tales are explicitly historical, like "The Maypole of Merrymount" and "The Gray Champion," with a very few exceptions, the most obvious of which is "Alice Doane's Appeal," they have moral overtones, are informed with moral meaning, are written from within a coherent moral tradition, which the tale assumes and which may be deduced from the tale. The novels likewise, and most obviously, are "moral romances"—*The Scarlet Letter* and *Blithedale*—or moral and theological—*The House* and *The Marble Faun*. But *The Ancestral Footstep* and *Dr. Grimshawe's Secret* are not, except sporadically and peripherally, moral at all. The moral meanings of *Septimius Felton* are incoherent, except on the subject of Hawthorne's old conviction that earthly "immortality," mere earthly deathlessness, would not be a blessing, and even there, feeling and thought tend, not surprisingly, to be at odds. The fragments of *The Dolliver Romance* are too incomplete for us to tell what that would have become, though what was written is in the old vein.

The late romances are in general not moral, they are Gothic, as *Fanshawe* and "Alice Doane's Appeal" are Gothic. They are personal, as those early works were. They are conventional, as those were. They are at the same time far more conventional and far more personal than *The Scarlet Letter* or *The House of the Seven Gables*, personal in their lack of distance from Hawthorne's private anguish, conventional in plot and incident and device. They are at once "expressionistic" and stereotyped; which is only to say that they fail completely as art. Their failure of meaning—again except in *Dolliver*—is everywhere so apparent that I shall give only two examples. In both *The Ancestral Footstep* and *Dr. Grimshawe's Secret* Hawthorne tried to use the "bloody footprint" legend he had picked up and recorded in his Notebooks in England. His past works are full of such Gothic "wonders"—men with glowing eyes, scarlet letters on the chest or in the sky, branches of trees that die when a handkerchief is tied around them, beautiful flowers that are deadly poison. But now he could see no meaning in his wonders, and that made all the difference. The bloody footprint as used in the late romances has no moral overtones whatever; it remains what it was when Hawthorne found it, a meaningless marvel. It was never transmuted by his imagination.

Again, Hawthorne tried to use in all of the late romances except *Dolliver* his memory of—or notes on—the giant spiders he had seen in the British Museum, but again he could do nothing with them. Though they are presented as though they were symbolic, a close reading of the passages in which they occur makes it perfectly clear that they symbolize nothing whatever. Dr. Grimshawe, who worked in his study beneath an enormous and repulsive spider, is not an evil man (in so far as he is sufficiently created so that we can judge him at all) merely crotchety and old and addicted to the bottle. The spider adds "atmosphere" but no meaning, and the "atmosphere" is finally useless. When we think of what Hawthorne had done with a cat and the hens in *The House of the Seven Gables*, or with a snake in "Egotism," or with a dog in "Ethan Brand," we see both the measure and the nature of his failure here. "What meaning?" Hawthorne asked himself repeatedly in his marginal notes on his manuscripts.

What meaning indeed! Hawthorne had not had to ask himself such a question when he was writing his great works. His grasp of an object and of its meaning had been simultaneous, and both "object" and "meaning"—to imply a separation that did not exist for him—had preceded the embodiment in a tissue of character and incident that made the tale out of a "moral idea." This had been Hawthorne's way of working, the only way he could work. Now he was searching out "marvels" and wondering desperately what meaning he could arbitrarily assign to them.

That this failure of his "particulars" to have meaning was in part a result of the weakening of Hawthorne's religious convictions seems to me very likely, though the evidence is not conclusive enough to convince anyone who prefers to believe that psychological factors alone are sufficient to account for the failure. One can only recall and weigh the significance of such matters as the implications of some of the imagery in *Blithedale* and the assigning of the function of guarding religious values in *The Marble Faun* chiefly to Hilda. Or one may ponder the significance of the fact that Septimius Felton, the last of the long line of secretive scholar-recluses created by Hawthorne as partial self-portraits, is made a materialistic naturalist who has "too profound a sense of the marvelous contrivance and adaptation of this material world to require or believe in anything spiritual." Hawthorne himself of course did, to the very end, believe in the significance of the spiritual. He was no materialist, now or ever. Felton's confidence in the self-sufficient completeness of the natural world was the very opposite of Hawthorne's view. Yet Felton is still recognizably a self-portrait. In rejecting his naturalistic views, Hawthorne is criticizing and rejecting a part of himself—the self that entertained the corrosive doubts.

Years before in "A Virtuoso's Collection" Hawthorne had written of another materialist that the most terrible consequence of his doom was that "the victim no longer regarded it as a calamity." Like Septimius Felton, the Wandering Jew found no reason to believe in anything spiritual. When told that the narrator would pray that he might be permitted to die, the earthbound creature had answered, as any of Hawthorne's scientific villains, his "empiricists," might have:

"Your prayers will be in vain," replied he, with a smile of cold triumph. "My destiny is linked with the realities of earth. You are welcome to your visions and shadows of a future state; but give me what I can see, and touch, and understand, and I ask no more."

"It is indeed too late," thought I. "The soul is dead within him."

Hubert Hoeltje has recently written of Hawthorne that his last years were serene, but I wonder whether it is not significant that while the Wandering Jew is not a self-portrait,

Septimius Felton is. We can only hope that Mr. Hoeltje is right, but many little pieces of evidence, each inconclusive in itself, point in the same direction: Hawthorne's last years were not serene, and one of the reasons they were not is that the "realities of earth" were coming to occupy a larger and larger place in his feelings. I think Hawthorne was aware of this change within him and *did* regard it as a calamity.

Hawthorne's faith in immortality had always rested primarily on his sense of the reality of evil, both moral and natural, man's guilt and his finiteness; and there is no evidence that he ever changed his *thinking* about the problem. In 1855 he wrote in his Notebook, "God himself cannot compensate us for being born for any period short of eternity. All the misery endured here constitutes a claim for another life, and, still more, *all the happiness*; because all true happiness involves something more than the earth owns, and needs something more than a mortal capacity for the enjoyment of it." Whatever change there is, is not one of "belief" as such but of the way in which belief is held, of the degree of conviction with which it is entertained.

At the same time that Hawthorne was becoming more aware of the newer currents of naturalistic thought, he was enduring the shock of conditions he observed in the slums of Liverpool. Concord and Salem had not prepared him for this. His contact with poverty and suffering such as he had never known, except theoretically, put his faith in Providence to the test. It survived the test, but only, perhaps, in a weakened form. It ceased, I suspect, to be a conviction and became instead the belief that conviction was necessary. Commenting, in *Our Old Home*, on the deformed, diseased, and filthy children he saw, children so naturally repellent to the senses that one was tempted to think of them as not human at all but some lower form of life, he wrote one of the most moving and meaningful passages he ever set down on the well-springs of his religious life. It reveals both the nature and depth of his faith and the extent of the threat to it:

It might almost make a man doubt the existence of his own

soul, to observe how Nature has flung these little wretches into the street and left them there, so evidently regarding them as nothing worth, and how all mankind acquiesce in the great mother's estimate of her offspring . . . Without an infinite faith, there seemed as much prospect of a blessed futurity for those hideous bugs and many-footed worms [that one finds under rotting plants] as for these brethren of our humanity and co-heirs of all our heavenly inheritance. Ah, what a mystery! Slowly, slowly, as after groping at the bottom of a deep, noisome, stagnant pool, my hope struggles upward to the surface, bearing the half-drowned body of a child along with it, and heaving it aloft for its life, and my own life, and all our lives. Unless these slime-clogged nostrils can be made capable of inhaling celestial air, I know not how the purest and most intellectual of us can reasonably expect ever to taste a breath of it. The whole question of eternity is staked there. If a single one of those helpless little ones be lost, the world is lost!

We note that Hawthorne attributes responsibility for this evil to Nature, not God; but who created nature? It would, he thinks, take an "infinite" faith to believe what must be believed, and Hawthorne had never thought of his own faith as "infinite." His final affirmation is existential in the purest sense, and as genuine and meaningful as a religious utterance could be; but it is clear that he finds no rational support for the belief he struggles to affirm—none, at least, except what is perhaps the best reason possible, that without this belief life does not seem to him to make any sense. If we compare the tone of this with that of "Sunday at Home," or even that of "Night Sketches," where the existence of evil is taken very seriously, we are likely to get the impression that the darkness was increasing the area of its dominion for Hawthorne in these late years.

The impression may be strengthened when we note the precise words he used in his well-known description of his last talk with Melville, who had stopped off at Liverpool to see his old friend before going on to the Holy Land. Alone together on the beach, the two talked for hours:

Melville, as he always does, began to reason of Providence and futurity, and of everything that lies beyond human ken, and informed me that he had "pretty much made up his mind to be annihilated"; but still he does not seem to rest in that anticipation, and, I think, will never rest until he gets hold of a definite belief.

It is strange how he persists—and has persisted ever since I knew him, and probably long before, in wandering to and fro over these deserts, as dismal and monotonous as the sandhills amid which we were sitting. He can neither believe, nor be comfortable in his unbelief; and he is too honest and courageous not to try to do one or the other.

If he were a religious man, he would be one of the most truly religious and reverential; he has a very high and noble nature and is better worth immortality than most of us.

Apart from the value of this as a wonderful revelation of Melville, there are in it, it seems to me, both overt and covert revelations of Hawthorne's own religious commitments. Overtly, he distinguishes his own position from that of Melville—from Melville's unbelief and from his continuing to speculate about what reason cannot determine. He himself, he implies clearly enough, *does* have hold of a definite belief and has *not* made up his mind to be annihilated. In contrast with Melville, he considers himself "a religious man."

But does one whose religious faith is very firm consider discussion of ultimate questions of faith to be like wandering over "deserts" that are "dismal" and "monotonous"? To be sure, Hawthorne had never thought pure reason could deal very profitably with such questions. His religion had always been existential, we should say; of the heart, he said. So that it might be argued that he found the discussion "dismal" only because Melville tried to "reason" about matters reason could not handle. Still, though it is easy to see why he might find such discussion profitless, he did not say it was "profitless" but "dismal"; more precisely, he did not even say the discussion itself was dismal, but the *subjects* of it. It seems to me there may well be an unintended revelation in the adjectives he chose to describe "Providence and futurity, and . . . everything that lies beyond human ken." A mood is revealed, at least. In 1857 he recorded in his English Notebooks (in a passage that Mrs. Hawthorne revised, to protect her husband's reputation for piety) that the fog obscured the statues of the saints on St. Paul's so that they looked down "dimly from their standpoint on high, faintest, as spiritual consolations are apt to be, when the world was darkest." I think it was his experience of this failure of "spiritual consolations" that lay behind an image that he worked into *Septimius Felton* and that is one of the half dozen or so happy strokes in that novel:

In short, it was such a moment as I suppose all men feel (at least, I can answer for one), when the real scene and picture of life swims, jars, shakes, seems about to be broken up and dispersed, like the picture in a smooth pond, when we disturb its tranquil mirror by throwing in a stone; and though the scene soon settles itself, and looks as real as before, a haunting doubt keeps close at hand, as long as we live, asking, "Is it stable? Am I sure of it? Am I certainly not dreaming? See; it trembles again, ready to dissolve."

Perhaps the sort of experience suggested by this image prompted the curious phrase—curious for Hawthorne—in *The Dolliver Romance*: "the old man, a hater of empiricism (in which, however, is contained all hope for man)." Hawthorne is speaking out directly as author here, not characterizing anyone by assigning a belief to him; and when we think of the meaning of "The Birthmark" and of much else that Hawthorne had written, the sense of the oddity of the statement grows. It seems unlikely that assigning a meaning of "trial and error" to the word *empiricism* removes all the oddity. Hawthorne's belief in immortality, his "higher hope," had never rested on empiricism, in any of that word's possible meanings.

4

Dr. Grimshawe's Secret contains several touches that remind us of the earlier writings without suggesting parody. One of them is the heart image that comes late in the first draft. It is worth quoting at some length:

There is—or there was, now (ages) many years ago, and a few years also, it was still extant—a chamber, which when I think of, it seems to me like entering a deep recess of my own consciousness, a deep cave of my nature; so much have I thought of it and its inmate, through a considerable period of my life ... (Compare it with Spenser's Cave of Despair. Put instruments of suicide there.) ... It was dim, dim as a melancholy mood ... The face of your familiar friend, or your dearest beloved one, would be unrecognizable across it . . . no windows were apparent; no communication with the outward day.*

The suggestion here of the increasing loneliness of the man who envisaged his own heart as dangerous and without communication with "the outward day," and the Colcord—Jesus relationship that is quite skillfully set up (but not developed) are, I think, the only things worth remembering in this novel on which Hawthorne worked harder and longer than he had on *The Scarlet Letter*.

Septimius Felton has, as Mark Van Doren has said, a number of good things in it. The killing of the young Englishman, the burial, some of Septimius' thoughts—these things and perhaps one or two others are memorable enough to deserve to be preserved, out of context, in a small anthology that could be made of the worthwhile passages in Hawthorne's last writings. But one significant thing about these passages is that they do not draw upon Hawthorne's recent experience at all but upon experience as old as the earliest of the tales. The material from the English Notebooks that he had tried so hard to work into *The Ancestral Footstep* and *Dr. Grimshawe's Secret* and the parallel between the Civil and the Revolutionary wars that he hoped to develop here were totally unsuccessful. There is, finally, a kind of ponderous humor that breaks into the work now and then, to remind us, almost, of the old Hawthorne. As Hawthorne had said

* Edward H. Davidson, ed., *Hawthorne's Dr. Grimshawe's Secret* (Cambridge, Massachusetts, Harvard University Press, 1954), p. 198. I have omitted not only several parts of the passage itself but Professor Davidson's indications of Hawthorne's revisions. For my purposes here, it would not be worth while first to explain and then to reproduce Professor Davidson's editorial markings.

long ago in "The Antique Ring," "There is a kind of play-fulness that comes in moments of despair."

What there is of *The Dolliver Romance* is good. Again, as on *Septimius Felton* and on the period of the late romances in general, Mark Van Doren is the most penetrating critic:

> By some miracle the pieces of it [Hawthorne] did produce came near to being the brightest and best of all his work. The surviving fragments of this fourth fragment . . . have an astonishing force, a reassuring grace . . . *The Dolliver Romance* is an intricate, a delicate, a cunning comment upon its author's developing senility. Dr. Dolliver, who lives beside a graveyard with his great-granddaughter Pansie and her kitten, is neither Mr. Kirkup of Florence nor Dr. Grimshawe of the black bottle and the bloated spiders; he is Hawthorne grown old, and the good wife Bessie who died so long ago is perhaps Sophia, and Pansie is certainly the Una of 1849 . . . Hawthorne is now free of his notebooks and his plans . . . The striking thing is Hawthorne's amusement. The self-portrait is not in the least line sentimental.*

All this and more that Mr. Van Doren says with his usual felicity, is very just. But the comment that Hawthorne is now free of his English Notebooks, though valuable, is insufficient as an explanation of why he is writing so very much better than he had for a long time. We shall never, I suppose, have a sufficient explanation of this remarkable resurgence of power in the last months of Hawthorne's life, when his physical powers were failing daily. But we may note that in addition to the self-portraiture in old Dr. Dolliver there is another element in the fragments, and that is by no means a product of Hawthorne's contemporary experience, but rather a group of symbols lifted bodily from his earliest writings. The child running toward the open grave, the flower, the coiled serpent, the glowing eyes, the sparkling elixirs, the villainous Colonel Dabney—these are all familiar ingredients handled in the old way. There is, in fact, except for the portrayal of senility, nothing new in *The Dolliver Romance*. The amazing thing is that what had once been Hawthorne's by right of creation has been recovered.

* *Nathaniel Hawthorne* (New York: Sloane, 1949), pp. 260-261.

And not by any "technical device," not because Hawthorne suddenly remembered what he had forgotten how to do. In the final months of his life, after he had lost all hope that his symptoms were temporary, it may be that he gained a fresh hold on, or a new vision of, those convictions, and the values and feelings attached to them, that had been his, despite his doubts and his questions, earlier in his life. A personality is not only a product of anterior and exterior forces. There is a very real and important sense in which it is self-created by the values it espouses. It seems probable that in his last years Hawthorne's hold on the only beliefs he could really accept, the only ones that, for him, could support the values he lived and wrote by, had been weakening, and imaginative writing had become impossible for him. Now at the end the old values seem to have reasserted themselves.

At any rate, some sort of "elixir of life" worked for Hawthorne's writing at the end: it returned to the manner and matter of his youth. From internal evidence alone we would have no way of knowing that *The Dolliver Romance* was not written a quarter of a century before it was. Here is a mystery unlike that of the failure of the other late writings: it does not seem to give promise of any definitive solution.

CHAPTER TEN

CONCLUSION

At the height of his career Hawthorne described himself as a man who had spent his creative life "burrowing, to his utmost ability, into the depths of our common nature, for the purposes of psychological romance,—and who pursues his researches in that dusky region, as he needs must, as well by the tact of sympathy as by the light of observation." For "the purposes of psychological romance": no such purpose in literature had been conceived, before Hawthorne conceived it; and no form of fiction appropriate to such a purpose existed, before he created it. In the deepest sense of the word Hawthorne was a creative writer.

He and Poe began creating an American fiction at the same time, under many of the same influences, and with results in many ways comparable. It seems to most critics today that Hawthorne had the richer imagination; yet whatever may be our judgment of the comparative merits of the two, it is clear that before them there was nothing in American fiction that either writer could take very seriously. Turning to European fiction, and especially to the Gothic tale, each of them in his own way, but particularly Hawthorne, took what served his needs and transformed it, to create a form, a language, and a meaning that had never before existed.

What Hawthorne had to do when he started writing was

more than just what any writer always has to do, to adapt a tradition to his individual sensibility and his talent and to his time. Hawthorne lived in an age of revolution both social and intellectual, which was also a time when fiction was beginning to take over functions previously fulfilled by other forms of literature or not fulfilled at all. No existing form of fiction very closely approached being suitable for his purposes. Perhaps traditional allegory, whether in prose or in verse, was more help to him than anything else. But the one thing most obviously demanded by allegory, a clear, fixed, publicly accepted scheme of values, was not available to Hawthorne. He was no philosopher; more relevantly, not a Christian in the sense that Bunyan and Spenser were, with their literal acceptance of the Bible as history. He was a man of the nineteenth century who had read and valued Voltaire when young, Christian in sympathy and conservative in temperament to be sure, with a kind of intuitive grasp of the essentials of Christian faith, a man who retained a tragic sense in an age of romantic primitivism and the religion of progress, but a man of the nineteenth century still. Allegory as it had been known and practiced was impossible to him in any but a limited and occasional and peripheral sense.

As for the Gothic novel and tale, these were at once more obviously available and finally less suitable. The amount of Hawthorne's indebtedness to the form has been explored in a learned volume.* But no one reading *The Castle of Otranto* or *The Monk* without preconceptions would be likely to see any but superficial resemblances between these or similar Gothic romances and Hawthorne's work. The matter can be stated very briefly: Hawthorne drew extensively upon this popular form, as Shakespeare used the revenge tragedy and James used the comedy of manners, but the form itself, as he found it existing, was not to his purpose. Taking from it certain elements and turning them to new purposes, he transformed what he used. Only an examination which artificially

* Jane Lundblad, *Nathaniel Hawthorne and the Tradition of the Gothic Romance* (Upsala, Sweden, 1946).

isolates form from meaning will fail to note the difference between the Gothic elements in Hawthorne's fiction and the same elements in the popular Gothic novel. The house of seven gables is first a decaying New England mansion and then the kind of edifice that pride always builds and finally an image of the human heart; its resemblance to a long line of castles in the Gothic novels is interesting but not of primary significance to one who is concerned with the meaning and value of this work. Hawthorne's use of the formulas of the Gothic romance is of much the same order as Robert Penn Warren's use, in *World Enough and Time*, of the currently popular form of the historical novel.

What we now think of as a main stream of the English novel from DeFoe and Fielding through Jane Austen to Scott and Dickens was realistic in intention, taking the cue for its form from the histories, journals, letters, and memoirs of "real life," or from the stage, and very largely divorced from the mythopoetic sources of modern fiction. That this tradition of the "novel," with its aim at realism and social criticism, as opposed to the "romance"' was unsuited to Hawthorne's sensibility and purposes is too clear to need extended comment, and that despite Hawthorne's occasional wish that he might write like Trollope. At least in the formative first twenty-five years of his writing career, Hawthorne had little desire to "picture" society; and at no time in his career did he have either the desire or—in his own opinion —the ability to "instruct," in the sense of urging appropriate courses of action as Dickens instructed, taking his reader by the elbow and pointing out abuses that needed correction.

Despite its tendency toward allegory, Hawthorne's work is not didactic in the usual sense of that word, but contemplative, aimed at the imagination and the understanding rather than at action. His own temperament was such that even in private life he could not readily bring himself to give advice, not even when his position seemed to make it appropriate that he do so. The reason he gives in *Our Old Home* for not "meddling" in the affairs of others while he was a consul at Liverpool suggests an attitude that would seem to militate against the writing of didactic fiction. "For a man, with a natural tendency to meddle with other people's business," he noted in his description of his consular experiences,

there could not possibly be a more congenial sphere than the Liverpool Consulate. For myself, I had never been in the habit of feeling that I could sufficiently comprehend any particular conjunction of circumstances with human character, to justify me in thrusting in my awkward agency among the intricate and unintelligible machinery of Providence. I have always hated to give advice, especially when there is a prospect of its being taken. It is only one-eyed people who love to advise, or have any spontaneous promptitude of action. When a man opens both his eyes, he generally sees about as many reasons for acting in any one way as in any other, and quite as many for acting in neither . . .

And his work had as little in common with the realistic aim of the contemporary novel as with the didactic. Both in theory and in practice, his work looks back to epic and romance and myth and forward to such writers as James, Conrad, Kafka, Faulkner. The gulf between it and the work of Fielding, Richardson, Smollett, Dickens, or even Scott, whose romances Hawthorne liked to read aloud to his family, is very great. One reason for this is surely that any "burrowing" that had been done in the main stream of the English novel up to Hawthorne's time had been quite incidental to other purposes.

When Hawthorne defined his purpose as a writer of "romances," his first care was to distinguish the romance from the novel.

When a writer calls his work a Romance, it need hardly be observed that he wishes to claim a certain latitude, both as to its fashion and material, which he would not have felt himself entitled to assume had he professed to be writing a Novel. The latter form of composition is presumed to aim at a very minute fidelity, not merely to the possible, but to the probable and ordinary course of man's experience. The former—while, as a work of art, it must rigidly subject itself to laws, and while it sins unpardonably so far as it may swerve aside from the truth of the human heart—has fairly a right to present that truth under circumstances, to a great extent, of the writer's own choosing or creation. If he think fit, also, he may so manage his atmospherical medium as to bring out or mellow the lights and deepen and enrich the shadows of the picture.*

We get the feeling when we reread Hawthorne's prefaces that he was groping toward a conception of fiction that was more novel than he realized. Others before him, from Fielding on, had wondered where to place fiction among the several kinds of literature, but Hawthorne's emphasis on it as an art form, his insistence that it be tested by laws appropriate to its mode of existence rather than its accuracy as document, clearly foreshadows James's thinking on the same problems. And his choice of painting as an analogy points in the same direction. But most important of all is his lifelong insistence that the kind of truth he wanted to portray was the "truth of the human heart," and that the best way to portray this is by the strategy of indirection. The truth so conceived is of a different order from the truth conveyed by ordinary didactic fiction, by philosophy (unless, with Whitehead, we conceive of philosophy as a kind of poetry), or by the univocal symbolism of the exact sciences. It is a truth that not only cannot be expressed except in the images of the imagination but, as Hawthorne himself thought, cannot be "grasped" except in such images. The most striking way in which Hawthorne's work is seminal for modern fiction is the mythopoetic aspect of both his theory and his practice.

2

But if Hawthorne conceived of his work as being more like poetry than like history or journalism, the question of how this general conception could be translated into actual works of fiction had still to be faced. For nearly forty years of active writing he experimented with various forms in an effort to find the one best suited to the composition of that natural history of the soul that he wished to write.

* From the Preface to *The House of the Seven Gables.*

Fanshawe was his experiment with the fictional formulas popular in the 1820's. Almost immediately recognizing the error of this, he turned to two forms that might be considered two versions of the opposite extreme: from the contrived plot, the exaggerated suspense, and the melodrama of the sentimental Gothic tale to a retelling of "true" tales from local history and to semifictional sketches. He felt at ease in both forms, but in the sketch in particular he felt that he could exercise his peculiar talent. Developing it out of the periodical essay of the preceding century as handled by writers of the romantic period who had given it a more personal cast, he valued the form because it allowed him to glimpse truth out of the corner of his eye and to give fancy full sway. And surely he was not wholly wrong. The essay has almost disappeared today as a literary form and we find it difficult to appreciate the sketches, or to avoid comparing them with the best of the tales, almost invariably to the disadvantage of the sketches. But he did some of his best work in them, and we need to read again not simply the several best but such seldom-read ones as "The Old Apple Dealer," "Night Sketches," "The Hall of Fantasy," "Main Street," "A Virtuoso's Collection," "P's Correspondence," and "The Intelligence Office."

But the sketch was not entirely suited to his purposes. Between it and the tale he contrived a sort of intermediate form having some of the characteristics of the older allegory and some of the features of the personal essay. "The Haunted Mind" is more nearly an essay than an allegory, "The Procession of Life" more nearly an allegory than an essay. The advantage of this intermediate form over the sketch lay in the greater opportunity it offered for objectification of feeling and thought in symbolic form. The disadvantage—from our point of view at least, since it is not clear that Hawthorne's consciousness of his purposes brought him to this point in analysis—the disadvantage lay in the inadequate autonomy of the symbols so created. The figures in "The Christmas Banquet" do not move by themselves in accordance with their own necessities but only as their very present creator moves them. "The Celestial Railroad" is saved from the subjectivity and inadequate, because wholly allegorical, meaning of "The Procession of Life" chiefly by Hawthorne's reliance on the structure of incident and value supplied him by Bunyan.

No sharp separation can be made between the allegorical "processions," the sketches with some narrative ingredients, and the "tales proper," as we think of the short story today. Is "Wakefield" a sketch or a story? Is "Earth's Holocaust" an essay, an allegory, or a tale? The unity of all of Hawthorne's work must not be forgotten while we categorize the diversity. Yet the impossibility of making neat distinctions should not obscure such important differences as those between, say, "Fancy's Showbox" and "Ethan Brand," or "The Christmas Banquet" and "Major Molineux." Between "The Man of Adamant," which Hawthorne called an apologue and we might be more likely to call an extended parable, and "The Wives of the Dead," which would appear to have no conceptual theme beyond what may be called a feeling for the "strangeness" of life, the opacity of experience, there are significant differences; but both grow out of history, both take the form of legends, and both are concerned only with the significance of history, not with history as fact. "The Gentle Boy" is comparatively "realistic" in its exploration of the theme of religious fanaticism through the Puritan persecution of the Quakers; "Young Goodman Brown" is comparatively allegorical in its treatment of the nature and consequences of the Puritan belief in the total depravity of man. The two stories are very different in their effect, and one of them, the more allegorical one, seems to most readers of Hawthorne today very much the greater of the two. (The other was a favorite of Hawthorne's contemporaries—and is in fact a very fine story. We need to reread it.) Yet it would be misleading to set up sharply contrasting categories, label them "realism" and "allegory," and assign the stories to them. What holds these two stories and the others together is the tendency of all them, even of those that are more nearly sketches than tales, to move toward the mythopoetic.

Some of Hawthorne's writing for children provides an interesting commentary on his assumptions and his procedure in the rest of his work. Grandfather's chair, for instance, in the book to which it supplies a name, is not an emblem or type of anything, in Hawthorne's usual sense of these words. If it is a symbol, it is not such a symbol as can be translated in abstract terms. Rather it is intended to be for Hawthorne's young readers what we might describe today in Eliot's phrase, an objective correlative: a formula for a particular set of emotions. Explaining his general purpose as that of retelling episodes from the American past in such a way as to create "picturesque sketches of the times," Hawthorne tells why he gives the chair so prominent a place in the book:

> There is certainly no method by which the shadowy outlines of departed men and women can be made to assume the hues of life more effectually than by connecting their images with the substantial and homely reality of a fireside chair. It causes us to feel at once that these characters of history had a private and familiar existence, and were not wholly contained within that cold array of outward action which we are compelled to receive as the adequate representation of their lives. If this impression can be given, much is accomplished . . . The human heart may best be read in the fireside chair.

Though this has its "dated" air, sounding perhaps to a generation suspicious of the simpler emotions a little rustic and naïve, there are some interesting assumptions behind it. The human heart cannot be read directly, nor can what Hawthorne wanted to say about history be said directly. For what Hawthorne wanted to say there was not a more "literal" language, indeed for precisely what he wanted to say, no language at all until he created it. And creating it involved finding the adequate symbols, whether emblems or types or objective correlatives or, in the larger sense of structure, significant form. Hawthorne realized that fiction is an art form long before James began to write in the Hawthorne tradition. He realized it when other writers thought of fiction as document or as the vehicle for something extraneous to

itself or as a harmless form of entertainment. Recalling what
he said about his attempt to understand Wakefield's vagary
and to realize aesthetically the negative character of the old
apple dealer, we see that his experiments with the various
forms and combinations of parable, allegory, legend, sketch,
tale, and romance were demanded by his attempt to accomplish a task not very different, despite the more abstractly
intellectual character of his art, from that William Faulkner
set before himself in the opening of his story of the man
called Monk:

I will have to try to tell about Monk. I mean, actually try—a
deliberate attempt to bridge the inconsistencies in his brief and
sordid and unoriginal history, to make something out of it, not
only with the nebulous tools of supposition and inference and
invention, but to employ these nebulous tools upon the nebulous
and inexplicable material which he left behind him. Because it
is only in literature that the paradoxical and even mutually
negativing anecdotes in the history of a human heart can be
juxtaposed and annealed by art into verisimilitude and credibil-
ity.

3

But it will not do to stress only Hawthorne's "modernity,"
the ties that link his work to that of such contemporaries as
Warren and Faulkner in an unbroken tradition in our
literature. Hawthorne is also very archaic. In saying so, I am
not intending to pass a value judgment. Hawthorne himself
liked what were for him the "old time" writers best, and
those who may follow him in this preference have no need
to apologize. But we should at least try to avoid the distortion of seeing in him only a reflection of our own image.
His style, for instance, was a little old-fashioned even when
he wrote it. It is slow-moving, with its pace slowed down still
further by his very heavy punctuation. It is rhetorical, in the
rhetorical fashion taught by the rhetoric books of his time,
a fashion thoroughly repudiated by modernism. It circles
around its subject, enveloping it in balanced clauses and
phrases that make qualification after qualification, often

returning at the end to where it began. It is marked by a strong preference for the abstract or generalized word over the concrete or specific one. It makes more frequent use of periodic structures than we are used to—though it generally combines them with loose word order to make a flowing, hesitating rhythm that is peculiarly Hawthorne's own. It is a formal, public, "literary" style, the style of a man of letters, quite different from the private, undressed, colloquial, imagistic style modern writing has taught us to prefer.

Two sentences quoted earlier for another purpose from "Sunday at Home" will illustrate a part of the point. In the first, Hawthorne writes two main clauses related in contrast by a "but" to make, as the over-all or enclosing pattern, a loose or colloquial structure; but he pauses after his conjunction to insert the qualifications he thinks he must make if the second clause is to be true, so that this basically loose sentence is at the same time strongly periodic in effect. In the second sentence we note the formally "correct" subjunctive verb:

> Doubts may flit around me, or seem to close their evil wings, and settle down; but, so long as I imagine that the earth is hallowed, and the light of heaven retains its sanctity, on the Sabbath—while that blessed sunshine lives within me—never can my soul have lost the instinct of its faith. If it have gone astray, it will return again.

When this sort of style works best for Hawthorne, it perfectly expresses his meanings, including that special form of irresolution of his, that double, ironic vision that we have come to recognize as characteristic. Its balanced clauses are never too rigidly balanced, too neatly rational or schematic. Its cadences are strong but irregular; they hesitate, pause, start again. The first sentence of "The Man of Adamant" is typical in the way it opens periodically, inverts the normal order of subject and verb, then closes with a loosely related modifier that returns us to where the sentence began: "In the old times of religious gloom and intolerance lived Richard Digby, the gloomiest and most intolerant of a stern brotherhood." Hawthorne's emphasis here is just where the story that follows shows he wanted it to be, on the nature of the age, on the man who typified it, and, subtly, on the basis of the story's condemnation of both man and age, that is, on *brotherhood.* The paradox in *"stern* brotherhood"— does not "brotherhood" imply love and tolerance rather than sternness?—already implies, in this first sentence, what we find to be the major paradox of the story, the fact that Digby's damnation springs from the very intensity of his search for salvation. The sentence works perfectly for Hawthorne's purposes but it is none the less old-fashioned. No writer today that I can think of would be likely to pick up and repeat in adjectival form, as Hawthorne does, that "gloom and intolerance" of his opening phrase, so that the sentence may end where it began, though it has traveled meanwhile.

But it is not only style in this narrow sense that keeps Hawthorne from seeming perfectly "one of us." His whole procedure as a fictionist is pre-Jamesian, which is to say pre-modern. If being present in his story in his own person, reminding the reader that it is, after all, just a story, and *he* is telling it to us, if this is a sin the writer of fiction must avoid, then Hawthorne can be thought of only as very inept or very archaic. He is one of the most regularly intrusive of intrusive authors. He takes us by the elbow, nudges us, tells us what we must attend to, offers interpretations, or confesses that he can't state all the meanings he somehow sees. Post-Jamesian fiction, in contrast, has as its most basic rule, "Don't tell, show!" Hawthorne of course does "show," at least in his better things, but the point is that he also "tells," not only at the end in the moral comment he often makes, but all the way through. In his normal practice he depends on both image and rhetoric to express his meanings.

After he has presented the image of Ethan Brand laughing, for instance, Hawthorne intrudes with a comment: "Laughter, when out of place, mistimed, or bursting forth from a disordered state of feeling, may be the most terrible modulation of the human voice." If something has been lost here in immediacy by the very fact of the intrusion, something has been gained in meaning. He has shown, now he will tell, in the hope of bringing out the meaning of his image. Later in the story, in his summary of Brand's career, he stops showing entirely and merely tells: "Thus Ethan Brand became a fiend . . . He had lost his hold of the magnetic chain of humanity."

The final effect of this archaic aspect of Hawthorne's technique is to confirm what we have come to know from other approaches to his work, that for him there is always something more important than the mere *facts* of life, the images. There is meaning, meaning which can perhaps best be found in and best conveyed *by* the images, but which may also, with varying degrees of adequacy, be *talked* about. Though he once made a spokesman character say he could not separate symbol and idea, Hawthorne in fact, in his most typical work, found he *could*—up to a point. His intrusive comments are generally intended to bring out the *meaning* of his symbols—not all the meaning, just that part that can be talked about in abstract language. To say this is another way of saying that though, as a writer, Hawthorne was a symbolist, he was not a modern symbolist. Treating him as though he was has accounted for a number of critical misinterpretations of his work.

4

The predominantly existential nature of Hawthorne's religion had a good deal to do with shaping his special blend of, and his alternations between, traditional allegory and modern symbolism. The relations of art and belief in Hawthorne's work are subtle, intricate, and very important. Searching for light in a dark world, he clung tenaciously to a few theological convictions while thoroughly distrusting theology. Believing that he could both discover and express in symbols what he could neither discover nor express as theory, he yet regularly commented in his stories on the truths his symbols enabled him partially to grasp. Holding that true religion must be unmediated and intuitive, "of the heart," he nevertheless called upon the head to support the findings of the heart whenever the head seemed likely to be effective in its support. "How difficult to believe . . . my hope struggles upward."

No wonder he frequently wrote allegory, but allegory generally so fluid and subjective that Bunyan might have recognized it only in those tales and sketches that today we like the least, and would not have recognized it at all in such things as "Roger Malvin's Burial." If Bunyan had read Hawthorne, he might have put him in one of his own allegories and called him Mr. Shaky-faith. We can imagine Bunyan recognizing the outlines of historic belief, presented in types and emblems and reinforced by Biblical allusions (Bunyan would surely catch more of these than we do, and understand them better), but also noting the hovering "as if" and disapproving it.

Hawthorne wrote "allegories of the heart," as he himself once called them, but the heart took its cue from the historic faith. Over and over again he retold the story of the Fall, and now and then he managed to imagine its sequel, the redemption effected by the Second Adam. Loss of innocence compelled his imagination. That man lived in darkness and separation seemed too obvious to be questioned. The light, whether from the heart or from above, had to be searched out and affirmed as real, just because it was not immediately "given," like the darkness. Retreat into fantasy would not do, cherishing dreams because while they lasted they had been delightful would not do: the man under the umbrella had to leave the snug comfort of his brightly lighted chamber and brave the discomforts of a dark, cold, and rainy world, to see the world at its worst, before he could affirm that a proper faith could be trusted to lead us home through the encompassing darkness. Mr. Shaky-faith: the doubt is real and the faith genuine. The two together, varying in their proportions but never ceasing to be in some sort of creative conflict, do more than anything else to give Hawthorne's work its distinctive shape and quality.

The faith of Bunyan and Spenser was less "reasonable" but their work was more "rational." There were more elements in their religious belief that modern man would have to label untrue, or not true in the way they took them to be, or even positively false. Hawthorne's faith was pared down, more skeptical: he was indeed, in a sense, the child of the Enlightenment, as all since then who are aware of history are. Knowing myth to be myth, he could not confuse faith and knowledge. If Genesis was shaky history but his deepest experience made its meaning seem to him in some sense still true, there was nothing he could do but reinterpret the Fall in terms the heart could understand. Man falls, whether Adam ever lived or not.

But if his way of presenting the faith was more *reasonable*, less offensive to modern reason, than Bunyan's and Spenser's, it was also less *rationalistic*. Their faith may have been "false" in some of its elements, but it was a public, shared faith assumed to be objectively true, not needing to be validated, except in some ultimate and strictly personal sense, by the heart. Unlike Hawthorne, they did not see heart and head as in inevitable and unceasing conflict. (Hawthorne thought redemption, wholeness, would come only when the conflict ceased, when the two co-operated; but this was a wished for, not an experienced, state.) They could write more objectively because the dream that shaped their works did not seem like a dream; they were quite sure, indeed, that much of it was fact, not dream at all. Their symbols could have the kind of objectivity that is provided by known public referents. They could be, in their own eyes and those of their contemporaries who shared their beliefs, men of reason without committing treason to the heart.

In Hawthorne's work at its best, on the other hand, the meanings of the images are partly determined by their analogy with historic myth, mostly Christian, and partly determined internally, by context. And always, again when he is writing at his best, they are to some degree ambiguous. That is why it remains possible for commentators so inclined to give narrowly, even reductively, psychological interpreta-

tions of some of his works, and for other commentators to
give strictly theological interpretations of the same works.
Often, both types of interpretation are "valid" but neither
is complete alone. What the "right" interpretation is cannot
be settled for Hawthorne's work in the same way it can
for Bunyan's. Symbols that often begin by being ambiguous
and end by being almost wholly contextually determined
are not "rational" in the sense that Spenser's political allegory is.

Of course Hawthorne's practice varied all the way from
the almost perfectly traditional (and "rationalistic") to the
almost mythic and archetypal in the modern sense. He wrote
"The Great Carbuncle" and also "Roger Malvin's Burial,"
"Lady Eleanor's Mantle" and also "My Kinsman, Major
Molineux." In "Young Goodman Brown" he called Brown's
wife Faith, as Bunyan might have done, but he also treated
the revelations in the forest more ambiguously than Bunyan
would have found aesthetically possible or religiously desirable. In "Rappaccini's Daughter" he exercises his privilege
as intrusive author to remind us of the parallels between
his story and the story of the expulsion from an earlier
Garden, but he so manipulates his archetype that in the
end it becomes impossible to draw any point-by-point allegorical analogy. Critics are likely to continue to differ on
just where to locate the center of Hawthorne's practice, but
that his special quality as a writer is a function of his unique
relationship to both the form and the content of traditional
Christian allegory on the one hand and to modern symbolism
on the other seems hardly open to question.

One thing seems certain in this whole difficult area. Where
Hawthorne's beliefs are surest, he writes most traditionally.
In effect this means that when his subjects have the strongest
theological implications, they are treated the most ambiguously, mythically, and subjectively; and when they are
moral in the most limited sense, they are clearest, most rational, and most traditional. Of course, the theological is
never without moral implication in Hawthorne, or the moral
without implied theological sanction and result. The distinc-

tion I am using is by no means absolute, or even clear-cut. But it is useful for the purpose at hand, which is to comment on the reason why so many of Hawthorne's most traditionally allegorical tales, like "Lady Eleanor's Mantle," are concerned with relatively simple moral problems—simple in the sense of not necessarily directly involving any ultimate religious beliefs.

Hawthorne thought he knew the moral meaning of pride. It was a sin, in some sense deadly—about this he had no doubt at all. He wrote "Lady Eleanor's Mantle" in a way that Bunyan would have understood and approved. He had clear and firm convictions about materialists and cynics, and produced "The Great Carbuncle." He had no doubt about where bigotry led—though he could see that it might have its origin in mixed motives, some of them good—and he wrote "The Man of Adamant." He disapproved of any monkish withdrawal from the world into ascetic purity: his disapproval is clearly and allegorically recorded in "The Canterbury Pilgrims."

On the other hand, how was he to take the Atonement, Unitarian that he was by family tradition if not by any sympathy with what seemed to him its greater follies? That man could not save himself by his own unaided efforts he felt rather sure, but clear orthodox Trinitarian he was not. "Roger Malvin's Burial" makes a sacrificial death the means of redemption, echoing, as it does so, both the Abraham and Isaac story and the story of Christ; but the rational clarity of allegory is wholly lacking in the tale, and it would be unwise to claim orthodoxy for Hawthorne on the basis of it. A better claim could be based on the much more allegorical episode of the birch cup filled with clear water offered to and refused by the man of adamant. Since the offer is made in terms that echo the liturgy, it seems impossible to rule out a reference to the Holy Communion here, however surprising the allusion may seem in a child of the Puritans who almost never went to church. But if this is a part of the meaning, it is only one part, and another emphasis is possible: Nature (the water from the spring) and Scripture (the cup) co-operate and agree in offering redemption, here as elsewhere in Hawthorne.

Clarity and ambiguity, allegory and myth, clear conviction and tentative belief. *The Scarlet Letter* is not, it seems to me, an allegory in the traditional mode, though it has often been so called and has many allegorical elements. But the deterioration of Chillingworth, his becoming a fiend and creeping along the ground like a snake, is allegorically handled. Hawthorne was perfectly clear in his mind about the moral status of revenge, or, more relevantly to Chillingworth, about the results of treating other people as though they were objects, using them to satisfy our curiosity, performing experiments on them, as Chillingworth did on Dimmesdale. But he was not sure about the mechanism of forgiveness or the machinery of redemption, any more than he was about the "machinery of Providence" into which he hesitated to thrust his awkward agency: the ultimate fate of Hester and Dimmesdale contains a certain ambiguity that is never dispelled, even by Hester's apparent halo or the minister's dying gestures and words, which are so recorded as to remind us of Christ on the cross. Indeed, the ambiguity is reinforced by the closing words of the novel, with their images of black, which counters the hope suggested by the Christ allusions of the last scaffold scene, and red, which is by this time thoroughly ambiguous.

The "ambiguity device" isolated and discussed so well years ago by Matthiessen is thus no mere "device" but an expression in technical terms of the essential condition of Hawthorne's belief. It is a method of blurring the clear eye, of refusing to specify how literally something should be taken, of believing in Providence while not pretending to understand its machinery. It is a method, we may say, of avoiding clarity—but the kind of clarity that is avoided is the kind Hawthorne thought either specious or irrelevant. Something supernatural seemed to have occurred; a natural explanation, or several natural explanations, could be given. But would the explanation, even if we could be sure it were true, render void the religious significance of the strange event? It is easy to imagine Hawthorne writing—in fact, he *should* have written, though I cannot recall that he ever did —"Whether Adam lived or no . . ."

If, as I have argued, the most important shaping force behind Hawthorne's art is the special character of his religious belief, it is not surprising that the so-called ambiguity device should be one of the most characteristic features of his writing and that a more generalized ambiguity should be so typical of it. For Hawthorne's religious belief was existentially oriented, not institutional or traditional. He found in his own *experience* reason for looking at life as the "old time" writers had, reason for believing the Scriptures would never be destroyed by the bonfires of reform. But religious experience—not doctrine or dogma but experience —is always, and necessarily, ambiguous. Did the god speak or did we merely imagine his voice? If he did really speak, it is clear that only the prepared, the imaginative ear could receive the words. It is possible to argue that only the Faithful saw the Risen Christ without intending to impugn the reality of the Resurrection.

The decision as to which is the true dream and which the false must be made by the individual in the depths of his inwardness. Hawthorne was not without his commitments, and in some areas of thought he was willing to declare them, preferably in allegorical form. But on matters closest to his heart he was either unable to attain commitment or reluctant to declare his commitments propositionally. His ambiguity, whether inseparable from the greatness of his finest writing or the mere idiosyncrasy it becomes in his poorest, is a translation of this aspect of his belief into art.

5

✓ Hawthorne was an Idealist who wrote in the age of philosophical Idealism. He did not seriously question the general philosophical assumptions of his age. When he defined the special area occupied by his writing as lying between the Real and the Ideal—or, when implicitly apologizing for the furry ears of Donatello, between the Real and the Fantastic —he was using the words in a sense it is easy to misunderstand today. He did not mean between the real and the unreal but between external and internal, between thing and idea, between meaningless fact and ungrounded meaning. The perennial battle between Realism and Idealism as philosophical positions is relevant to his meaning. Idealism locates reality in the nature of the knowing mind, Realism in the nature of the thing known. One reason why philosophers today often do not feel required to take a stand for one position or the other is that, even if they do not see such problems as insoluble, mere verbal problems, they are inclined to see the dichotomy as a false one, with both camps right and both wrong. Existentially, we cannot separate knower and known so clearly.

It would certainly be essentially misleading to try to make a case for Hawthorne as a philosopher, and I have no intention of doing so. But one of the implications of his work is that he anticipated contemporary philosophy (without thinking the issues through philosophically, needless to say) in refusing the Idealist-Realist choice. Between Emerson, who thought the world plastic to mind and recommended the Ideal theory because it fitted our needs and desires, and later realists, who stressed nature's intractible and even alien aspects, Hawthorne took his stand. Fact, he implied, was of no use until interpreted by mind; but mind must always return to fact to keep in touch with reality. Less the idealist (to drop a strictly philosophical sense and turn to a more popular one) than Emerson, he thought he knew some unpleasant facts we must take account of whether we liked them or not. Any theory which ignored them could not be true. But he did not think we were bound to take the apparent meaninglessness of nature at face value: if some dreams were mere figments, others were true.

He invented an art form about halfway, at its center, between pure interpretation, or mind triumphant, and uncreative recording, or mind in abdication—between allegory and the naturalistic record. (Both these extremes are mere

whipping boys for critics, of course; neither, if pure, would
be art at all; neither is perhaps even possible, whether we
call the result art or not.) Unlike Bunyan, he would not
write simply to teach, to convey meanings: he would render
scenes, as James would say later. But he would render them
clarified, purified of irrelevant detail. He would use facts,
but *meaningful* facts, facts taken into heart and mind and
seen humanly.

"Night Sketches" begins with mind triumphant in daydream, moves to the shock of the initial confrontation with
the impenetrable void of meaningless nature, and ends with
the darkness illuminated with the true light, meaninglessness shaped into sufficient meaning by the true dream. In
religious terms, Hawthorne seemed to find himself faced
with a choice between Bunyan's faith and utter meaninglessness, which is what a completely naturalistic outlook would
have meant to him. He refused the choice. The true faith,
he seems to have thought, would be more like Bunyan's in
general outline than like Emerson's, but it would take account of things Bunyan did not know. The faith could perhaps be preserved if its form were purified.

For the man this meant validating the religious vision
of his favorite Christian authors by expressing that vision
in the language and concepts of a new age, without committing himself to their religious literalism, their confusion
of history and myth. For the artist, it meant transforming
traditional allegory into a mythopoetic art sometimes close
to Bunyan and Spenser, sometimes close to Faulkner, but
at its best in an area all its own. For both man and artist it
meant devising a way of distinguishing false lights from
true by observing their effects in the night. It meant, ultimately, correcting the dream in order to conserve it. Both
as man and as artist, Hawthorne knew how to value the
little circle of light in the darkness of human life.

Index

INDEX

Adam: "Rappaccini's Daughter," 115, 117; *The House,* 171; *The Marble Faun,* 209, 210, 213; and myth, 264

Aesthetics (Hawthorne's): imagination, 29; matter and manner, 30-44; distance, 67-69; thinking in images, 75-77; image, symbol, myth, 105-106; relation to the didactic, 249-251

Aiken, Conrad, 71

"Alice Doane's Appeal," 10, 46, 48-56; and laughter, 57, 59; and guilt, 65, 67, 111, 205; in relation to the late romances, 229, 230, 236, 237

Alienation (isolation, "insulation"): Hawthorne's, 1-11, 233-236, 243; of the artist, 32-34; as a theme, 4, 76; "Alice Doane's Appeal," 52-56; "My Kinsman," 59; "The Man of Adamant," 107-111; "Wakefield," 75-76

Allegory, 124-125, 248-255; ambiguity, 258-264; realism, 38-44; symbolism, 71-104; "The Canterbury Pilgrims," 78-90; "The Man of Adamant," 106-111; *The Scarlet Letter,* 126ff.; *The Marble Faun,* 224

Ambiguity, 250, 258-264; "My Kinsman," 56-64; Hawthorne's style, 172-174; *The Scarlet Letter,* 135-138, 141, 150, 154-159; *The House,* 177; *Blithedale,* 204-205

American Renaissance, 72, 263

"American Scholar, The," 21, 46

Ancestral Footstep, The, 226-246, *passim*

"Antique Ring, The," 77, 245

Antirationalism (Hawthorne's): and mystery, 11; and Hawthorne's faith, 14-16, 250, 258-266; head and heart, 22-23; and the role of the artist, 32-37; and myth, 214-220. See *Libido sciendi* and religion

Arcadia, 1, 70, 196, 211, 216-217, 228

"Artist of the Beautiful, The," 15

Austen, Jane, 249

"Bartleby the Scrivener," 218

Bible, The: Hawthorne's belief in, 14, 15, 22, 28-29, 248, 260-264; "My Kinsman," 60-63; "Roger Malvin's Burial," 92-98; "The Man of Adamant," 108-111; *The Scarlet Letter,* 145, 149, 154-159; *The House,* 185-187; *The Marble Faun,* 209-211, 213-215

"Billy Budd," 236

"Birthmark, The," 4, 108, 201-202, 243

Blithedale Romance, The, 4, 188-208, 236, 237, 239; external evidence of intended meaning, 27; Gothic aspects, 64; Eden imagery, 229; and death, 230

Book of Common Prayer, The, 109

Brook Farm, 4, 6, 16, 70, 188, 191

Bryant, William Cullen, 21

"Buds and Bird Voices," 42

Bunyan, John, 36, 43, 44, 233; and "The Celestial Railroad," 18, 253; difference between his practice and Hawthorne's, 99, 106, 248, 259-261, 266

Bushnell, Horace, 16

"Canterbury Pilgrims, The," 77, 78-90, 98-104, 112, 185; origin of, in Hawthorne's experience, 39-42; and "The Maypole of Merrymount," 156-157; and Hawthorne's antiasceticism, 262

Carlyle, Thomas, 19

Castle of Otranto, The, 248

"Celestial Railroad, The," 11, 17-19, 178, 221, 253

Cervantes, 233

Channing, Ellery, 19

Channing, W. E., 17

"Chiefly About War Matters," 200

Chillingworth, 33, 51, 59, 72, 126-159, *passim*

Christ: Hawthorne's attitude toward, 13, 14, 16, 220, 262-264;

"Roger Malvin's Burial," 98; "The Man of Adamant," 109-110; and Dimmesdale, 149; and the theme of *The Scarlet Letter*, 155; Hawthorne's comment on Sodoma's fresco of, 220; *Dr. Grimshawe's Secret*, 244

Christian civilization, 113, 114, 117, 123, 151

"Christmas Banquet, The": and Hawthorne's self-portrayal, 4, 205, 229; as allegory, 99, 252, 253; and *Blithedale*, 196

Cilley, Jonathan, 7

Civil War, 70, 232

Classical civilization: "Rappaccini's Daughter," 112-117, 123; *The Scarlet Letter*, 151, 158

Clifford, 72, 163-187, *passim*

Conrad, Joseph, 250

Conservatism (Hawthorne's), 11, 248; and Brook Farm, 6; "Earth's Holocaust," 19-23; compared with Dr. Johnson's, 24-25; and progress, 168-170, 178-187; *The House*, 168-170, 178-187; *Blithedale*, 189-190, 199-202, 204-208

Coverdale, 25, 27, 59, 188-208, *passim*

Dante, 20, 43, 112, 117, 217, 233

Darkness (Hawthorne's): and death, 23-26, 230; and light, 26-30; "Night Sketches," 34-38; *The Scarlet Letter*, 127-129, 135, 154-155, 159; *The House*, 181-184; *Blithedale*, 195, 199-204; *The Marble Faun*, 219-220, 224-225; and the problem of evil, 240-241; and Hawthorne's religion, 242-243, 245, 258-259, 266

Davidson, Edward H., 227, 244

Death: Hawthorne's premonition of, 1, 226, 230; his preoccupation with, 23-26, 42, 52, 54, 56, 231, 236; *The Scarlet Letter*, 129, 159; *The House*, 161-162; *Blithedale*, 204-207; *The Marble Faun*, 216-217, 219, 220, 225

DeFoe, Daniel, 249

Dickens, Charles, 249, 250

Didacticism, 249-250, 258-264, 266

Dimmesdale, 72, 97, 126-159, *passim*, 201

Divine Comedy, The, 112, 117, 217

Dr. Grimshawe's Secret, 135, 226-246, *passim*

"Dr. Heidegger's Experiment," 111, 230

Dolliver Romance, The, 226-246, *passim*

Donatello, 173, 209-225, *passim*

Donne, John, 24

"Earth's Holocaust," 11, 17, 19-23, 42, 253; and death, 26; in relation to the theme of *Blithedale*, 27-28, 189, 203, 207; and Revelation, 29; in relation to *The Marble Faun*, 221

Eden: as a theme in Hawthorne's work, 1, 42, 259, 261; "Rappaccini's Daughter," 111-124; *The Scarlet Letter*, 157-159; *The House*, 171-172, 175, 180-181, 186; *Blithedale*, 196, 202; *The Marble Faun*, 209-225; the late romances, 228, 229, 230, 236

Edwards, Jonathan, 111

"Egotism, or the Bosom Serpent,": the happy ending, 66; relation of the story to the Notebook entry, 73, 238; its triadic structure and texture, 103; love and reason together as redemptive, 111, 154; the fountain, 167

Emerson, R. W., 2, 19, 25, 46; Hawthorne's partial disagreement with, 12, 21, 38, 75, 265, 266; Hawthorne's partial agreement with, 15-16, 29-30, 265; and Hester, 146; his style compared with Hawthorne's, 172

Empiricists, 15-16, 123, 239, 243

English Traits, 25

"Ethan Brand," 4, 238, 253; "I-Thou" and "I-It," 33; Hawthorne's use of present experience, 41, 44; Gothic elements in, 64; theme of community, 76; the journey plot, 101; Brand's sin, 142; and Hawthorne's technique, 257-258

Evangeline, 3

Faerie Queene, The, 99
Fall of Man, the: Hawthorne's sense of man as fallen, 1, 52-55, 227-230, 259, 264; the locus of evil, 22-23; "My Kinsman," 56-64; "Roger Malvin's Burial," 91-98; "Rappaccini's Daughter," 111-124; *The House*, 171-172, 180-181, 186; as a theme in Hawthorne's work, 209-211; *The Marble Faun*, 209-225

"Fancy's Show Box," 11-17, 51, 53, 253

Fanshawe, 25, 45, 53, 227, 237, 252

Fate: Hawthorne's feeling of, 10, 11, 12-13, 42, 50, 51, 66, 230-231; as a theme in the works: "Wakefield," 76; "Roger Malvin's Burial," 96, *The House*, 177-178

Faulkner, William, 250, 255, 266

Fielding, Henry, 249, 250, 251

"Fire Worship," 182

"Flowering Judas," 71

Form and Fable in American Fiction, 57

Fortunate Fall, 211-225, *passim*

Fountains (and springs): "The Canterbury Pilgrims," 80-81, 89-90; "Rappaccini's Daughter," 112-114; *The House*, 167, 174, 177; "The Man of Adamant," 262-263

French Revolution, The, 19

Freud, Sigmund, 233

Fuller, Margaret, 188

"Gentle Boy, The," 106, 108, 253

Gothic (aspect of Hawthorne's work): *Fanshawe*, 25, 45, 46, 53; in general, 43, 64, 247, 248-249, 252; "Alice Doane's Appeal," 54; *Blithedale*, 188, 192, 208; the late romances, 228, 237

Grandfather's Chair, 254

"Gray Champion, The," 237

"Great Carbuncle, The," 72, 99, 111, 125, 261, 262

Guilt: Hawthorne's feeling of, 10, 12-13, 23, 26, 44, 65, 121, 233-236, 259; "The Hollow of the Three Hills," 47; "Alice Doane's Appeal," 50-56, 67; "My Kinsman," 60, 62; "Roger Malvin's Burial," 92-98; "Rappaccini's Daughter," 121; *The Scarlet Letter*, 129

"Hall of Fantasy, The," 183, 207, 252

"Haunted Mind, The," 8-11, 26, 125, 205, 252

Hawthorne, Elizabeth, 48, 52

Hawthorne, Sophia, 42, 187, 245; as editor, 2, 3, 87, 243; as the inspiration: for Priscilla, 27; for Phoebe, 170; for Eve, 209; for Hilda, 213-214, 221

Hawthorne, Una, 72, 152, 170, 245

"Hawthorne as Poet," 105

Hawthorne's Dr. Grimshawe's Secret, 244

Hawthorne's Last Phase, 227

"Hawthorne's 'Man of Adamant': A Spenserian Source Study," 109

"Hawthorne's Unfinished Works," 233

Head, the (in Hawthorne's head and heart dichotomy): "Night Sketches," 35ff.; "shrewdness" as a theme in "My Kinsman," 56ff.; Rappaccini, 114-115, 117-118, 119, 121, 123-124; rationalism and empiricism in Giovanni ("Rappaccini's Daughter"), 123, 239; Chillingworth, 144, 145-146, 150; *The House*, 163, 167; the Wandering Jew, 239

Head and the heart, the (relations of), 3-4, 8-11, 26-30, 48, 259; "Night Sketches," 34-38; *The House*, 167, 175-176, 182

Heart, the: definition of, in "The Haunted Mind," 9ff.; as locus of evil in "Earth's Holocaust," 22-23; and guilt, 47; *The Marble Faun*, 47, 221, 224; implicit heart imagery in "The Hollow of the

Three Hills," 47, 221; the heart and the unconscious in "Alice Doane's Appeal," 48-56; "Roger Malvin's Burial," 92, 97; and allegory, 106; as a cavern, 106ff.; as a fountain (pure hearts), 112-113; hearts of pure young girls, 129; *The Scarlet Letter*, 133-134, 141-145, 147, 150, 153; *The House*, 163, 167; *Blithedale*, 190, 195, 196, 197, 203; as a fireplace, 235; as a chamber, 244; the truth of, 251; reading the meanings of, 254; the heart and religious truth, 259

Hemingway, Ernest, 43

Hepzibah, 72, 160-187, *passim*, 224

Hester, 10, 14, 68, 126-159, *passim*, 224

Hilda, 10, 73, 209-225, *passim*, 230

Hoeltje, Hubert, 14, 45, 239, 240

Hoffman, Daniel G., 57, 62

Holgrave, 166, 167, 176, 182, 185-187

Hollingsworth, 190-191, 193, 194, 195, 202, 204

"Hollow of the Three Hills, The," 64; witchcraft, 46; expression of Hawthorne's central themes, 47; the use of the past, 48; and symbolism, 111; heart imagery in, 221; death, 230

House of the Seven Gables, The, 160-187, 194, 230, 237, 238, 251; Hawthorne's belief in freedom, 10; compared with *The Scarlet Letter*, 27, 127, 159; "fact" and "truth" in the Preface, 37; as an expression of hopefulness, 66; and allegory, 72; as a product of Hawthorne's conscious beliefs, 125; Hawthorne's belief in immortality, 200; Phoebe compared with Priscilla, 202; compared with *Blithedale*, 203; compared with *The Marble Faun*, 210, 211, 221; compared with the late romances, 229

"Howe's Masquerade," 125

Hutchinson, Ann, 158

Idealism (Hawthorne's), 28-34, 68, 183, 239, 264-266

Imagination (in Hawthorne's thought and his work): its role in religion, 29; its parallel role in art, 30-38; its relation to the artist's creativity, 32; its realm in relation to reality, 34; Hawthorne's, and Niagara Falls, 43; its relation to the heart, 55-56; its need of distance, 68

Immortality (Hawthorne's belief in): *The House*, 180, 185; in relation to the tone of *Blithedale*, 200-202; *The Marble Faun*, 217, 220; in relation to Eden, 230; in the Notebooks, 231; Septimius Felton, 231, 237; the Wandering Jew, 233; faith and doubt, 239-243

Initiation (as a theme in Hawthorne's work): Robin in "My Kinsman," 56-64, 221-223; Giovanni in "Rappaccini's Daughter," 117; Beatrice in "Rappaccini's Daughter," 121; false or misleading initiation, in "Young Goodman Brown," 14, 92, 101, 209-210; denial of the need for initiation, young girls, 222; Donatello in *The Marble Faun*, 209-225, *passim*; initiation and the Fall, 259

"Inscription for the Entrance to a Wood," 21

"Intelligence Office, The," 113, 252

Inward Sky: The Mind and Heart of Nathaniel Hawthorne, 14

Irving, Washington, 3, 8, 46-47

Isolation—see Alienation

James, Henry, 161, 248, 257, 266; James's idea of "the alchemy of art" and Hawthorne's idea in "The Old Apple Dealer," 32; James and Hawthorne on the difficulties facing the American novelist, 46; art and life, 67; James commenting on *The House*, 175; Coverdale as a Jamesian character, 208; Hawthorne's anticipations of, 223, 250, 251, 254

Johnson, Samuel, 24, 43, 70, 189, 231, 233
Joyce, James, 174

Kafka, Franz, 71, 250
Keats, John, 9, 179
Kenyon, 212-225, *passim*

"Lady Eleanor's Mantle," 99, 161, 229, 261, 262
Lamont, Dr. John H., 52, 233
Lathrop, C. P., 40
Lawrence, D. H., 158
Leavis, Q. D., 57, 105
Legends of New England in Prose and Verse, 47
"Legends of the Province House," 125
Libido sciendi (the lust for knowledge, or excessive rationalism in Hawthorne's thought and work): Aylmer, 4; Ethan Brand, 4, 142; Hawthorne's antirationalism compared with Emerson's, 15-16; resulting in isolation or alienation, 33, 258; Rappaccini, 114-115, 117-119, 121, 123-124; Chillingworth, 147, 150
Life of Franklin Pierce, 200
Light, the (in Hawthorne's thought and work): Melville's view of Hawthorne's darkness, 26; Hawthorne's intention to affirm the light, 26-30, 258, 259, 266; *The Scarlet Letter,* 126-159, *passim,* esp. 137, 159; *The House,* 160-187, *passim,* esp. 170-171; *The Marble Faun,* 209-225, *passim,* esp. 217-220, 225
Light and Dark, balance of, 266; relation to the head and the heart, 26-30; Hawthorne's special kind of balance maintained in "Night Sketches," 34-37; "The Canterbury Pilgrims," 89; lack of that balance in *The Scarlet Letter,* 156, 159; the balance again in *The House,* 160, 170-171, 175
"Little Daffydowndilly," 3

"London" (Johnson's poem), 24
Longfellow, H. W., 2, 3, 7, 105
Lowell, J. R., 2
Lundblad, Jane, 248

Macaulay, T. B., 8
"Main Street," 101, 106, 252
"Man of Adamant, The," 99, 101, 106-111; as implying Hawthorne's view of the Puritans, 16, 155; the Bible, 63, 155; its artfulness, 124, 125; the man of adamant and Hilda, 222; compared with "The Wives of the Dead" as an indication of the range of Hawthorne's practice, 253; the style, 256-257; its clarity as allegory, 262
Marble Faun, The, 46, 66, 202, 209-225, 229, 233, 237, 265; use of Notebook material in, 41; the catacombs as a dream, 47; the catacombs as a heart, 48; Gothic elements in, 64; Hilda as an emblematic character, 73; compared with *The Scarlet Letter,* 100; the circles of history and man's destiny, 173; death, 230; as a revelation of Hawthorne's religion, 239
Mark Twain, 2, 187
Matthiessen, F. O., 72, 120, 263
"Maypole of Merrymount, The," 106, 156, 237
Melville, Herman, 41, 88, 150; his view of Hawthorne's darkness, 26, 30; compared with Hawthorne, 36, 61, 236, 242; Hawthorne's green shrub in *The Marble Faun* and Melville's green grass in "Bartleby," 218; visit to Hawthorne in Liverpool, 241ff.; religious views compared with Hawthorne's, 241-243
Mesmerism, 181, 194, 208
Milton, 105, 233
"Minister's Black Veil, The," 101, 106, 111, 201
Miriam, 10, 73, 209-225, *passim,* 230

"Mr. Higginbotham's Catastrophe," 100
Moby Dick, 160, 174
Monk, The, 248
"Monk" (Faulkner's story), 255
Murray, Henry A., 236
"My Kinsman, Major Molineux," 56-64, 90, 91, 253; Hawthorne's religion, 13; the past and distance, 48, 67; compared with "Alice Doane's Appeal," 65; the hopeful ending of, 66; the journey plot, 100; the Bible in, 108-109; passive sensibility, 111, 125; as a story of a fortunate fall, 209-210; Robin compared with Hilda, 222; Eden and the Fall, 229; as myth, 261
"My Visit to Niagara," 43
Myth, 106, 261, 266; "My Kinsman," 56-64; "Roger Malvin's Burial," 91-98; Prometheus and the little reptile, 113; Vertumnus and Pomona, 113-114, 117; Adam in the Garden ("Rappaccini's Daughter"), 111-125; The Marble Faun, 209-225; passim, esp. 215-217; Hawthorne's use of the word myth, 215-216; the serpent in the Garden, 112, 216. See Arcadia and Eden

Nathaniel Hawthorne and the Tradition of the Gothic Romance, 248
Nature: as the language of the General Revelation, 28-29, 63, 77; as dead, or the realm of death, 36, 114, 266; portrayed in "Buds and Bird Voices," 42; as agreeing with Scripture, 63, 108-111, 156, 186, 262-263; as promoting "romance," 80-81; man's transcendence of, 116-117, 120, 121; The Scarlet Letter, 138ff.; as unillumined by Revelation, 141; as compared with the moral, 148ff.; nature and love, 155; and true religion, 63, 108-111, 156; The House, 162ff., 177, 183-184;

nature and Grace, 177; its voice as unintelligible, 186; The Marble Faun, 211-220, passim, esp. 215-217; and the problem of evil, 240-241
"New Adam and Eve, The," 209, 229
"Night Sketches: Beneath an Umbrella," 34-38, 252; "justification by grace through faith," 13, 63; compared with "My Kinsman," 63; compared with the revelations gained by Clifford and Hepzibah in their flight, 182, 184; the darkness of, compared with the darkness in Blithedale, 201; compared to The Marble Faun, 219; and the sense of evil, 241; and Hawthorne's affirmation of the light, 266
Notebooks, 4, 7, 11, 41; Mrs. Hawthorne's revisions of, 2, 87, 243; barrenness of the English Notebooks, 39; use of the material in, 44, 48, 223-224, 244; French and Italian, 68, 69; general relation to the fiction, 73-74, 106, 215, 223, 224, 228, 245; American, 87, 88; English, 109, 228, 229, 230, 234-235, 240, 243

Oedipus, 98
"Old Apple Dealer, The," 31-34, 252
Organicism (Hawthorne's), 30-34
Original Sin: as a theme in "Roger Malvin's Burial," 92-98; as a theme in The House, 161, 180ff.; The Marble Faun, 209-225. See also Adam, Eden, and the Fall of Man
Our Old Home, 67, 69, 240, 249; compared with Emerson's English Traits, 24-25; its connection with the Eden-Arcadia themes, 229
Ovid, 113

Passive sensibility, 9, 61, 125
Past, the: usefulness of, to Hawthorne, 7, 31, 45-70, 91, 125; Hawthorne's view of its relation

to the imagination, 55; fate and freedom, 66, 76, 160-187, *passim;* Hawthorne's feeling for his own and New England's past (*see also* Puritanism), 1, 107, 161, 228-229, 233; the meaning of the past in *The House,* 160-187; Hawthorne's reaction to English antiquities, 168

Pearl, 72, 126-159, *passim,* 170

Phoebe, 10, 72, 163-187, *passim,* 230

Pierce, Franklin, 5, 200

Pierre, 236

Pilgrim's Progress, 17, 18

Plato, 30

Poe, E. A., 24, 25, 46, 247

Politics (Hawthorne's), 161, 207

Pomona (in classic myth), 113

Porter, Katherine Anne, 71

Priscilla, 27, 190-203, *passim,* 230

"Procession of Life, The," 101, 252, 253

Progress (as a theme, and Hawthorne's views on), 248; "The Celestial Railroad," 17-19; "Earth's Holocaust," 19-23; *The House,* 176-184; *Blithedale,* 199-202, 204-208

Prometheus, 113

Providence: Hawthorne's belief in, 14, 218, 241-242, 263; our inability to understand, 68-69, 201, 241-242, 250, 263

Psychoanalysis (depth psychology): "Earth's Holocaust," 23; Hawthorne's personality, 52, 54-55, 233-236; "Alice Doane's Appeal," 53, 61; Hawthorne's feeling about the past, 65-66; *The Scarlet Letter,* 151; *The House,* 174; *The Marble Faun,* 224; the late romances, 233-236; Hawthorne's definition of his role as artist, 249

Puritanism (and the Puritans, in Hawthorne's view): predestination, 12-15; Hawthorne's partial agreement with, 13-15, 62; Calvinism, 17, 54; Hawthorne's differences with, 13-15, 31, 262; the

Puritans as bigots, lacking love ("The Man of Adamant"), 106-111, 256-257; other negative judgments of, 106-111, 127-128, 139, 142, 155-156, 157-159, 253; as portrayed in *The Scarlet Letter,* 127-129, 139, 142, 155-156, 157-159; Hilda as a daughter of the Puritans, 222; "Young Goodman Brown" and belief in total depravity, 253

"P's Correspondence," 252

"Rappaccini's Daughter," 111-125; Rappaccini as a character, 4, 51, 59; initiation as a theme, 62; the rich texture of, 90-91, 106; the role of Beatrice, 111-125, *passim,* 148; classical and Christian worlds, 151, 157, 158; Eden, 209, 229, 261; the Fall, 210, 229, 261

Rasselas, 70, 189, 190

Reform, 17, 19-23, 178-184, 188-208, 264. *See also* Progress

Religion (Hawthorne's), 2, 3, 248; paradoxes of, 6-7; repent and hope for forgiveness ("Fancy's Show Box"), 12-17; "justification by grace through faith," 13, 62; moral problems not solved by progress ("The Celestial Railroad"), 18-19; the progress of knowledge makes the Scriptures shine all the more brightly ("Earth's Holocaust"), 19-23; Hawthorne's religion compared with Dr. Johnson's, 24; through nature to God ("Sunday at Home"), 28-30; mechanism and mystery: man not a machine ("The Old Apple Dealer"), 30-34; the light of faith in a dark world ("Night Sketches"), 34-38; no salvation by "works," or by mind alone—"shrewdness" ("My Kinsman"), 63; "the magnetic chain" of love, 68-69; fanaticism, bigotry, and love ("The Man of Adamant"), 109; Hawthorne's Protestantism, 14, 141;

the humanistic emphasis, 159; history and myth, 212; a religion "of the heart," existentially, rather than doctrinally or institutionally, oriented, 214-215, 217-219, 258-264, 266; faith, and man's mortality, 220, 225; the light of faith, 225; immortality, 231; doubt, 238-243; possible final resurgence of faith, 245-246; Providence, 250

Revelation (in the Bible): the Scriptures inspired but needing criticism, 22; Revelation as offering guidance and support to man, 28; and imagination, 29; the Bible illuminated, 61-63; interpretation of, 108, 155; directly to the heart, 113; light as a symbol of Revelation, 133, 134-135, 136; support by General Revelation (Nature), 186, 263-264

Revelation, the General (all Nature, as interpreted by reason and intuition, seen with an imaginative vision): and imagination, 28-29; nature corroborates Scripture, 62-63, 108-111, 155, 186; the light of nature as an image of the light of Revelation, 133; a sacrament at once natural and supernatural, the "birchen cup" of "The Man of Adamant," 262-263

Richardson, Samuel, 250

Robinson, E. A., 51

"Roger Malvin's Burial," 90-98; lack of Gothic elements, 64; lack of explicit statement of theme, 77; lack of outward action, 99, 100; triadic structure, 103-104; ambiguity, 106; its exemplification of one pole of the range of Hawthorne's practice, 111, 261; its mythic suggestions, 124-125; its expression of Hawthorne's tragic vision, 150; a Sin more Original than specific and actual, 210-211; the loss of innocence, 229; its relation to Bunyanesque

allegory, 259; its retelling of the story of Abraham and Isaac, 262

Romance, the (Hawthorne's conception of): vision and artistry, 30-31; the nature of "the imaginative vision," 32; the necessity of mystery, 34; the "romance" and the "novel," 37-38, 164, 173-174, 187, 247, 249, 250-251

Romanticism, 3, 8-9, 23, 29; and the haunted mind, 61; Hawthorne's romanticism and his antiromanticism, 79-81, 82, 86, 89; romance and irony in "The Canterbury Pilgrims," 78-90; romanticism and "the truth of the human heart," 232-233

St. Matthew, 145

St. Paul, 15, 108, 154

Salem, 1, 3, 5, 49, 53, 240

Sargent's New Monthly Magazine, 30, 31

Scarlet Letter, The, 1, 126-159, 168, 197, 199, 227, 237, 244; its immediate success, 5; working in the Custom House, 6; the judgment of the Puritan Society, 14; the darkness of the ending, 27; the fact of adultery, 31; the Gothic elements, 64; the lack of hope, 66; Hawthorne's "research" for, 68; Spenserian emblematic characters, 72; the explicit moral, "Be true!" 95, 201; lack of action, 100; the Puritans as men of adamant, 107; compared with The House, 125, 176, 185; Hawthorne's emotional involvement with his story, 160; Pearl and Una, 170; the first chapter compared with the first chapter of The House, 175; compared with Blithedale, 194; compared with The Marble Faun, 221; comparative lack of Eden imagery, 229; relation to "the twilight of romance," 233; not allegory, 263

Scott, Sir Walter, 43, 44, 233, 249, 250

Septimius Felton, 226-246, *passim*
"Seven Tales of My Native Land," 49
"Shaker Bridal, The" 88
Shakers, 4, 39-41, 78ff., 156
Shakespeare, 105, 150, 233, 248
Shroeder, John W., 109, 190
"Sinners in the Hands of an Angry God," 111
Sketches, 8-44, 207
"Sketches from Memory," 43
Smollett, Tobias, 250
"Snow Image, The," 3
Snow Image and Other Twice-Told Tales, The, 38
Spenser, Edmund: as defining Hawthorne's "tradition," 43; Matthiessen on Spenser's influence, 72, 73; the nature of Hawthorne's allegory compared with Spenser's, 99, 106, 260, 261, 266; as a favorite author, 105, 233; Hawthorne's debt to him in "The Man of Adamant," 109; what the Cave of Despair meant to Hawthorne, 244
Spiritualism, 181
Stevens, Wallace, 36
Stewart, Randall, 2, 3, 50, 51, 87
Study of Hawthorne, A., 40
Style (Hawthorne's), 101-104, 172-173, 255-258
"Sunday at Home," 28-30, 63, 241, 256
Supernaturalism of New England, 47
Symbolism: the relations of fantasy, imagination, and fact, 37-41; abstract conceptual thought and thinking in images, 71-104; three kinds of visual images in *The Scarlet Letter*, 130-138; the symbols in the sketches compared with those in the fiction, 252-255; symbolism, allegory, and the nature of Hawthorne's religious belief, 258-264. *See also* Allegory, the Romance, and Myth

" 'That Inward Sphere': Hawthorne's Heart Imagery and Symbolism," 190
Thoreau, H. D., 16, 42, 88
Tillich, Paul, 16
Transcendentalism, 3, 13, 14, 15-16, 18, 30, 207-208
Trollope, Anthony, 38, 233, 249
Two types of meaning, 26-28
Typee, 236

Van Doren, Mark, 231, 232, 244, 245
"Vanity of Human Wishes, The," 24, 189
Vertumnus (in classic myth), 112, 113, 114, 117
Villains (Hawthorne's), 51, 59, 142
Virgil, 20
"Virtuoso's Collection, A," 29, 37, 239, 252
Voltaire, 248

"Wakefield," 75-77, 255; as a study in alienation (isolation), *passim*; and fate, 51; as an example of Hawthorne's procedure as an artist, *passim*; as undeveloped fiction, 98; its lack of action, 100, 253
Warren, Austin, 116
Warren, Robert Penn, 180, 249, 255
Westervelt: his sin, using people as objects, 4; laughter as a "terrible modulation of the human voice," 59, 194; his name, 191; his false teeth as a mask, 194; his relation to Coverdale, 196; his profusion of masks, 199. *See also Libido sciendi*, Antirationalism, and Empiricists
Whitehead, Alfred North, 251
Whitman, Walt, 7, 25
Whittier, J. G., 47, 63
Winters, Yvor, 147
Witchcraft, 46, 47, 48-56, 59
"Wives of the Dead, The," 64, 72, 111, 253
World Enough and Time, 249

"Young Goodman Brown": implied judgment of the Puritans on the doctrine of total depravity, 14; compared with Poe's Roderick Usher, 25; fate, 59; dream, 60; Gothic elements, 64; the meaning of, 66; as a false initiation, 92; its lack of action, 100; compared with the sketches, 101; its style, 103; witchcraft, 119; Brown as an Innocent, 120; the story evaluated, 125; the forest as a heart image, 143; Brown as a partial self-image of Hawthorne, 205; as a treatment of the theme of the Fall, 209-210, 211; as allegory, 253, 261

Zenobia, 188-208; *passim*, 224, 230

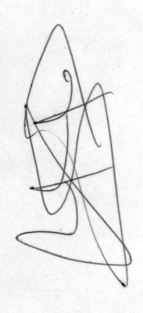

EVERY MOUNTAIN
MADE LOW

ALEX WHITE

First published 2016 by Solaris
an imprint of Rebellion Publishing Ltd,
Riverside House, Osney Mead,
Oxford, OX2 0ES, UK

www.solarisbooks.com

ISBN: 978 1 78108 466 3

10 9 8 7 6 5 4 3 2 1

A CIP catalogue record for this book is available
from the British Library.

Designed & typeset by Rebellion Publishing

Printed in the US